# Inflation

A National Bureau
of Economic Research
Project Report

# Inflation: Causes and Effects

Edited by Robert E. Hall

The University of Chicago Press

*Chicago and London*

ROBERT E. HALL is professor in the Department of Economics and Senior Fellow of the Hoover Institution, Stanford University. He also serves as director of the Research Program on Economic Fluctuations and the Project on Inflation of the National Bureau of Economic Research and as chairman of the NBER's Business Cycle Dating Group.

The University of Chicago Press, Chicago 60637
The University of Chicago Press, Ltd., London
© 1982 by The National Bureau of Economic Research
All rights reserved. Published 1982
Printed in the United States of America
89 88 87 86 85 84 83 82   5 4 3 2 1

*The Library of Congress Cataloging in Publication Data*
Main entry under title:

Inflation, causes and effects.

(A National Bureau of Economic Research project report)
  1. Inflation (Finance)—Addresses, essays, lectures.
2. Inflation (Finance)—United States—Addresses,
essays, lectures.   I. Hall, Robert Ernest, 1943–
II. Series: Project report (National Bureau of Economic Research)
HG229.I4512   1982        332.4'1        82-10932
ISBN 0-226-31323-9

## Relation of the Directors to the
## Work and Publications of the
## National Bureau of Economic Research

1. The object of the National Bureau of Economic Research is to ascertain and to present to the public important economic facts and their interpretation in a scientific and impartial manner. The Board of Directors is charged with the responsibility of ensuring that the work of the National Bureau is carried on in strict conformity with this object.

2. The President of the National Bureau shall submit to the Board of Directors, or to its Executive Committee, for their formal adoption all specific proposals for research to be instituted.

3. No research report shall be published by the National Bureau until the President has sent each member of the Board a notice that a manuscript is recommended for publication and that in the President's opinion it is suitable for publication in accordance with the principles of the National Bureau. Such notification will include an abstract or summary of the manuscript's content and a response form for use by those Directors who desire a copy of the manuscript for review. Each manuscript shall contain a summary drawing attention to the nature and treatment of the problem studied, the character of the data and their utilization in the report, and the main conclusions reached.

4. For each manuscript so submitted, a special committee of the Directors (including Directors Emeriti) shall be appointed by majority agreement of the President and Vice Presidents (or by the Executive Committee in case of inability to decide on the part of the President and Vice Presidents), consisting of three Directors selected as nearly as may be one from each general division of the Board. The names of the special manuscript committee shall be stated to each Director when notice of the proposed publication is submitted to him. It shall be the duty of each member of the special manuscript committee to read the manuscript. If each member of the manuscript committee signifies his approval within thirty days of the transmittal of the manuscript, the report may be published. If at the end of that period any member of the manuscript committee withholds his approval, the President shall then notify each member of the Board, requesting approval or disapproval of publication, and thirty days additional shall be granted for this purpose. The manuscript shall then not be published unless at least a majority of the entire Board who shall have voted on the proposal within the time fixed for the receipt of votes shall have approved.

5. No manuscript may be published, though approved by each member of the special manuscript committee, until forty-five days have elapsed from the transmittal of the report in manuscript form. The interval is allowed for the receipt of any memorandum of dissent or reservation, together with a brief statement of his reasons, that any member may wish to express; and such memorandum of dissent or reservation shall be published with the manuscript if he so desires. Publication does not, however, imply that each member of the Board has read the manuscript, or that either members of the Board in general or the special committee have passed on its validity in every detail.

6. Publications of the National Bureau issued for informational purposes concerning the work of the Bureau and its staff, or issued to inform the public of activities of Bureau staff, and volumes issued as a result of various conferences involving the National Bureau shall contain a specific disclaimer noting that such publication has not passed through the normal review procedures required in this resolution. The Executive Committee of the Board is charged with review of all such publications from time to time to ensure that they do not take on the character of formal research reports of the National Bureau, requiring formal Board approval.

7. Unless otherwise determined by the Board or exempted by the terms of paragraph 6, a copy of this resolution shall be printed in each National Bureau publication.

*(Resolution adopted October 25, 1926, as revised through September 30, 1974)*

# Contents

# Acknowledgments

The National Bureau of Economic Research's Project on Inflation was supported by the National Science Foundation. We are grateful to Louise Sherman for administrative help in all aspects of the project and in the preparation of this volume.

Robert E. Hall

# Introduction

Robert E. Hall

The essays in this volume are the product of the NBER's Project on Inflation and reflect a dozen diverse views on one of the nation's central economic problems. Our emphasis here is on diagnosis of the causes of inflation and a description of the effects of inflation, not on specific policy recommendations to end inflation. Many of us have views on what to do about inflation and have not hesitated to speak up in public about those views, but our papers here are not advocating those views. Instead, we are trying to illuminate some of the economic and political processes involving inflation.

The twelve papers in this volume fall into four general categories. Two papers—those of Robert J. Gordon and Thomas J. Sargent—find dramatically different answers to the central question of what would happen to output and employment if inflation were brought to an end. Two other papers deal with the types of change in economic institutions that might contribute to limiting inflation. Robert J. Barro points to the need for a monetary standard that stabilizes some dollar-denominated quantity in the economy as the key feature of an economy with stable prices. Robert E. Hall pursues this idea, presenting an example of a monetary standard which borrows from the gold standard yet tries to avoid some of its pitfalls. Seven of the remaining papers deal with one or another way that inflation has changed the economy or how the economy has reacted to inflation. Jeremy I. Bulow reports, surprisingly, that inflation has brought large capital gains to the private pension system. Dennis W. Carlton argues that inflation has changed the character of certain types of

Robert E. Hall is professor in the Department of Economics and Senior Fellow of the Hoover Institution, Stanford University. He also serves as director of the Research Program on Economic Fluctuations and the Project on Inflation of the National Bureau of Economic Research and as chairman of the NBER's Business Cycle Dating Group.

markets, encouraging standardized products and limiting the marketing of highly specialized products. Martin Feldstein investigates the joint effects of inflation and the tax system on the incentives for capital accumulation. Stanley Fischer shows that the private economy has adapted partially to inflation by changing the form of financial instruments like mortgages and by indexing some forms of income. Jacob A. Frenkel discusses the relation between domestic monetary instability, inflation, and the international value of the dollar. Douglas A. Hibbs, Jr., a political scientist, shows how the public rates the problem of inflation compared to other social problems and how this rating responds to the actual state of the economy. Jeremy I. Bulow and John B. Shoven take a look at the distortions that inflation brings to the measurement of the earnings of corporations; they conclude that correction of the distortion actually raises corporate earnings. Finally, in a category of its own is Alan S. Blinder's examination of the volatile inflation of the 1970s and its relation to shocks in energy and food markets.

The papers by Gordon and by Sargent provide an interesting contrast. Both look to historical data on disinflation to draw conclusions about the likely effects of a move against inflation today. But they reach dramatically different conclusions. Gordon's paper, "Why Stopping Inflation May Be Costly: Evidence from Fourteen Historical Episodes," warns that ending inflation could decrease output and increase unemployment. His evidence, from a study of historical episodes in the United States, Germany, Switzerland, France, Japan, Italy, Brazil, and Israel, is not unanimous, however. Not every episode shows that ending inflation has an adverse effect on employment. He points out that there was a spectacular turnaround in inflation just after World War I in the United States, when inflation dropped from 20% to minus 26% in just a year and a half. The end of the inflation after World War II was also reasonably favorable, accompanied as it was by only a relatively mild recession. But more recent experience in the United States indicates that recessions have weak anti-inflationary effects. "The puzzling aspect of 1970–71 is the failure of the recession, which brought the level of real output from 4 percent above trend to 2.5% below trend, to have any effect at all in dampening inflation." Gordon finds that other countries too have succeeded in limiting recent bursts of inflation only by tolerating reduced output and employment. Germany has pursued a successful anti-inflation policy, says Gordon, but "the cost of this policy was relatively slow output growth of only 2.3% between 1973 and 1979, compared to 2.8% in the United States." Earlier, German growth had been well above United States growth. And in Switzerland, according to Gordon, literal price stability was achieved in the 1970s "by creating a veritable depression in real output." There are a few episodes during which inflation has been brought under control without deep recession: France and Italy in the mid-1960s and Japan in the late 1970s. Gordon concludes that contractions in demand, especially "cold turkey" policies, bring substantial likelihood of depressed employment and output, though they will succeed in cooling inflation.

In Sargent's paper, "The Ends of Four Big Inflations," a review of history indicates the opposite conclusion. Inflation raged in four European nations—Austria, Hungary, Poland, and Germany—in the aftermath of World War I. Once-and-for-all fiscal reforms proved to be the key to successful control of inflation in all four cases. These episodes are laboratories for studying changes in policy regimes and shed a good deal of light on the kind of policy that could eliminate current United States inflation, even though it is nowhere near as serious as the inflations studied here.

The major common features in the four cases are: (1) Each country persistently ran enormous budget deficits during the inflations. (2) Deliberate and drastic fiscal and monetary measures ended the hyperinflations almost overnight. (3) There were large increases in the money stock in the months and years after rapid inflation ended. This evidence counters Gordon's view, a view that has become common among economists: Inflation has a stubborn, self-sustaining momentum, not susceptible to cure by conventional measures of monetary and fiscal restraint. In this view, eradicating inflation would have a prohibitively high cost in widespread and sustained unemployment. Sargent favors an alternative view, associated with the hypothesis of rational expectations, that denies that there is any inherent momentum in the process of inflation. Were the government to adopt a comprehensive change in fiscal and monetary policy, inflation could end quickly, as it did in the four countries studied, according to Sargent's thinking.

Barro's and Hall's papers are complementary, on the other hand. Barro spells out the requirements for price stability in general terms, and Hall provides a quite specific example of the type of stable system Barro has in mind. Barro's paper, "United States Inflation and the Choice of Monetary Standard," points out that money growth and inflation are strongly positively correlated over long periods of time but are less closely associated from year to year. One source of short-run divergence between money and prices is a shift in the demand for money that is induced by a change in inflationary expectations. Variations in long-term inflationary expectations are mirrored in observable long-term interest rates, and these rates have become far more volatile in recent years. Barro estimates that each percentage point movement in these rates is associated—via higher monetary velocity—with a rise of about four percentage points in the inflation rate. The heightened volatility of interest rates and underlying expectations of money and price change reflects a movement away from a regime that provided some restraint on long-run monetary expansion. Some remnants of the gold standard and fixed exchange rates imposed these constraints even as recently as 1971. Under the present setup with paper money, future money and prices depend on the cumulated discretion of the Federal Reserve—the system possesses no nominal anchor, says Barro.

Commodity standards like the gold standard provide a nominal anchor by pegging the prices of particular goods. Although the commodity base can be expanded beyond gold, the limited potential coverage would allow for substantial variations in the general price level. The gold standard also entails direct resource costs. Further, at least under a fractional-reserve banking system, the history of gold standards indicates substantial room for economic contractions.

A monetary constitution that precommits the long-term path of nominal aggregates avoids many of the problems of commodity standards. Milton Friedman's constant-growth-rate rule is a regime of this type. What is key is not the constancy of the growth rate or the particular number for the rate or the precise definition of the monetary aggregate, but rather the commitment to and hence anchor on some future nominal values. We have substantial historical experience with regimes with nominal anchors that are of the gold standard type, but not with monetary constitutions in a paper money environment.

Hall's paper, "Explorations in the Gold Standard and Related Policies for Stabilizing the Dollar," pursues the idea of a nominal anchor achieved through a commodity standard. His paper explores the good and bad features of the gold standard and its generalization, the commodity standard, without taking a stand for or against the idea. A properly managed commodity standard emerges as a potential competitor to a properly managed fiat money system as a way to achieve price stability. Both systems require good management. Simply switching from our existing badly managed fiat money to a badly managed commodity standard might well be a step backward.

Hall reports that during the years of the gold standard in the United States (1879–1914), inflation was kept to reasonable levels but cumulated over decades so that the long-run purchasing power of the dollar declined by 40%. The gold standard does not meet the requirement of long-run stabilization of the real value of the dollar. Moreover, recent instability in the world gold market would have brought alternating periods of severe inflation and deflation had the United States been on the gold standard.

Hall finds that an acceptable commodity standard could be based on a package of several commodities, chosen so that the historical association of the price of the package and the cost of living has been close. An example of such a package contains ammonium nitrate, copper, aluminum, and plywood. But even with the best choice of a commodity standard, it is necessary to redefine the standard periodically. Monthly changes in the commodity content of the dollar could be used according to a fixed rule. Such a rule can promise almost exact long-run stability in the cost of living. Whatever type of commodity standard is adopted, it would function more effectively if the government did not hold reserves of the commodity. Manipulation of reserves and intervention in commodity markets defeat the anti-inflationary purpose of the commodity standard. Finally, Hall comments that, although a good commodity standard would have been far superior to the actual monetary policy of the past two decades, better management of the existing system based on fiat money might have done as well or better. The commodity standard is not inherently superior to fiat money as a way to stabilize the cost of living. The commodity standard is just as subject to abuse as is the existing system.

Among the papers dealing with the impact of inflation on the workings of the United States economy, Jeremy Bulow's "The Effect of Inflation on the Private Pension System" is one of the most surprising. Private pension plans are accumulating surpluses of tens of billions of dollars, thanks to inflation. According to Bulow, inflation raises the interest rates earned by pension funds, but does not raise the pensions of most retired workers. As a result, "Workers have lost out to both firms and the Pension Benefit Guaranty Corporation." Most private pensions are set in dollar terms at the time of retirement and do not rise with inflation after that time, in contrast to social security benefits. Bulow finds that, because of the enormous expense involved, it is unlikely that private pensions will be indexed to inflation in the future. Even indexing for 4 or 5% inflation, far below current rates, "could easily double the value of a plan's vested benefits." To finance indexing of benefits, either current workers would have to accept a large reduction in wages or retirees would have to settle for much smaller initial pensions.

Dennis Carlton's paper, "The Disruptive Effect of Inflation on the Organization of Markets," asks what has happened to the organization and efficiency of individual markets in the United States under the transition to rapid inflation over the past two decades. Carlton suggests that inflation has pushed markets toward uniform products traded in highly organized markets and away from custom products. He shows that businesses relied heavily on unchanging prices for individual products in the bygone era of a stable dollar. In today's economy, all prices must be revised frequently. Customers must spend more effort in gathering information about prices. Carlton pointed to the explosion in the number and level of activity of organized commodity markets in the years since inflation became a serious problem. The number of contracts traded in the Chicago Mercantile Exchange rose by a factor of nearly 20 between 1955 and 1978, according to Carlton. He concludes that the "disruption of transaction, consumption, and production patterns . . . helps explain the hostility the public justly holds towards inflation."

Martin Feldstein's "Inflation, Capital Taxation, and Monetary Policy" points out the adverse effects on the United States economy of the interaction between inflation and tax rules. Because accounting definitions embodied in tax laws do not measure income flows appropriately under inflation, the effective tax rate on the earnings of capital has risen dramatically over the past decade. Feldstein gives the example of an individual in the 30% marginal tax bracket who earned 12% interest in 1979. After taxes, the apparent earnings are 8.4%, but after adjusting for the diminished value of the dollar, the real after-tax earnings are minus 4.6%. Feldstein observes, "The small saver was thus penalized rather than rewarded for attempting to save."

Feldstein notes the decline in the fraction of total national income devoted to net investment in nonresidential capital and blames it in large part on the increases in effective tax rates on capital brought about by inflation. He also observes that high nominal interest rates associated with inflation may have confused monetary policymakers into thinking that policy was contractionary when in fact it was quite inflationary.

Stanley Fischer's "Adapting to Inflation in the United States Economy" shows that the past decade has seen the United States economy undergo a variety of adjustments to high and variable inflation. The major adjustments are in the financial sector, particularly in mortgage financing. New mortgage instruments have been introduced, particularly in California: the graduated payment mortgage (GPM), the variable rate mortgage (VRM), and the rollover mortgage. Half the FHA mortgage applications in California in 1979 were for GPMs. The secondary market for mortgages is now well established as a major source of funds for the mortgage-lending institutions. Money market certificates and other new liabilities have substantially reduced the probability of future episodes of disintermediation.

The Depositary Institutions Deregulation and Monetary Control Act of 1980 will eliminate interest ceilings by 1986 and overrides state usury statutes. Corporations have shifted to debt from equity financing and have shortened the maturity of their outstanding debt. There is some indexing of life insurance contracts but very little indexing of private pensions. There has been increasing indexation of labor contracts, but cost of living clauses cover only a small part of the labor force. The federal government has made few adjustments to inflation aside from indexation of social security benefits and some other transfer payments. In particular, inflation substantially affects the taxation of capital.

Complete indexation would make the economy virtually impervious to inflations caused purely by expansion of the money supply and would make the inflation rate fall more rapidly in response to disinflationary policy (as well as rise more rapidly in response to inflationary policy). But an economy that is only partially indexed, as is the United States economy, may be more seriously affected by inflation than one that is not indexed at all. In a partially indexed economy, the burden of adjustment to inflation is spread more unevenly than in a nonindexed economy, according to Fischer's analysis.

Jacob A. Frenkel's "United States Inflation and the Dollar" asks whether a return to a fixed exchange rate would eliminate the wild swings in the international value of the dollar that have contributed to inflation since 1973. In Frenkel's view, the foreign exchange market is like the stock market, responding instantly to all types of new information, including changing expectations about United States policy and the policies of other affluent nations. Restoration of the purchasing power of the dollar at home would strengthen the external value of the dollar and limit its fluctuations. Moreover, says Frenkel, a floating exchange rate would help insulate the United States from misguided foreign monetary policies.

Douglas A. Hibbs, Jr., in his "Public Concern about Inflation and Unemployment in the United States: Trends, Correlates, and Political Implications" points out that not since the Great Depression of the 1930s and the immediate post-World War II reconversion scare has the state of the economy occupied such a salient place on the public agenda. In every year since the United States withdrawal from Vietnam more than 70% of the American public had identified inflation or unemployment as "the most important problem facing the country today."

Hibbs's paper analyzes opinion poll data on the public's relative concern about inflation and unemployment over the period from 1970 to 1980. He investigates trends and fluctuations in public concern about these problems in the light of recent macroeconomic events. The analysis shows that public opinion responds in a systematic way to macroeconomic developments: high and rising rates of inflation cause upward movements in the public's concern about inflation relative to unemployment, and rising unemployment rates cause upward movements in the public's concern about unemployment relative to inflation. The opinion data indicate that when unemployment is stable, a solid majority of the public typically is more concerned about inflation than unemployment *if* inflation is running higher than 5%.

Hibbs also discusses the political implications of public reactions to inflation and unemployment. His evidence shows that macroeconomic performance systematically affects mass political support for the President. Finally, according to Hibbs, opinion data show that although the public agrees with the economics profession's diagnosis of the proximate sources of inflation (excessive monetary growth rates stemming in part from high deficits), the public's preferred policy response is wage and price controls, even if this means real wage sacrifices.

Jeremy I. Bulow's joint paper with John B. Shoven, "Inflation, Corporate Profits, and the Rate of Return Capital," looks at the distorting effect of inflation on measured profits. A common view holds that the accounting procedures of corporations overstate true profits under inflation. Not so, say Bulow and Shoven. True, inflation enlarges reported profits by depressing depreciation deductions below their proper economic level, but there is an equally important bias from inflation in the opposite direction. When prices are rising, corporations repay their debts in dollars of reduced value, and this reduction adds to their true economic profits. According to Bulow and Shoven, corporate profits reported by the government for the years since 1973 "have understated our real current cost income figures by a total of about $160 billion."

Alan S. Blinder's "The Anatomy of Double-Digit Inflation in the 1970s" finds that the episodes of double-digit inflation in 1974 and 1979–80 have much in common: both were precipitated by food and energy shocks, and both were accompanied by substantial changes in relative prices. The dramatic acceleration of inflation between 1972 and 1974 can be traced mainly to three shocks—rising food prices, rising energy prices, and the end of the Nixon wage-price controls program—each of which required rapid adjustments of some relative prices. The equally dramatic deceleration of inflation between 1974 and 1976 can be traced to the simple fact that the three factors just named were not repeated. In other words, double-digit inflation went away by itself.

Blinder finds that the state of demand had little to do with either the acceleration or the deceleration of inflation between 1972 and 1976. This is not to say that aggregate demand management was irrelevant to inflation, but only that its effects were minor compared to the supply shocks. While the rate of inflation as measured in the CPI rose about nine percentage points between 1977 and early 1980, the baseline or underlying rate may have risen by as little as three percentage points. The rest of the inflationary acceleration came from special factors. The initial impetus for accelerating inflation in 1978 came mainly from the food sector, with some help from mortgage interest rates. The further acceleration into the double-digit range in 1979 mainly reflected soaring energy prices and, once again, rising mortgage rates. Finally, mortgage interest carried the ball almost by itself in early 1980.

Blinder emphasizes that the 1970s really were different from the 1950s and 1960s. Energy shocks are quite clearly a product of the post–OPEC world. Food shocks are not new, but we somehow managed to get away without them in the 1950s and 1960s. The role of special factors in the recent burst of inflation suggests that inflation will spend itself naturally. It thus seems reasonable to expect a substantial slowing of inflation even without contractionary monetary and fiscal policies.

The volume as a whole is not an encyclopedia on inflation. We found we had very little to say, for example, on one of the central aspects of inflation in the longer run, the behavior of the money wage rate. Instead, we offer twelve essays on aspects of the problem we do feel we understand.

# 1     Why Stopping Inflation May Be Costly: Evidence from Fourteen Historical Episodes

Robert J. Gordon

Politicians looking forward to the next election, upon learning from pollsters that the public believes inflation to be the nation's most important economic problem, should be observed without exception to espouse and implement measures to eliminate inflation. Since inflation is defined as growth in the dollar (or "nominal") value of aggregate spending that exceeds the growth of real output, those measures would appear to involve achieving slower growth of nominal expenditures through budget cuts, tax increases, and tight monetary policy. If restrictive demand management policy were like a headache remedy that delivered an instant cure with no side effects, it would elicit little controversy and would be observed to be always and everywhere in place in any nation experiencing even a small amount of inflation. But the failure of most industrial nations consistently to pursue a restrictive policy suggests that a better analogy would be a powerful anticancer drug that has long-lasting and painful side effects.

Any reduction in the growth of nominal spending, no matter how it is achieved, must by definition be divided between a decline in the rate of inflation and a decline in the growth of real output. The success of restrictive demand policies depends largely on the speed with which inflation responds to a sustained reduction in nominal spending growth. An instant and complete response means that real output is insulated from the policies. But a slow and partial response means that real output must take up the slack, with a resulting drop in production, accompanying layoffs and unemployment, and bankruptcies of some individuals and firms. These painful side effects dampen the enthusiasm of politicians for

Robert J. Gordon is with the National Bureau of Economic Research and the Department of Economics, Northwestern University.

This research has been supported by the National Science Foundation and the John Simon Guggenheim Memorial Foundation. George Kahn assisted with the data.

restrictive policies and lessen the chances that they will actually be implemented. Often the temptation has been to avoid a painful cure for the basic causes of the inflation disease and instead to dull its pain with remedies, including financial reforms and indexation, that are aimed at reducing its costs rather than reducing its magnitude.

How does inflation respond to nominal spending changes? Pessimists assert that the first-year degree of responsiveness is only 10%; a deceleration of nominal spending growth from 10 to 0% would initially cause a 1% deceleration of inflation and a 9% drop in the growth of real output (Okun 1978). It is easy for proponents of this "1-to-9 split" to show that a serious attempt to stop inflation with restrictive demand management policy could involve more than $1 trillion in lost output. In contrast some argue that inflation can be stopped at a much lower cost. Fellner (1979) claims that inflation will respond more promptly to a "credible" (i.e. consistent and sustained) demand restriction than to the inconsistent and short-lived restrictions observed in historical data. Sargent (chapter 2 of this volume) points to the abrupt halt of four hyperinflations as evidence that drastic changes in policy can achieve instant results.

This paper assembles a wide variety of historical evidence on the speed and extent of response of the inflation rate to temporary and permanent changes in the growth rate of nominal spending. Rather than weaving a web of econometric equations to explain the data (a task performed elsewhere), we limit ourselves to a pictorial history that illustrates the highly divergent responses of inflation in six United States episodes since 1916, and in eight countries since the mid-1960s (West Germany, Switzerland, France, Japan, the United States, Italy, Brazil, and Israel). The primary purpose of the paper is to present the data in a novel graphical format in order to inform public discussion; a secondary purpose is to determine major differences among the fourteen examples that may help to identify those most relevant to the likely behavior of the United States in the 1980s.

## 1.1    Identities Linking Nominal Demand, Inflation, and Output

A few simple identities help to clarify the necessary relationship between price adjustment and the evolution of real output. Throughout we take the exogenous nominal aggregate demand variable to be nominal GNP. By definition the log of nominal GNP ($Y$) must be divided between the log of the GNP deflator ($P$) and the log of real GNP ($Q$):

(1)    $$Y \equiv P + Q.$$

Taking the derivative of (1) with respect to time and using the notation that percentage changes per unit of time are designated by lowercase letters, we have

(2) $\qquad y \equiv p + q,$

which states that any change in nominal GNP must be divided between a change in the aggregate price level and a change in real GNP. Next we subtract from both sides of equation (2) the trend, or "natural," growth rate of real GNP $(q^*)$ and use a "hat" to designate variables defined as the net of that trend growth rate of real output:

(3) $\qquad y - q^* \equiv p + (q - q^*);$
$\qquad\qquad \hat{y} \equiv p + \hat{q}.$

Thus any excess of nominal GNP growth over the trend growth of real output $(\hat{y})$, which we call "adjusted" nominal GNP growth, must be accompanied by some combination of inflation $(p)$ and a deviation of real output from trend $(\hat{q})$. Since the latter must be zero in the long run, any permanent acceleration or deceleration of adjusted nominal GNP growth must be accompanied by exactly the same acceleration or deceleration of inflation (we neglect any feedback from output or price fluctuations to the natural growth rate of output). To the extent that the long-run growth rate of the money supply is the basic determinant of the long-run behavior of nominal GNP, and both money and nominal GNP are exogenous, equation (3) is a way of restating the claim that *in the long run* "inflation is always and everywhere a monetary phenomenon" (Friedman 1963).

Over shorter business-cycle frequencies, equation (3) states that fluctuations in nominal GNP growth must be divided between price and output fluctuations. Real GNP can be stable only if price changes exactly mimic the proportional change in nominal GNP, and any tendency for prices to adjust only partially to nominal GNP cycles *must* imply procyclical fluctuations in real GNP. For instance, if the rate of change of prices over the business cycle is always equal to some constant fraction $(\alpha)$ of the adjusted nominal GNP movement, then deviations of real GNP from trend must soak up the remaining fraction $(1 - \alpha)$:

(4) $\qquad p = \alpha\hat{y},$
$\qquad\quad \hat{q} \equiv \hat{y} - p = (1 - \alpha)\hat{y}.$

Can one proceed from the identity expressed in (4) to the significant proposition that an economy with relatively sticky prices (a small $\alpha$) must exhibit correspondingly larger fluctuations in real output? That would follow, other things being equal, except insofar as the responsiveness of prices themselves influenced the amplitude of fluctuations in nominal GNP.

## 1.2   A Graphical Representation of Alternative Adjustment Paths

Because the top line of equation (4) is a relation between only two variables, the inflation rate $(p)$ and adjusted nominal GNP growth $(\hat{y})$, it can be displayed on a simple diagram that plots $p$ on the vertical axis and $\hat{y}$ on the horizontal. If the price adjustment coefficient ($\alpha$) were unity, then inflation would respond instantly and completely to changes in the growth of aggregate spending, and the locus of inflation rates accompanying different rates of demand growth would appear to lie along a 45 degree line, as in figure 1.1a. Because inflation would absorb all of the variation in nominal demand, there would be no divergence of real output from its trend growth path ($\hat{q} = 0$). In contrast figure 1.1b plots a completely unresponsive inflation rate that remains at zero whether adjusted demand growth is $+ 5$, $- 5$, or 0%. Because the adjustment coefficient ($\alpha$) is zero, equation (4) states that all variations in nominal demand growth are completely absorbed in deviations of real GNP from trend. The vertical distance between the 45 degree line and the horizontal line in figure 1.1b shows changes in detrended output growth. For instance, a 5% growth rate of adjusted nominal GNP would be reflected in 5% growth of

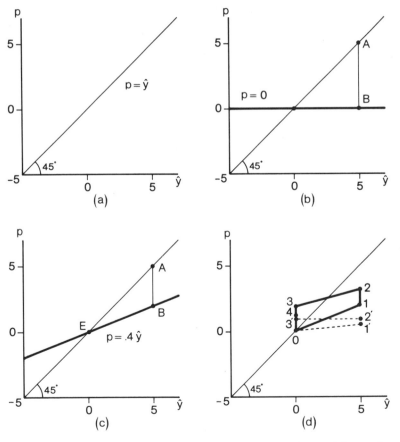

**Fig. 1.1**    Hypothetical relations between inflation and demand growth.

real output in excess of its trend, as represented by the line segment marked $AB$.

An intermediate case depicted in figure 1.1c exhibits partial price adjustment, with the coefficient $\alpha$ equal to 0.4 rather than unity or zero. From an initial situation at point $E$ with both inflation and adjusted nominal demand growth equal to 0%, a temporary acceleration of demand growth to 5% would raise inflation to 2% at point $B$, with the remaining 3% absorbed by real output growth in excess of trend (this is the distance $AB$). Similarly, negative demand growth would be split between negative inflation (an actual drop in the price level) and a decline in real output relative to trend.

So far we have examined only *instantaneous* responses to inflation—with a complete response in figure 1.1a, no response in figure 1.1b, and a partial response in figure 1.1c. More realistic is an adjustment that is both partial and gradual, with the response in the initial period augmented by a further reaction in the second and subsequent periods if demand growth remains above its initial level. A simple dynamic adjustment process, that allows inflation fully to absorb all of nominal demand growth in the long run, can be written

$$(5) \qquad p_t = \alpha \hat{y}_t + (1 - \alpha)p_{t-1},$$

where the subscripts distinguish variables measured in the current period ($t$) from those applying in the last period ($t - 1$). Equation (5) states that current inflation is a weighted average of this period's adjusted nominal demand growth and last period's inflation rate, with weights adding up to unity. In one extreme case when $\alpha = 1$, inflation responds completely to current demand growth, past inflation is irrelevant, and the inflation-demand relation lies along the 45 degree line, as in figure 1.1a. In the opposite extreme case when $\alpha = 0$, inflation stays at the same rate forever and demand growth is irrelevant, as in figure 1.1b. Between the extremes inflation exhibits a gradual and delayed adjustment to changes in demand. If, for instance, $\alpha = 0.4$ and demand growth temporarily were to increase from 0 to 5% for two periods and then return to zero, we would have the situation shown in table 1.1.

This gradual adjustment path is plotted as the solid line in figure 1.1d, and the numbers on the solid line indicate the economy's location in each of the first four time periods. The column in table 1.1 labeled $\hat{q}_t$ shows the detrended growth rate of real output, i.e. adjusted nominal demand growth minus inflation, and $\hat{Q}_t$ shows the cumulative departure of real output from its trend ($\hat{Q}_t$ is the log of a ratio and thus equals zero when output is on its trend). The temporary acceleration of nominal GNP growth causes above-normal output growth, followed by below-normal output growth, that eventually returns the level of output to its trend. Now compare the "box" formed by the solid line in figure 1.1d with an

Table 1.1          Response of Inflation to a Temporary
                   Acceleration in Nominal Demand Growth

| Time Period | $\hat{y}_t$ | $p_t$ | $\hat{q}_t$ | $\hat{Q}_t$ |
|---|---|---|---|---|
| 0 | 0.0 | 0.0 | 0.0 | 0.0 |
| 1 | 5.0 | 2.0 | 3.0 | 3.0 |
| 2 | 5.0 | 3.2 | 1.8 | 4.8 |
| 3 | 0.0 | 1.9 | −1.9 | 2.9 |
| 4 | 0.0 | 1.2 | −1.2 | 1.7 |
| . | ... | ... | ... | ... |
| . | ... | ... | ... | ... |
| ∞ | 0.0 | 0.0 | 0.0 | 0.0 |

alternative box formed by the dotted lines that represent the adjustment to the same nominal demand disturbance when $\alpha$ is set at 0.1 instead of 0.4. The larger is $\alpha$ and thus the more complete is the short-run response of inflation, the steeper are the top and bottom sides of the box.

An important failing of the adjustment equation (5) is that it allows output to depart permanently from trend when there is a permanent acceleration or deceleration in demand growth. Consider a case in which adjusted nominal GNP growth accelerates permanently from 0 to 5%, roughly what occurred in the United States in the 1960s. At first, according to (5), inflation will accelerate by less than 5% , but eventually will reach a 5% rate. This means that initially output grows faster than its trend, eventually reaching its trend, but never falls below trend. Thus the *level* of output remains permanently above trend by an amount which equals 7.5% in this example when $\alpha = 0.4$. In short, equation (5) violates the "natural rate hypothesis" that the level of real output is independent in the long run of the rate of growth of nominal demand.

A more realistic adjustment equation would allow inflation to respond not only to the rate of growth of nominal demand but also to last period's deviation of real output from trend:

(6)          $p_t = \alpha\hat{y}_t + \beta\hat{Q}_{t-1} + (1 - \alpha)p_{t-1}.$

The adjustment of inflation to a permanent increase in the rate of nominal demand growth includes a temporary period of overshooting during which inflation exceeds its long-run value and real output growth falls below its trend, thus eliminating the initial bulge in the level of output.

## 1.3    Stopping Inflation in Pictures

Since the main interest of United States policymakers is in stopping an ongoing inflation of about 10%, let us examine alternative paths of adjustment of inflation to a permanent drop in adjusted nominal demand growth from 10 to 0%. If the adjustment parameter α were equal to unity, inflation would respond instantly and completely, and there would be no deviation of output from trend. Any value of α below unity, however, causes output to fall temporarily below trend, and causes the negative detrended level of output to pull down inflation by an amount which depends on the β coefficient in equation (6).

Two basic approaches have been suggested to stop inflation through restrictive demand management policy. The first, sometimes called the "big bang" or "cold turkey" technique, would instantly drop adjusted nominal demand growth to zero, the rate compatible with stable prices in the long run. Such an approach would eventually bring the inflation rate to zero, according to equation (6), but would impose a cost in lost output if the adjustment coefficient (α) were less than unity. Let us imagine that the response of inflation to an output gap (β) is 0.2 and the length of a time period is a year, so that a 5% shortfall of output below trend would cause a one percentage point slowdown in the inflation rate each year. For any given value of this β coefficient, the speed of the economy's adjustment to the "cold turkey" remedy would then depend on the value of α. Table 1.2 shows for two sample values of α (0.4 and 0.1) the enormous difference in the economy's adjustment path when adjusted demand growth is held at zero from the first year onward.

The "cold turkey" policy cures inflation quickly in both cases, in the third and fourth years, respectively. But the output cost is severe, with a maximum drop of the detrended output level of 8.2 and 16.7%, respectively, from the initial period. And worse yet, the apparently stable policy of maintaining nominal demand growth at zero creates enormous instability in the economy, with continuing cycles in inflation and real output. When α = 0.4 these cycles damp out after a decade, but when α = 0.1 the inflation rate overshoots to a value of *minus* 7 percent in year 7, and the enormous shortfall of inflation below nominal demand growth propels

**Table 1.2**    **Economy's Adjustment Path in Response to "Cold Turkey" Nominal Demand Policy**

|  | α = 0.4 | | | α = 0.1 | | |
|---|---|---|---|---|---|---|
|  | Year | $p_t$ | $\hat{Q}_t$ | Year | $p_t$ | $\hat{Q}_t$ |
| First period | 1 | 6.0 | −6.0 | 1 | 9.0 | −9.0 |
| Period of minimum output ratio | 3 | −0.2 | −8.2 | 4 | −1.2 | −16.7 |
| Period of maximum overshooting of $p_t$ | 5 | −2.3 | −4.1 | 7 | −7.0 | 1.1 |
| Period of maximum overshooting of $\hat{Q}_t$ | 10 | −0.0 | 1.4 | 10 | −1.4 | 12.6 |

real output into an enormous boom that pushes it from 16.7% below trend in year 4 to 12.6% below trend in year 10, comparable to the 1939–43 explosion of real output in the United States.

The smaller the α adjustment coefficient, the greater the degree of instability created by a "cold turkey" policy, and hence the less likely that any such policy will actually be implemented. A less drastic alternative would be a "gradualist" policy that reduces the rate of nominal demand growth by, say, two percentage points a year, from an initial 10% to 0% in year 5. As shown in figure 1.2 (which continues to assume that β = 0.2), the relatively high α adjustment coefficient of 0.4 in the upper frame makes the inflation rate "cling" relatively closely to the 45 degree line and minimizes the output cost of stopping inflation. The maximum output shortfall below trend in the top frame is 6.7% in year 5, less than with the "cold turkey" policy; the cost of this advantage is a two-year delay in achieving zero inflation. Along the dotted line in the bottom frame, where α = 0.1, the maximum output loss reaches − 14.2%, the inflation rate overshoots to − 5.6% in year 9, and the output ratio overshoots to + 10% in year 12.

### 1.4    The Scissors of Demand and Supply

Economists are used to treating every economic relationship as involving a trade-off between benefits and costs. From the point of view of policymakers, however, figures 1.1 and 1.2 illustrate that the phenomenon of gradual inflation adjustment (a small α) involves only costs, no benefits. Even for society as a whole, the benefits are obscure. Some

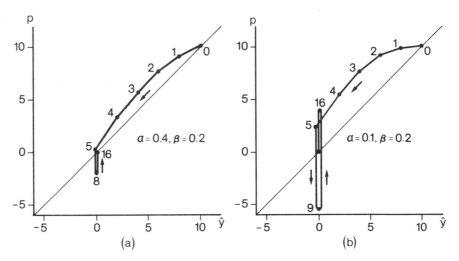

**Fig. 1.2**          Alternative responses to gradualist disinflationary policy.

analysts trace gradual price adjustment in the United States to three-year staggered union wage contracts, in which case the benefits might appear to be a reduction in the costs of negotiations and strikes, but there is ample evidence that the phenomenon long antedates modern labor contracting institutions (Gordon 1981*a*).

The historical examples presented in the next sections suggest that prices exhibit a speed of adjustment that varies over time and across countries. In some examples it is possible to discern patterns that display striking similarities to the simple examples displayed in figures 1.1 and 1.2. But other patterns appear as well. In the 1970s the inflation rate in the United States and some other countries exhibited variations that cannot be attributed solely to prior changes in the rate of demand growth. Imagine a situation in which an increase in the relative price of oil temporarily boosts the inflation rate while policymakers adopt a "neutral" policy stance, maintaining a constant rate of nominal GNP growth. The plot of the inflation-demand relation in our diagram would exhibit a vertical movement, first north and then south. Similarly, the imposition of price controls together with a neutral demand policy would cause a vertical movement to the south, and then back to the north if prices rebounded after controls were abandoned.

Other patterns are possible as well. Monetary accommodation in response to a supply shock would lead to an initial movement to the northeast, moving along the 45 degree line itself in an economy like Israel with very rapid price adjustment. The opposite of accommodation, an extinguishing monetary policy, would lead to a northwest movement following an oil shock, as in the United States in 1973–74, and a southeast movement following the imposition of price controls, as in the United States in 1971–72. Graphs for the 1970s in the United States are strikingly different in appearance from those in earlier decades and in the hypothetical cases of figures 1.1 and 1.2, providing vivid evidence that the inflation experienced by the United States during the past decade must be understood as resulting from an interaction of supply and demand shocks, not as a delayed adjustment to demand shocks alone.

## 1.5    Examples from United States History

There are no examples in United States history before the 1950s of a conscious attempt by policymakers to stop an ongoing inflation. Nevertheless earlier episodes are of interest, since they reveal evidence of the same basic obstacle facing current United States policymakers—the phenomenon of gradual price adjustment. For each period since 1916 during which there was important variability of the inflation rate, we display graphs arranged like figures 1.1 and 1.2. All the plotted figures for the United States are four-quarter moving averages of quarterly data; e.g.

the first observation plotted in figure 1.3 represents a rate of growth for the GNP deflator of 6.7% and for adjusted nominal GNP of 14.0%, respectively, in the four quarters ending in the first quarter of 1916, "1916:1" (these pre-1947 quarterly data are developed and analyzed in Gordon 1981*b*, and Gordon and Wilcox 1981; all figures use as the output trend the "natural output" series from Gordon 1981*c*, appendix B).

1. *A unique example of rapid price adjustment, 1916–24.* The plot of the 1916–24 experience in figure 1.3 combines several different subepisodes, but the major impression is of extremely flexible prices. The plotted four-quarter rates of inflation varied from + 24.3 to − 21.7%, an enormous range, and the economy in both the peak and trough quarters for inflation adhered quite closely to the 45 degree line. In just a year and a half, between 1920:1 and 1921:3, the four-quarter inflation rate fell from + 20 to − 26% and real output fell only 8% relative to trend, so that about 85% of the drop in nominal GNP was absorbed by lower prices and only the remaining 15% by lower real output. Another period with very

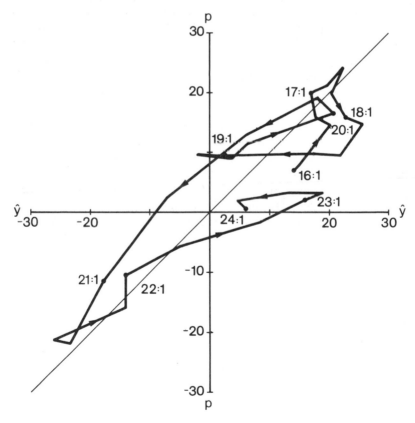

**Fig. 1.3**             United States, 1916–24.

flexible prices was between 1916:1 and 1917:3, when the path traced by the observations in figure 1.3 is actually *steeper* than a 45 degree line.

Between the 1916–17 increase in inflation and the 1920–21 collapse in prices, there was an intermediate period that reflects government intervention in the price-setting process. Beginning in early 1918 partial price controls were implemented (Rockoff 1980), and this pushed the adjustment path in a vertical downward direction. Then in 1919 as the rate of nominal demand growth fell rapidly, the inflation rate remained almost constant, probably reflecting a partial postcontrols "rebound" effect, as occurred again in 1946 and 1974.

Starting in early 1922, the price adjustment path becomes visibly flatter. between 1922:1 and 1923:2 inflation absorbed only 40% of changes in nominal demand, against expressed as four-quarter changes, and over the following three quarters only 20%. As we shall see, these flat partial adjustment paths have been typical of United States experience since 1922 (and also before 1916—see Gordon 1981*b*). The 1916–22 experience of rapid price adjustment seems to be a historical aberration, reflecting the ability of economic agents to change their price-setting practices when they are universally aware of a special event (wartime government purchases and deficit spending) that has a common effect on costs and prices. The 1920–21 decline in price presumably reflects a widespread belief that the wartime price "bubble" had ended as occurred after the War of 1812 and the Civil War. Price behavior returned to its usual gradual adjustment path after 1922, reflecting a general belief that normal peacetime conditions had returned and that local industry-specific disturbances to costs and prices were now large relative to any common aggregate disturbance.

2. *The Great Depression, 1929–37.* During the dramatic years that followed 1929, the four-quarter rate of adjusted nominal GNP growth was even more variable than during World War I and ranged from − 36% in 1932:2 to + 26% in 1934:1. Yet the response of inflation was much more like the peacetime expansion of 1922–23 than the World War I experience. The four quarters of maximum nominal spending decline (ending in 1932:2) were accompanied by a "price absorption" amounting to only 33%, with 67% absorbed by real output. Over the entire period of fourteen quarters between the economy's 1929:3 peak and 1933:1 trough, prices absorbed only 38% of the nominal spending decrease. The plot in figure 1.4 thus appears to resemble the hypothetical cases drawn in figure 1.1*c* and 1.1*d*, which assume an absorption of 40%.

Just as the inflation rate displayed vertical jumps in 1918 when price controls were introduced, so the inflation rate jumped in the last half of 1933 as a consequence of the National Recovery Act. The southeast movement of the plotted line between mid-1934 and late 1935 can be interpreted as the gradual elimination of the initial impact of the NRA,

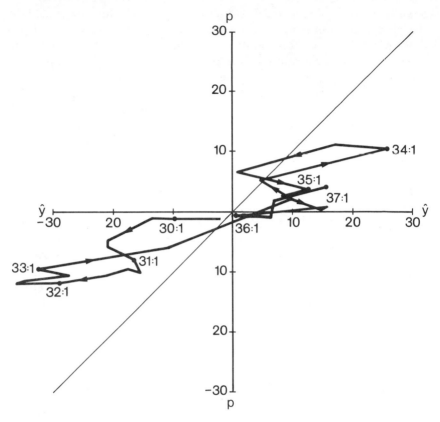

**Fig. 1.4**          United States, 1929–37.

which was declared unconstitutional in mid-1935. Price adjustment continued to be gradual after the "price blip" connected with the NRA had faded away; adjusted nominal GNP growth in the four quarters ending in 1937:1 of 15.4% was reflected in an inflation rate of only 4.1%.

3. *World War II and its aftermath, 1940–49.* During the early period of accelerated United States war production, between early 1940 and early 1941, there was virtually no response of inflation to the spending boom, as illustrated in figure 1.5. In fact it is interesting to compare, as is done in table 1.3 two four-quarter periods in World Wars I and II having virtually identical rates of adjusted nominal GNP growth. The small response of inflation in late 1940 and early 1941 may provide evidence supporting an adjustment mechanism like equation (6) above, in which both the rate of nominal GNP growth and the level of the output gap have independent effects on the inflation rate. In the subsequent year ending in 1942:1, as a rapid expansion in output quickly eliminated the output gap, inflation surged ahead, absorbing 75% of adjusted nominal spending growth.

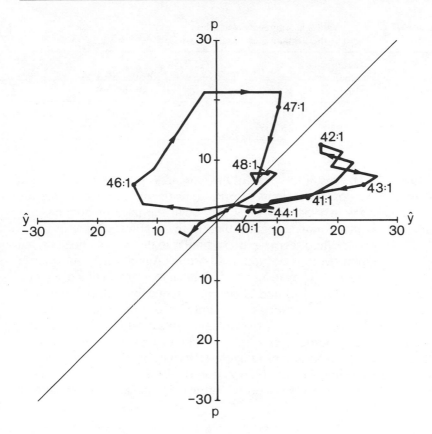

**Fig. 1.5**          United States, 1940–49.

After 1942:1 the economy was pushed in a southeastern direction in figure 1.5, reflecting the operation of stringent wartime price controls. Inflation was held below 5% in each four-quarter period between 1943:2 and 1945:4. Then prices exploded when the wartime controls were ended, rising at an annual rate of 52% in a single quarter, 1946:3. The 1946–47 price bulge was a much more extreme episode than 1919 and early 1920, reflecting the greater impact of price controls during World War II. But perhaps a more interesting difference between the two postwar periods lies in the more modest extent of the 1949 recession in nominal spending growth as compared to 1920–21, and in the relatively small 33% absorption of spending decline by price decline in the four quarters ending in 1949:4.

4. *The "flat fifties," 1953–59.* We skip the Korean War period, with its speculative boom in late 1950 and its amazingly low inflation rates in 1951–53 (the latter representing some combination of price-control effects and the end of the speculative commodity bubble). The next plot

Table 1.3               Values of Aggregate Variables
                        at the Beginning of Two Wartime Episodes

| | Four Quarters Ending | $\hat{y}_t$ | $p_t$ | $\hat{q}_t$ | $\hat{Q}_t$ at Start of Interval |
|---|---|---|---|---|---|
| | 1916:2 | 14.8 | 7.7 | 7.1 | −9.0 |
| | 1941:1 | 15.2 | 3.9 | 11.3 | −22.9 |

(figure 1.6a) begins at the peak of the Korean War boom in 1953:2 and illustrates the low coefficients of price adjustment observed during the two recessions in 1954 and 1958. Although the pace of nominal GNP growth was much more irregular than in the simple example of figure 1.1d, it is possible to discern a pattern similar to the dotted "box" in that earlier diagram, with its flat top and bottom. Again using four-quarter changes, there was a drop in adjusted nominal GNP growth of 9.6 percentage points between 1953:2 and 1954:2, but a reduction in the inflation rate of only 0.7 points (an "absorption" of only 7%). In the next five quarters there was an increase of 11.7 percentage points in adjusted nominal GNP growth but a response in the inflation rate of only 1.1 points. Then a lagged adjustment began, as in figure 1.1d, pushing the economy above the 45 degree line in late 1956 and early 1957. In the five quarters following 1957:1, there was a drop in adjusted nominal GNP growth of 6.6

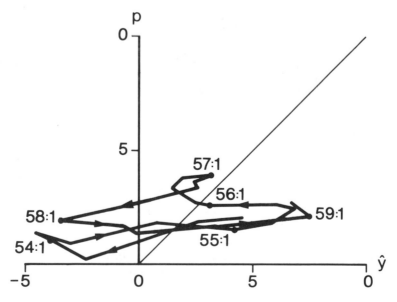

Fig. 1.6              (a) United States, 1953–59. (b) United States, 1959–71. (c) United States, 1971–80.

percentage points, and in inflation of 2.1 points, for an absorption ratio of 32%, closer to the experience of 1923 and the 1930s than to 1953–55. Finally, there was little change in the four-quarter inflation rate between early 1958 and early 1959, perhaps reflecting the offsetting impacts of positive adjusted nominal demand growth and a negative output gap.

5. *The classic period of gradual adjustment and overshooting, 1959–71.* The bulk of the existing econometric evidence on price adjustment in the

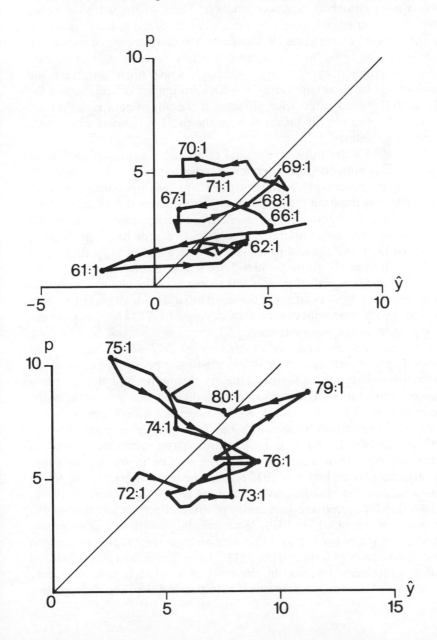

postwar United States is based on a statistical analysis of the period between 1953 and the present. The overwhelming consensus is that inflation adjusts very slowly to nominal demand shocks. It is easy from our diagrams to see that this pessimistic message is not an artifact of statistical technique but rather is embedded in the data, particularly for the interval between 1953 and 1971. Of the 11.3 percentage point swing in nominal GNP growth between 1959:2 and 1961:1, only 1.8 percentage points were absorbed in slower inflation. Then, of the 9.1 point swing from 1961:1 to 1965:4, only 1.9 points were absorbed in faster inflation. In the period between late 1962 and late 1965 any impact of the output gap in slowing inflation was completely offset by the impact of positive adjusted nominal GNP growth. Although some might interpret the 1963–65 evidence as supporting a downward impact on inflation of the Kennedy-Johnson wage-price guidelines, the adjustment paths do not seem to be appreciably different from the pre-1963 period when there were no guidelines.

After 1965:4 the inflation-demand relationship drifts upward in response to continued positive rates of adjusted nominal GNP growth, reflecting the process of lagged adjustment implied by equation (6). After early 1969 the inflation rate "overshot," rising above the 45 degree line, just as the adjustment process in the hypothetical cases of figure 1.2 carried the economy temporarily below the 45 degree line. The puzzling aspect of 1970–71 is the failure of the recession, which brought the level of real output from 4% above trend to 2.5% below trend, to have any effect at all in dampening inflation. It was the despair of the Nixon administration's economy policymakers at the rapid inflation rate of early 1971 that caused the startling policy reversal of 15 August 1971, when comprehensive price controls were introduced.

6. *Untangling demand and supply shocks, 1971–80.* Unlike the previous diagrams, where a clear southwest-to-northeast alignment of the plotted points can be discerned, the graph for the past decade has a chaotic appearance. The decade can be divided into two main parts, according to the main direction of movement, with a northwest-to-southeast orientation dominating the four-quarter periods between 1971:3 and 1976:1, and a "normal" southwest-to-northeast orientation occurring from then until late 1979. The decline in the inflation rate during late 1971 and most of 1972 reflects the initial impact of the Nixon controls, and the standard interpretation of 1972–76 (Gordon 1977*a*; Blinder 1979) is that the temporary positive effect on inflation of the postcontrol "rebound" in 1974–75 was combined with two other supply shocks that temporarily raised the inflation rate: the 1972–73 increase in the relative price of food and the 1973–74 increase in the relative price of oil. A permanent increase in the *level* of a relative price may only temporarily raise the inflation rate if its impact is dampened by restrictive

nominal demand policy and if the extent of cost-of-living escalators in wage contracts is relatively minor, both of which were conditions that were satisfied in the United States 1972–76. A contrasting situation is observed below for some foreign countries, where supply shocks have permanently raised the inflation rate.

The 1977–80 episode displays a pattern that exhibits some similarity to 1967–70. The upward drift of the inflation-demand plot in 1979–80 to some extent reflects the impact of the second OPEC oil shock, but also may provide evidence that the level of real output consistent with a stable inflation rate has been exaggerated by some investigators, including the Council of Economic Advisers. If this "natural" rate of output is overstated, then the corresponding "natural" unemployment rate may have been understated. My present estimate of a natural unemployment rate of 5.6% in 1979 (1981c, appendix B) may be understated by as much as a percentage point. A resolution of this issue depends on further econometric work that disentangles supply factors in the 1979–80 acceleration of inflation from the respective roles of the rate of growth and level of demand.

## 1.6    The Speed of Adjustment in Other Countries

The speed and extent of inflation's response to changes in nominal demand growth differs markedly across countries. We shall see that, in general, the inflation-demand relation clings more closely to the 45 degree line in foreign countries than in the United States. Before this evidence can be used to make a case that the rapid conquest of inflation is possible in the United States, however, we must determine whether the conditions necessary for fast responsiveness can be imported from abroad and whether this would require major changes in United States institutions.

Although a scattering of data is available that suggests a more rapid response of European than American prices during the interwar years (Gordon and Wilcox 1981), we limit the scope of the present paper to a study of foreign data since 1965 (or 1963 in cases where inflation decelerated between 1963 and 1965). The countries selected are the five major industrial nations besides the United States (Japan, Germany, France, Italy, and the United Kingdom), one small nation that has experienced very low rates of inflation in recent years (Switzerland), and two nations that have experienced relatively high rates of inflation (Brazil and Israel).[1] Annual rather than quarterly data are plotted, and the method of detrending real output growth is extremely crude—one trend is calculated for 1960–73 and a second trend for 1973–79. To the extent that the low 1973–79 trends in some countries reflect underutilization of resources rather than a slowdown in productivity growth, our calculations tend to understate the shortfall of output below trend experienced since 1973. An important corollary is that a faster "true" output trend would shift observations that presently lie on the 45 degree line west of that line and might change our conclusion of easy painless adjustment to one of prolonged and painful adjustment.

7. *West Germany, 1965–80.* Economists in most industrial countries envy the low inflation rates experienced in West Germany in the last half of the 1970s. Although the success of restrictive monetary policy in the first few years of the flexible exchange rate era has been much discussed, an earlier episode of anti-inflationary restrictive policy in 1965–67 deserves attention as well. In a famous conference in June 1965, German trade unions and employers' associations made a tripartite "social contract" with the then-new Council of Economic Advisers that called for a coordinated slowdown in the growth of nominal wages by two percentage points by 1967, and an accompanying slowdown in the growth of government expenditure and the money supply that would be consistent with a two percentage point slowdown in inflation. As shown in figure 1.7a, the inflation target was almost precisely met; the previous "problem" rate, which was 3.0% in 1964 and 3.5% in 1965, was reduced to 1.4% in 1967. Economic historians sometimes fail to point out that there was a substantial output cost, due partly to the rejection by the government of the scenario for its own actions laid out by the council. Herbert Giersch has called the actual policy response a "Teutonic big bang." Nominal GNP growth came almost to a dead halt in 1967, and our measure of adjusted

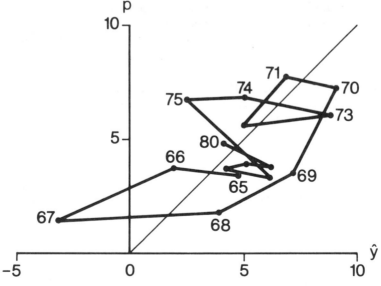

**Fig. 1.7**     (*a*) West Germany, 1965–80. (*b*) Switzerland, 1965–79. (*c*) France, 1963–80.

nominal GNP growth fell to $-3.2\%$. The economy's movement in figure 1.7a displays the same "flat" appearance as most United States episodes. The absorption of the 1965–67 deceleration of nominal GNP growth in slower inflation was just 26%, and of the 1967–69 acceleration just 20%.

The 1970 and 1971 experience can be interpreted as a lagged adjustment involving overshooting to the rapid demand growth of 1968–70 similar to that predicted by the inflation response mechanism written as

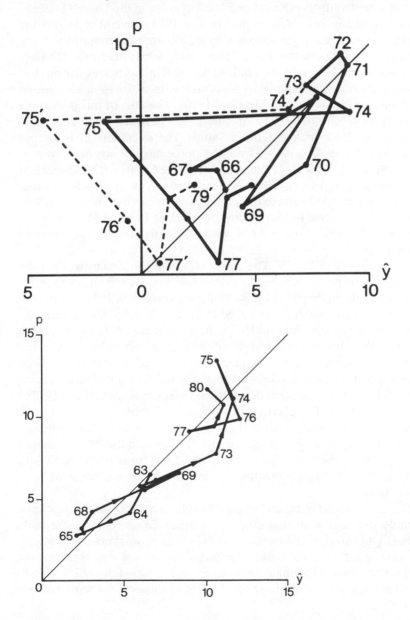

equation (6) above. While in 1972 and 1973 the economy adhered fairly closely to the 45 degree line, movements since 1973 display the north-west-to-southeast orientation that is expected when supply shocks are resisted by monetary policy. The loop that occurred in 1973 through 1976 appears to be almost identical to that in the United States but with a peak inflation rate of only 7% compared to the United States 1975 calendar-year peak of 9.3%. The difference partially reflects the absence in Germany of a postcontrols price rebound, as occurred in the United States in 1974–75, and the beneficial impact of the 1973 movement to floating exchange rates, which was followed by a 20% appreciation of the mark against the dollar between late 1972 and mid-1976. After 1976 the German experience is notable in contrast to the United States for modest growth in nominal GNP, allowing the economy to maintain itself close to the 45 degree line for most of the late 1970s. The cost of this policy was relatively slow output growth of only 2.3% between 1973 and 1979, compared to 2.8% in the United States. The deceleration in output growth as compared to 1960–73 was 2.2 percentage points in Germany, compared to 1.4 percentage points in the United States. The absence of any marked acceleration of inflation in Germany in 1979, when output growth was 4.5%, suggests that Germany may have operated beneath its "natural" level of real output throughout the late 1970s and that points in figure 1.7a for 1977–80 should be shifted slightly west of their plotted position.

8. *Switzerland, 1965–79.* The Swiss experience is similar to the German in most respects. Among the differences are the milder Swiss recession in 1967, the higher peak rates of inflation reached in 1971–72, and the much sharper recession experienced in 1975. The adjustment paths for Switzerland between 1965 and 1973 adhere quite closely to the 45 degree line, with the ratio of output to its trend ranging only between 97.1 and 101.6%. This story of stability ended after 1973 with a period of extreme monetary restriction when Swiss M1 actually fell in nominal terms during both 1974 and 1975; inflation decelerated from a peak of 9.7% in 1972 to only 0.4% in 1977. The cost of this "cold turkey" remedy was an incredible reduction in output which is disguised by the negative 1973–79 output trend used in figure 1.7b. Calculated with reference to the 1965–73 output trend of 4.0%, the ratio of output to trend fell from 100% in 1973 to 74.4% in 1979. Calculated with reference to a 3% trend, the same ratio fell to 80%.

Thus Switzerland managed to cure its inflation problem by creating a veritable depression in real output, an achievement that was feasible politically because of the freedom to export guestworkers back to Italy and other southern countries. The Swiss depression was considerably more severe than in Germany, where the output ratio fell to 87% in 1979 calculated at the 1965–73 trend and to 93% calculated at a more reasonable 3% trend. On the same basis the respective United States ratios in 1979 were 94 and 99%. The plotted points after 1974 in figure 1.7*b* may make the Swiss adjustment process appear to have been deceptively painless, because they employ a *negative* rate of trend output growth of − 0.3% per annum. If we substitute instead the German 1973–79 trend of + 2.3% per annum, the Swiss experience follows the path of the dashed line after 1973, and we observe a continued failure to achieve trend output growth despite an acceleration of inflation from zero percent in 1977 to 4% in 1979.

9. *France, 1963–79.* Although much of the French literature on inflation minimizes the causal role of changes in the growth rates of nominal money and spending, and treats inflation entirely as the result of a struggle over income shares, the inflation-demand relation displayed in figure 1.7*c* clings more tightly to the 45 degree line than in any of the episodes discussed so far. As must occur by definition when a plot of inflation and nominal demand growth moves back and forth along the 45 degree line, the growth of real output in each year remains very close to its trend. Between 1960 and 1973 the French output trend grew at 5.6% per annum, and there was no year in which the actual growth rate of output fell short of 4.3% or exceeded 6.7%.

A close correlation between nominal demand and price changes does not imply that the direction of causation necessarily runs from the former to the latter. The regular relation observed between 1963 and 1973 in figure 1.7*c* might simply reflect autonomous changes in the rate of inflation due to variations in the intensity of the battle over income shares (or, more specifically, the timing of episodes of "wage push"), followed by prompt monetary accommodation of these pressures. In the language that I have used elsewhere, a "demand for inflation" may bring forth its own "supply of inflation" (Gordon 1975).

However plausible, the price-leads-nominal demand direction of causation is not supported by the evidence. The first episode of decelerating inflation between 1963 and 1965, roughly two years in advance of the similar German experience, was the direct result of a ceiling imposed on the rate of growth of bank credit between mid-1963 and mid-1965. The growth rate of French M1 dropped from 18% in 1962 to 8% in 1964. The inflation rate followed along a year later and fell by more than half, from 6.4% in 1963 to 2.7% in 1965. In a statistical study that attempted to allocate credit for this deceleration between monetary policy and incomes policy (of which a mild version was in effect in 1964 and 1965), I found a strong role for the former and almost no impact of the latter (Gordon 1977*b*).

The best-known single episode in the history of postwar French inflation occurred in June 1968, when the Protocole de Grenelle between the government and unions allowed manufacturing wages to jump. Yet this clear episode of wage push was not backed by an accommodative monetary policy. After an initial burst of spending and inflation in 1969, as workers consumed their newly won gains, monetary policy turned quickly toward restriction (M1 actually fell in 1969). As a result, spending growth fell in 1970 and 1971 by enough to bring the economy back to the 45 degree line.

The evolution of the French economy in the 1970s exhibits interesting differences from the United States, German, and Swiss experiences. There was a modest accommodation of the first OPEC oil shock, with M1 growth jumping from 10% in 1973 to 15 and 12.5% in 1974 and 1975, respectively. Inflation doubled from 1973 to 1975, whereas inflation remained roughly at the same level in Germany and fell in Switzerland. The French authorities avoided an output bloodbath, as in Germany and Switzerland, and as a result endowed the economy with an inflation of about 10% during the 1976–80 period. The diagram of the French experience may give a misleading impression of an effortless adjustment, since the output trend used in the calculations dropped from 5.6% for 1960-73 to only 3.0% for 1973–79. The parallel upward movement of inflation and nominal demand growth between 1977 and 1979 does not suggest a major underutilization of capacity, however, if equation (6) has any relevance as a description of the French economy.

10. *Japan, 1965–80.* The Japanese export and productivity miracles have recently been joined by the Japanese inflation miracle; the GNP deflator rose only 2% in 1979 and by about the same amount in 1980. The plot of Japanese data in figure 1.8a illustrates a continual tilting of the inflation-demand relation, from a virtually horizontal slope in the expansion of nominal GNP growth between 1965 and 1970, to a slight upward tilt in the cycle between 1970 and 1972, to a 45 degree relation since then. Previous analyses of Japanese monetary policy in the fixed-exchange-rate era support an interpretation of an activist policy that promptly reduced the growth of the money supply in response to accelerations in output growth and deteriorations in the balance of payments. There was almost no response of the inflation rate to marked drops in nominal GNP growth in 1965 and again in 1971, and increases in the GNP deflator remained within the narrow range of 4.4 to 5.5% in every year between 1963 and 1972, with the single exception of 1970.

Japanese inflation broke out of its stable mold only once in the last two decades, when a 25% wage increase was granted in the 1974 spring wage offensive (Sachs 1979). While inflation ballooned in 1975, there was no monetary accommodation of the combined wage-oil shock. M1 growth dropped from 30% in 1970 to 11% in both 1974 and 1975. As in the case of Germany and Switzerland, the introduction of flexible exchange rates in 1973 allowed the Japanese to regain control of their money supply. The impact of restrained monetary growth on the exchange rate, which appreciated against the dollar by 52% between 1972 and late 1978, helps to explain why the inflation rate in Japan continued to slow down while growth in real output proceeded at a steady 5.5 to 6.5% pace beginning in 1976. A remaining puzzle is how the Japanese avoided any acceleration of inflation as a consequence of the decline in the yen by roughly 10% between the last half of 1978 and the last half of 1980. A possible explanation is that the 4% rate of output growth used in figure 1.8*a* for the period 1973–79 (compared to 10.2% for 1960–73) substantially understates the true trend and that the deceleration of inflation in the late 1970s reflects a continuing adjustment to an underutilization of resources. Another possibility is that Japanese unions are exhibiting deliberate restraint now to avoid an inflationary response to the second 1979–80 oil shock (*Wall Street Journal*, 6 February 1981).

11. *United Kingdom, 1965–80.* Although a band of monetarists fights a rearguard action, nowhere as in Britain is the view so entrenched that inflation results from an autonomous struggle over income shares. Perry (1975) and I (1977*b*), in econometric equations that allow for an impact of aggregate demand on wages, have found convincing evidence of an alternating series of episodes of incomes policy followed by autonomous wage push. In the 1965–72 period the British inflation-demand relation marched quite firmly along the 45 degree line in figure 1.8*b*, with only minor fluctuations in the growth rate of output. Since there was no lag between demand and inflation (as in France in 1963–65 or Germany in 1965–69), it is plausible to conclude that monetary policy accommodated an autonomous inflation cycle caused by wage push and an accelerating inflation in world traded goods prices. The institutions of British monetary control (or "noncontrol") were firmly wedded to pegging interest rates and allowed monetary accommodation to occur without much thought about alternative responses.

Of all the cases studied thus far, the British shows the clearest evidence that the 1974–75 oil shock was accommodated. M1 growth jumped from 5% in 1973 to 19% in 1975, and nominal GNP growth (unadjusted) jumped from 10% in 1972 to 24% in 1975. This experience can be compared to unadjusted 1975 nominal GNP growth rates of 8% in the United States, 5% in Germany, and − 1% in Switzerland. The movement down the 45 degree line in 1975 through 1978 reflects a coordinated policy reminiscent of Germany in 1965, with unions accepting lower wage increases under a "social contract," while monetary growth was decelerated under pressure from the International Monetary Fund. Monetary restriction in turn spurred a recovery in the value of the pound sterling from its low reached in October 1976, and the ensuing reduction in the inflation rate of import prices helped the social contract to remain in place until 1978. Finally, the 1979–80 acceleration of inflation traces a pattern in figure 1.8*b* that suggests a partial accommodation of supply shocks,

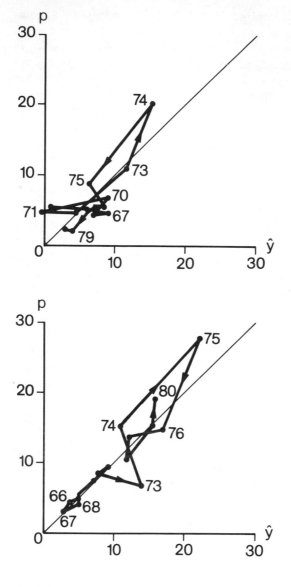

**Fig. 1.8**          (*a*) Japan, 1965–80. (*b*) United Kingdom, 1965–80.

consisting of excessive public-sector wage agreements granted by the departing Labor government in early 1979 and large increases in indirect taxes introduced by the new Conservative government in late 1979. These influences appear to have swamped the beneficial impact on inflation of the 30% appreciation in the pound sterling that occurred between mid-1978 and mid-1980.

12. *Italy, 1963–80.* The history of postwar Italian inflation is full of references to two major episodes of wage push, a so-called wage explosion in 1963 and a period of labor strife called "the hot autumn of 1969." My previous study (1977*b*) of quarterly wage and monetary change data found significant evidence of autonomous movements in wage rates in 1963 and the beginning of 1970. An important similarity between the two episodes was the anti-inflationary reaction of monetary policy, with the growth rate of M1 falling by more than half between 1962 and 1964, and by one-third between 1970 and 1971. The downward response of the inflation rate in 1963–66 in figure 1.9 follows a classic "loop" like those drawn in figure 1.2, with a cumulative decline in output relative to a trend of about 4.5%. In 1971–72 the response of inflation was almost nonexistent, possibly because of the ongoing acceleration of world traded goods prices. As a result the cumulative decline in detrended output between 1969 and 1972 amounted to about 6%.

Since 1973 Italy has moved back and forth along the 45 degree line in figure 1.9, with its rapid adjustment facilitated by the interaction of wage indexation (the *scala mobile*), flexible exchange rates, and monetary accommodation. The Italian response to the first oil shock of 1973–74 shows the permanent acceleration of inflation that we expect to occur when a supply shock strikes an economy that has a high degree of wage indexation. Several of the details of the Italian response after 1973 duplicate the British, so much so that in 1977 the *Economist* labeled Italy "Europe's other Britain." The inflation rate decelerated in both countries from a peak in 1975 to a trough in 1978, partly under pressure from the International Monetary Fund, and both experienced another acceleration of inflation in 1979 and 1980. In the case of Italy the 1979–80 acceleration was accommodated by monetary policy, perhaps reflecting the political weakness of the government, whereas the strong Parliamentary position of the Thatcher government allowed a partially successful attempt to slow down monetary growth. It will be interesting over the next two years to learn whether this political divergence between Britain and Italy will also cause a growing and permanent divergence in their inflation rates.

13. *Brazil, 1960–80.* The 1960–70 cycle in Brazil provides an example of a classic money-fueled aggregate demand inflation. After remaining in a range of 12 to 16% from 1947 to 1958, inflation began to accelerate in response to the heavy money-financed requirements of Kubitschek's 1959 "Target Plan." Although the source of accelerating inflation was recognized, no government before the April 1964 revolution had the political courage to carry out an effective stabilization plan for fear of causing recession, unemployment, and a drop in the growth rate of real income. There was also a belief that inflation was an effective mechanism for transferring savings to the industrial sector (Syvrud 1974). The output

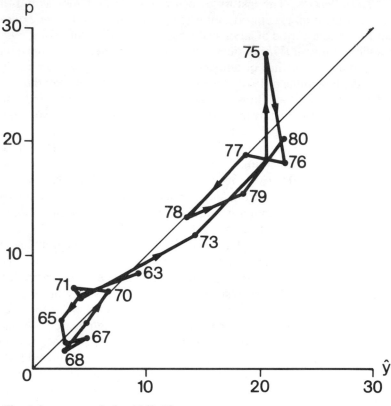

**Fig. 1.9**          Italy, 1963–80.

recession which actually occurred can be divided into two stages, an
initial period before the 1964 revolution during which the nation's international bankruptcy, as well as the inefficiency caused by a near 100%
inflation rate, had undermined the operation of the economy, and a
second stage in which monetary and credit restriction led to bankruptcies
and liquidity crises. Over the five years between 1963 and 1967 real GNP
fell cumulatively 19.7% below its 1960–73 trend. This shortfall was
gradually made up during 1968–73, when double-digit rates of real output
growth were achieved in all years but one. The cost of the Brazilian
experiment in price stabilization appears to be deceptively small in figure
1.10, but this reflects the enormous variance of inflation and correspondingly large scale of the diagram. After 1971 inflation steadily accelerated.
Initially this may have occurred as a result of the exuberant growth of real
output in 1972 and 1973, but since that year must have reflected (as in
Italy) the insidious interaction of supply shocks, wage indexation, flexible
exchange rates, and monetary accommodation.

    14. *Israel, 1965–79.* As is well known, Israel recently entered the

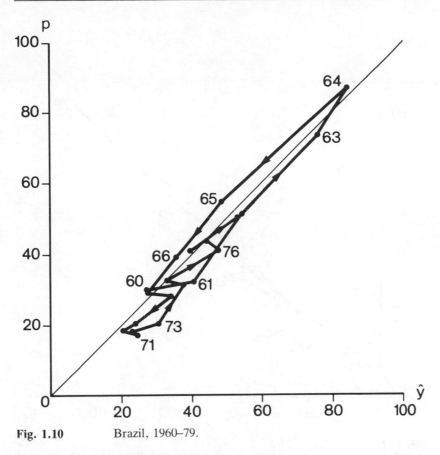

**Fig. 1.10**        Brazil, 1960–79.

territory of triple-digit inflation. This continues an acceleration process that began in 1970 and has been interrupted since then only during 1976. Figure 1.11 illustrates an interesting change from the flat adjustment relation displayed for 1965–69 to the 45 degree relation displayed since 1970. As in Brazil and Italy, the supply shocks of the 1970s, when combined with a high degree of wage indexation and flexible exchange rates, have forced governments to choose between large output losses and a continuing acceleration of inflation. The process will end only when politicians can convince their constituents to accept a decline in real income, as occurred in 1974–75 when Germany, Switzerland, and the United States used monetary restriction to battle the permanent inflationary consequences of supply shocks.

## 1.7  Conclusion

Throughout the twentieth century, with a single exception during and after World War I, United States inflation has responded slowly to

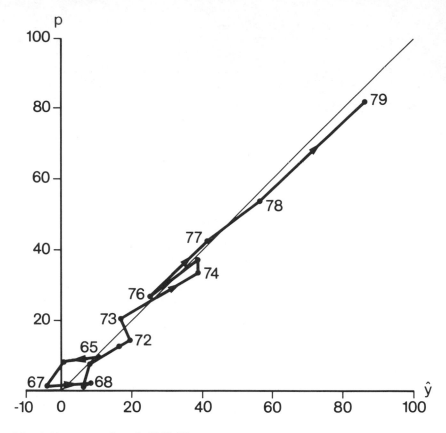

**Fig. 1.11**        Israel, 1965–79.

changes in the growth of nominal aggregate demand. Many commentators—including Fellner (1979) with his "credibility hypothesis," Lucas
(1978) and his followers with their "policy ineffectiveness proposition,"
and some advisers to the new administration—accept as an article of faith
that inflation will decelerate promptly in response to a sustained slowdown in the growth of nominal spending. Yet the wide variety of evidence
for the United States arrayed in figures 1.3–1.6 demonstrates that the
phenomenon of partial and gradual price adjustment transcends changes
in "policy regimes" and has characterized the United States in every
episode from Coolidge to Carter.

There is a widespread impression that inflation is more responsive to
demand disturbances in foreign countries than in the United States. Yet
there are only four episodes of those surveyed in this paper that exhibit all
of the following characteristics: (*a*) a marked slowdown of inflation, (*b*)

achieved by restrictive demand policy, (c) and with only a "minor" loss in output:

1. United States, 1920–22 (where the price level itself was reduced)
2. France, 1963–66
3. Japan, 1976–80
4. Italy, 1963–68

There are no such episodes in the United States since 1922, and instead abundant evidence that only 10 to 40% of nominal demand changes are absorbed by the inflation rate in the first year after such changes. A more surprising conclusion is that there are no other examples of such success-ful low-cost episodes of stopping inflation in other countries. Restrictive policy slowed down inflation in Germany in 1965–67 and 1973–76, but only at the cost of a substantial loss in real output. The Swiss policy of tight money may seem socially costless to first-time tourists, but the 17% decline in manufacturing employment between 1974 and 1978 and the − 0.3% annual real GNP trend recorded between 1973 and 1979 imposed a substantial cost on both current Swiss residents and now-departed guest workers. The Brazilian struggle to bring inflation from 90% in 1964 to 17% in 1971 required output to fall about 20% below trend during the period of adjustment. While the United Kingdom episode between 1975 and 1978 might be cited as a successful experiment, restrictive demand management policy was combined with a "social contract" between the Labor government and its labor union supporters; the relevance of this linkage for current United States policymakers, who are uniformly opposed to government intervention in the wage-price process, seems dubious at best. Finally, the experience over the past decade of France, Italy, Brazil, and Israel provides no guidance for stopping inflation, since all four countries accommodated the first OPEC oil shock and are still experiencing the permanent acceleration of inflation that resulted from their earlier policy decisions.

Not only are there few successful anti-inflationary episodes in the available historical evidence, leaving aside the hyperinflations reviewed by Sargent, but each of the four listed above has limited relevance to the United States in 1981. Our own experience during 1916–22 predated the advent of three-year staggered union wage contracts, which has intro-duced an extra delay into the responsiveness of the United States infla-tion process. The success of Japan since 1976 has resulted from a union bargaining structure in which contracts last only a year and expire simul-taneously and in which unions appear to have entered into an implicit social contract with the monetary policy authorities. This would appear to leave the experience of France and Italy in the early 1960s as the last refuge of the optimist.

# Note

1. Data through 1979 for other countries come from the *International Financial Statistics*, and 1980 estimates for some countries are from the *OECD Economic Outlook*, December 1980.

# References

Blinder, A. S. 1979. *The great stagflation*. New York: Academic Press.
Fellner, W. 1979. The credibility effect and rational expectations. *Brookings Papers* 10, no. 1: 167–78.
Friedman, M. 1963. *Inflation: Causes and consequences*. New York: Asia Publishing House.
Gordon, R. J. 1975. The demand for and supply of inflation. *Journal of Law and Economics* 18 (December): 807–36.
———. 1977a. Can the inflation of the 1970s be explained? *Brookings Papers* 8, no. 1: 253–77.
———. 1977b. World inflation and the sources of monetary accommodation: A study of eight countries. *Brookings Papers* 8, no. 2: 409–68.
———. 1981a. Output fluctuations and gradual price adjustment. *Journal of Economic Literature* 19 (June): 492–528.
———. 1981b. Price inertia and policy ineffectiveness. *Journal of Political Economy*, forthcoming. NBER Working Paper no. 744.
———. 1981c. *Macroeconomics*, 2d ed. Boston: Little, Brown.
Gordon, R. J., and Wilcox, J. A. 1981. Monetarist interpretations of the Great Depression: Evaluation and critique. In. K. Brunner, ed., *The Great Depression revisited*, pp. 49–107. Boston: Martinus Nijhoff.
Lucas, R. E., Jr. 1978. Unemployment policy. *American Economic Review* 68 (May): 353–57.
Okun, A. M. 1978. Efficient disinflationary policies. *American Economic Review* 68 (May): 348–52.
Rockoff, H. 1980. Price controls in World War I and II. Working paper.
Sachs, J. D. 1979. Wages, profits, and macroeconomic adjustment: A comparative study. *Brookings Papers* 10, no. 2: 269–319.
Syvrud, D. E. 1974. *Foundations of Brazilian economic growth*. Stanford: Hoover Institution Press.

# 2 The Ends of Four Big Inflations

Thomas J. Sargent

## 2.1 Introduction

Since the middle 1960s, many Western economies have experienced persistent and growing rates of inflation. Some prominent economists and statesmen have become convinced that this inflation has a stubborn, self-sustaining momentum and that either it simply is not susceptible to cure by conventional measures of monetary and fiscal restraint or, in terms of the consequent widespread and sustained unemployment, the cost of eradicating inflation by monetary and fiscal measures would be prohibitively high. It is often claimed that there is an underlying rate of inflation which responds slowly, if at all, to restrictive monetary and fiscal measures.[1] Evidently, this underlying rate of inflation is the rate of inflation that firms and workers have come to expect will prevail in the future. There is momentum in this process because firms and workers supposedly form their expectations by extrapolating past rates of inflation into the future. If this is true, the years from the middle 1960s to the early 1980s have left firms and workers with a legacy of high expected rates of inflation which promise to respond only slowly, if at all, to restrictive monetary and fiscal policy actions. According to this view, restrictive monetary and fiscal actions in the first instance cause substantial reduc-

Thomas J. Sargent is with the Federal Reserve Bank of Minneapolis and the Department of Economics, University of Minnesota.

The views expressed herein are solely those of the author and do not necessarily represent the views of the Federal Reserve Bank of Minneapolis or the Federal Reserve System. Helpful comments on earlier drafts of this paper were made by Preston Miller, John Kennan, Peter Garber, and Gail Makinen. General conversations on the subject with Michael K. Salemi and Neil Wallace were most helpful. Gail Makinen directed the author's attention to the unemployment figures for Poland. Carl Christ of the NBER reading committee made several comments that improved the manuscript.

tions in output and employment but have little, if any, effects in reducing the rate of inflation. For the economy of the United States, a widely cited estimate is that for every one percentage point reduction in the annual inflation rate accomplished by restrictive monetary and fiscal measures, $220 billion of annual GNP would be lost. For the $2,500 billion United States economy, the cost of achieving zero percent inflation would be great, indeed, according to this estimate.

An alternative "rational expectations" view denies that there is any inherent momentum in the present process of inflation.[2] This view maintains that firms and workers have now come to expect high rates of inflation in the future and that they strike inflationary bargains in light of these expectations.[3] However, it is held that people expect high rates of inflation in the future precisely because the government's current and prospective monetary and fiscal policies warrant those expectations. Further, the current rate of inflation and people's expectations about future rates of inflation may well seem to respond slowly to isolated *actions* of restrictive monetary and fiscal policy that are viewed as temporary departures from what is perceived as a long-term government *policy* involving high average rates of government deficits and monetary expansion in the future. Thus inflation only *seems* to have a momentum of its own; it is actually the long-term government policy of persistently running large deficits and creating money at high rates which imparts the momentum to the inflation rate. An implication of this view is that inflation can be stopped much more quickly than advocates of the "momentum" view have indicated and that their estimates of the length of time and the costs of stopping inflation in terms of foregone output ($220 billion of GNP for one percentage point in the inflation rate) are erroneous. This is not to say that it would be easy to eradicate inflation. On the contrary, it would require far more than a few temporary restrictive fiscal and monetary actions. It would require a change in the policy *regime*: there must be an abrupt change in the continuing government *policy*, or *strategy*, for setting deficits now and in the future that is sufficiently binding as to be widely believed. Economists do not now possess reliable, empirically tried and true models that can enable them to predict precisely how rapidly and with what disruption in terms of lost output and employment such a regime change will work its effects. How costly such a move would be in terms of foregone output and how long it would be in taking effect would depend partly on how resolute and evident the government's commitment was.

This paper describes several dramatic historical experiences which I believe to be consistent with the "rational expectations" view but which seem difficult to reconcile with the "momentum" model of inflation. The idea is to stand back from our current predicament and to examine the measures that successfully brought drastic inflations under control in several European countries in the 1920s. I shall describe and interpret events in Austria, Hungary, Germany, and Poland, countries which experienced a dramatic "hyperinflation" in which, after the passage of several months, price indexes assumed astronomical proportions. The basic data to be studied are the price indexes in figures 2.1–2.4. These data are recorded in a logarithmic scale, so that they will fit on a page. For all four countries, and especially Germany, the rise in the price level was spectacular. The graphs also reveal that in each case inflation stopped abruptly rather than gradually. I shall also briefly describe events in Czechoslovakia, a country surrounded by neighbors experiencing hyper-inflations, but which successfully achieved a stable currency itself. My reason for studying these episodes is that they are laboratories for the study of regime changes. Within each of Austria, Hungary, Poland, and Germany, there occurred a dramatic change in the fiscal policy regime which in each instance was associated with the end of a hyperinflation. Further, though it shared some problems with its four neighbors, Czechoslovakia deliberately adopted a relatively restrictive fiscal policy regime, with the avowed aim of maintaining the value of its currency.

While there are many differences in details among the Austrian, Hungarian, Polish, and German hyperinflations, there are some very important common features. These include the following:

i) The nature of the fiscal policy regime in effect during each of the hyperinflations. Each of the four countries persistently ran enormous budget deficits on current account.

ii) The nature of the deliberate and drastic fiscal and monetary mea-sures taken to end the hyperinflations.

iii) The immediacy with which the price level and foreign exchanges suddenly stabilized.[4]

iv) The rapid rise in the "high-powered" money supply in the months and years after the rapid inflation had ended.

I shall assemble and interpret the facts in the light of a view about the forces which give money value and about the way the international monetary system worked in the 1920s. Before interpreting the historical facts, I now turn to a brief description of this view.

## 2.2 The Gold Standard

After World War I, the United States was on the gold standard. The United States government stood ready to convert a dollar into a specified amount of gold on demand. To understate things, immediately after the war, Hungary, Austria, Poland, and Germany were not on the gold standard. In practice, their currencies were largely "fiat," or unbacked. The governments of these countries resorted to the printing of new

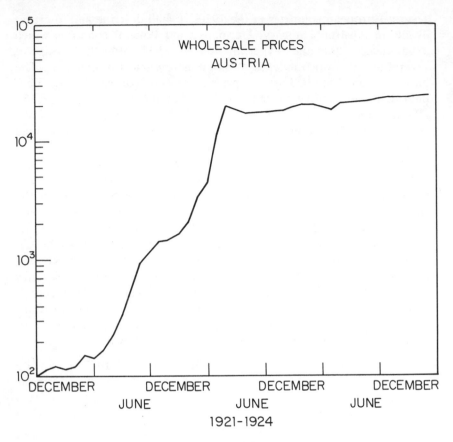

WHOLESALE PRICES
AUSTRIA

DECEMBER          DECEMBER          DECEMBER          DECEMBER

JUNE          JUNE          JUNE

1921-1924

**Fig. 2.1**          Wholesale prices in Austria.

unbacked money to finance government deficits.[5] This was done on such a scale that it led to a depreciation of the currencies of spectacular proportions. In the end, the German mark stabilized at 1 trillion ($10^{12}$) paper marks to the prewar gold mark, the Polish mark at 1.8 million paper marks to the gold zloty, the Austrian crown at 14,400 paper crowns to the prewar Austro-Hungarian crown, and the Hungarian krone at 14,500 paper crowns to the prewar Austro-Hungarian crown.[6]

This paper focuses on the deliberate changes in policy that each of Hungary, Austria, Poland, and Germany made to end its hyperinflation, and the deliberate choice of policy that Czechoslovakia made to avoid inflation in the first place. The hyperinflations were each ended by restoring or virtually restoring convertibility to the dollar or equivalently to gold. For this reason it is good to keep in mind the nature of the restrictions that adherence to the gold standard imposed on a government. Under the gold standard, a government issued demand notes and

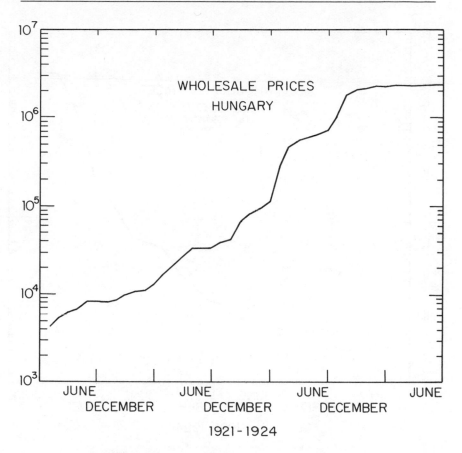

Fig. 2.2         Wholesale prices in Hungary.

longer-term debt which it promised to convert into gold under certain specified conditions, i.e. on demand, for notes. Presumably, people were willing to hold these claims at full value if the government's promise to pay were judged to be good. The government's promise to pay was "backed" only partially by its holding of gold reserves. More important in practice, since usually a government did not hold 100% reserves of gold, a government's notes and debts were backed by the commitment of the government to levy taxes in sufficient amounts, given its expenditures, to make good on its debt. In effect, the notes were backed by the government's pursuit of an appropriate budget policy. During the 1920s, John Maynard Keynes emphasized that the size of a government's gold reserve was not the determinant of whether it could successfully maintain convertibility with gold: its fiscal policy was.[7] According to this view, what mattered was not the current government deficit but the present value of current and prospective future government deficits. The government was

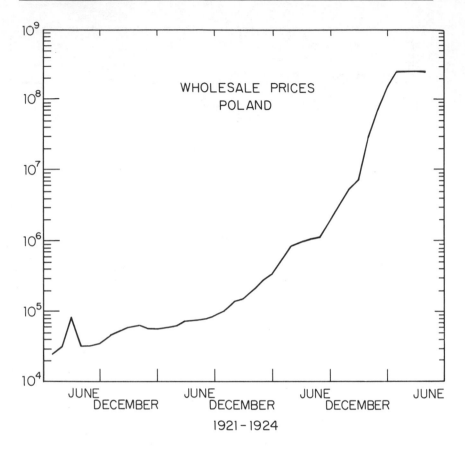

**Fig. 2.3**          Wholesale prices in Poland.

like a firm whose prospective receipts were its future tax collections. The value of the government's debt was, to a first approximation, equal to the present value of current and future government surpluses. So under a gold standard, a government must honor its debts and could not engage in inflationary finance. In order to assign a value to the government's debt, it was necessary to have a view about the fiscal policy regime in effect, that is, the rule determining the government deficit as a function of the state of the economy now and in the future. The public's perception of the fiscal regime influenced the value of government debt through private agents' expectations about the present value of the revenue streams backing that debt.[8] It will be worthwhile to keep this view of the gold standard in mind as we turn to review the events surrounding the ends of the four hyperinflations.[9]

However, it will be useful first to expand a little more generally on the distinction between the effects of isolated *actions* taken within the context

**Fig. 2.4**          Wholesale prices in Germany.

of a given general strategy, on the one hand, and the effects of choosing among alternative general strategies or rules for repeatedly taking actions, on the other. The latter choice I refer to as a choice of regime. The values of government expenditures and tax rates for one particular quarter are examples of actions, while the rules, implicit or explicit, for repeatedly selecting government expenditures and tax rates as functions of the state of the economy are examples of regimes. Recent work in dynamic macroeconomics has discovered the following general principle: whenever there is a change in the government strategy or regime, private economic agents can be expected to change their strategies or rules for choosing consumption rates, investment rates, portfolios, and so on.[10] The reason is that private agents' behavior is selfish, or at least purposeful, so that when the government switches its strategy, private agents usually find it in their best interests to change theirs. One by-product of this principle is that most of the empirical relations captured in standard econometric models cannot be expected to remain constant across contemplated changes in government policy regimes. For this reason, predictions made under the assumption that such relations will remain constant across regime changes ought not to be believed. The estimate that a 1% reduction in inflation would cost $220 billion GNP annually is one example of such a faulty prediction. When an important change in regime occurs, dynamic macroeconomics would predict that the entire pattern of correlations among variables will change in quantitatively important ways.

While the distinction between isolated actions and strategy regimes is clear in principle, it is an admittedly delicate task to interpret whether particular historical episodes reflect isolated actions within the same old rules of the game or whether they reflect a new set of rules or government strategies.[11] All that we have to go on are the recorded actions actually taken, together with the pronouncements of public officials, laws, legislative votes, and sometimes constitutional provisions. Out of this material we are to fashion a view about the government strategy being used. Common sense suggests and technical econometric considerations confirm the difficulties in making such interpretations in general. Having said this, I believe that the examples discussed below are about as close to being laboratories for studying regime changes as history has provided.

## 2.3   Austria

At the end of World War I, the Austro-Hungarian empire dissolved into a number of successor states, of which Austria was one. From having been the center of an empire of 625,000 square kilometers and 50 million inhabitants, Austria was reduced to a mere 80,000 square kilometers and 6.5 million inhabitants. Having suffered food scarcities during the war that were produced by an effective Allied blockade, Austria found itself confronted with new national borders and trade barriers that cut it off from the food sources formerly within its empire. Further, the government of Austria reabsorbed a large number of Austrian imperial bureaucrats who were no longer welcome in the other successor states. Austrians also faced a large-scale unemployment problem stemming from the need to reconvert the economy to peaceful activities and to adjust to the new national borders. If this were not enough, as a loser of the war Austria owed the Reparation Commission sums that for a long time were uncertain in amount but were presumed eventually to be substantial. The Reparation Commission, in effect, held a blanket mortgage against the assets and revenues of the Austrian government.

Austria responded to these pressing problems by making large expenditures in the form of food relief and payments to the unemployed. In addition, the state railroads and monopolies ran deficits, as taxes and prices were kept relatively low. The government did not collect enough taxes to cover expenditures and so ran very substantial deficits during the years 1919–22 (see table A1). As table A1 shows, in these years the deficit was typically over 50 percent of the total government expenditures. The government financed these deficits by selling treasury bills to the Austrian section of the Austro-Hungarian bank. The result was a very rapid increase in the volume of "high-powered" money, defined as the notes and demand deposit obligations of the central bank (see table A2). As the figures in table A2 indicate, between March 1919 and August 1922 the total note circulation in Austria[12] of the Austro-Hungarian bank increased by a factor of 288. This expansion of central bank notes stemmed mainly from the bank's policy of discounting treasury bills. However, it also resulted partly from the central bank's practice of making loans and discounts to private agents at nominal interest rates of between 6 and 9% per annum, rates which by any standard were far too low in view of the inflation rate, which averaged 10,000% per annum from January 1921 to August 1922 (table A3).[13]

In response to these government actions and what seemed like prospects for their indefinite continuation, the Austrian crown depreciated internationally and domestic prices rose rapidly (see tables A3 and A4). While between January 1921 and August 1922 the note circulation of the central bank increased by a factor of 39, the retail price index increased by a factor of 110 (see tables A3 and A4) so that the real value of the note circulation diminished during the currency depreciation.[14] The "flight from the crown" occurred as people chose to hold less of their wealth in the form of the rapidly depreciating crown, attempting instead to hold foreign currencies or real assets.[15] From the viewpoint of financing its deficit, the government of Austria had an interest in resisting the flight from the crown, because this had the effect of diminishing the resources that the government could command by printing money. Therefore the government established a system of exchange controls administered by an agency called the Devisenzentrale. The essential function of this

Table A1    Austrian Budgets, 1919–22 (in millions of paper crowns)

|  | Receipts | Expen-ditures | Deficit | Percentage of Expenditures Covered by New Issues of Paper Money |
|---|---|---|---|---|
| 1 January–30 June 1919 | 1,339 | 4,043 | 2,704 | 67 |
| 1 July 1919–30 June 1920 | 6,295 | 16,873 | 10,578 | 63 |
| 1 July 1920–30 June 1921 | 29,483 | 70,601 | 41,118 | 58 |
| 1 January–31 December 1922 | 209,763 | 347,533 | 137,770 | 40 |

Source: Pasvolsky [25, p. 102].

Table A2          Total Note Circulation of Austrian Crowns
                  (in thousands of crowns)

| | | | | | |
|---|---|---|---|---|---|
| 1919 | January | — | | May | 397,829,313 |
| | February | — | | June | 549,915,678 |
| | March | 4,687,056 | | July | 786,225,601 |
| | April | 5,577,851 | | August | 1,353,403,632 |
| | May | 5,960,003 | | September | 2,277,677,738 |
| | June | 7,397,692 | | October | 2,970,916,607 |
| | July | 8,391,405 | | November | 3,417,786,498 |
| | August | 9,241,135 | | December | 4,080,177,238 |
| | September | 9,781,112 | 1923 | January | 4,110,551,163 |
| | October | 10,819,310 | | February | 4,207,991,722 |
| | November | 11,193,670 | | March | 4,459,117,216 |
| | December | 12,134,474 | | April | 4,577,382,333 |
| 1920 | January | 13,266,878 | | May | 4,837,042,081 |
| | February | 14,292,809 | | June | 5,432,619,312 |
| | March | 15,457,749 | | July | 5,684,133,721 |
| | April | 15,523,832 | | August | 5,894,786,367 |
| | May | 15,793,805 | | September | 6,225,109,352 |
| | June | 16,971,344 | | October | 6,607,839,105 |
| | July | 18,721,495 | | November | 6,577,616,341 |
| | August | 20,050,281 | | December | 7,125,755,190 |
| | September | 22,271,686 | 1924 | January | 6,735,109,000 |
| | October | 25,120,385 | | February | 7,364,441,000 |
| | November | 28,072,331 | | March | 7,144,901,000 |
| | December | 30,645,658 | | April | 7,135,471,000 |
| 1921 | January | 34,525,634 | | May | 7,552,620,000 |
| | February | 38,352,648 | | June | 7,774,958,000 |
| | March | 41,067,299 | | July | 7,995,647,000 |
| | April | 45,036,723 | | August | 5,894,786,367 |
| | May | 45,583,194 | | September | 7,998,509,000 |
| | June | 49,685,140 | | October | 8,213,003,000 |
| | July | 54,107,281 | | November | 8,072,021,000 |
| | August | 58,533,766 | | December | 8,387,767,000 |
| | September | 70,170,798 | 1925 | January | 7,902,217,000 |
| 1922 | January | 227,015,925 | | February | 7,957,242,000 |
| | February | 259,931,138 | | March | 7,897,792,000 |
| | March | 304,063,642 | | April | 7,976,420,000 |
| | April | 346,697,776 | | | |

Source: Young [36, vol. 2, p. 292].

agency was to increase the amount of Austrian crowns held by Austrians, which it accomplished by adopting measures making it difficult or illegal for Austrians to hold foreign currencies and other substitutes for Austrian crowns.[16] Despite these regulations, it is certain that Austrian citizens were holding large amounts of foreign currencies during 1921 and 1922.

Table A4 reveals that the Austrian crown abruptly stabilized in August 1922, while table A3 indicates that prices abruptly stabilized a month

**Table A3**          **Austrian Retail Prices, 1921–24**

|      |           | Retail Price Index, 52 Commodities |
|------|-----------|-----------|
| 1921 | January   | 100 |
|      | February  | 114 |
|      | March     | 122 |
|      | April     | 116 |
|      | May       | 121 |
|      | June      | 150 |
|      | July      | 143 |
|      | August    | 167 |
|      | September | 215 |
|      | October   | 333 |
|      | November  | 566 |
|      | December  | 942 |
| 1922 | January   | 1,142 |
|      | February  | 1,428 |
|      | March     | 1,457 |
|      | April     | 1,619 |
|      | May       | 2,028 |
|      | June      | 3,431 |
|      | July      | 4,830 |
|      | August    | 11,046 |
|      | September | 20,090 |
|      | October   | 18,567 |
|      | November  | 17,681 |
|      | December  | 17,409 |
| 1923 | January   | 17,526 |
|      | February  | 17,851 |
|      | March     | 18,205 |
|      | April     | 19,428 |
|      | May       | 20,450 |
|      | June      | 20,482 |
|      | July      | 19,368 |
|      | August    | 18,511 |
|      | September | 20,955 |
|      | October   | 21,166 |
|      | November  | 21,479 |
|      | December  | 21,849 |
| 1924 | January   | 22,941 |
|      | February  | 23,336 |
|      | March     | 23,336 |
|      | April     | 23,361 |
|      | May       | 23,797 |
|      | June      | 24,267 |

Source: Young [36, vol. 2, p. 293].

Table A4          Exchange Rates, Austrian Crowns
                  per United States Dollar, in New York Market

|           | 1919   | 1920   | 1921     | 1922      | 1923      | 1924      |
|-----------|--------|--------|----------|-----------|-----------|-----------|
| January   | 17.09  | 271.43 | 654.00   | 7,375.00  | 71,500.00 | 70,760.00 |
| February  | 20.72  | 250.00 | 722.50   | 6,350.00  | 71,150.00 | 70,760.00 |
| March     | 25.85  | 206.66 | 676.00   | 7,487.50  | 71,000.00 | 70,760.00 |
| April     | 26.03  | 200.00 | 661.00   | 7,937.50  | 70,850.00 | 70,760.00 |
| May       | 24.75  | 155.83 | 604.00   | 11,100.00 | 70,800.00 | 70,760.00 |
| June      | 29.63  | 145.00 | 720.00   | 18,900.00 | 70,800.00 | 70,760.00 |
| July      | 37.24  | 165.00 | 957.00   | 42,350.00 | 70,760.00 | 70,760.00 |
| August    | 42.50  | 237.14 | 1,081.50 | 77,300.00 | 70,760.00 | 70,760.00 |
| September | 68.50  | 255.00 | 2,520.00 | 74,210.00 | 70,760.00 | 70,760.00 |
| October   | 99.50  | 358.33 | 4,355.00 | 73,550.00 | 70,760.00 | 70,760.00 |
| November  | 130.00 | 493.66 | 8,520.00 | 71,400.00 | 70,760.00 | 70,760.00 |
| December  | 155.00 | 659.40 | 5,275.00 | 70,925.00 | 70,760.00 | 70,760.00 |

Source: Young [36, vol. 2, p. 294].

later. This occurred despite the fact that the central bank's note circulation continued to increase rapidly, as table A1 indicates. Furthermore, there occurred no change in currency units or "currency reform," at least not for another year and a half.

The depreciation of the Austrian crown was suddenly stopped by the intervention of the Council of the League of Nations and the resulting binding commitment of the government of Austria to reorder Austrian fiscal and monetary strategies dramatically. After Austria's increasingly desperate pleas to the Allied governments for international aid had repeatedly been rejected or only partially fulfilled, in late August 1922 the Council of the League of Nations undertook to enter into serious negotiations to reconstruct the financial system of Austria. These negotiations led to the signing of three protocols on 2 October 1922 which successfully guided the financial reconstruction of Austria. It is remarkable that even before the precise details of the protocols were publicly announced, the fact of the serious deliberations of the Council brought relief to the situation. This can be seen in tables A3 and A4, and was described by Pasvolsky as follows:

> The moment the Council of the League decided to take up in earnest the question of Austrian reconstruction, there was immediately a widespread conviction that the solution of the problem was at hand. This conviction communicated itself first of all to that delicately adjusted mechanism, the international exchange market. Nearly two weeks before Chancellor Seipel officially laid the Austrian question before the Council of the League, on August 25, the foreign exchange rate ceased to soar and began to decline, the internal price level following suit three weeks later. The printing presses in Austria were

still grinding out new currency; the various ministries were still dispersing this new currency through the country by means of continuing budgetary deficits. Yet the rate of exchange was slowly declining. The crisis was checked.[17]

The first protocol was a declaration signed by Great Britain, France, Italy, Czechoslovakia, and Austria that reaffirmed the political independence and sovereignty of Austria.[18] The second protocol provided conditions for an international loan of 650 million gold crowns to Austria. The third protocol was signed by Austria alone and laid out a plan for reconstruction of its fiscal and monetary affairs. The Austrian government promised to establish a new independent central bank, to cease running large deficits, and to bind itself not to finance deficits with advances of notes from the central bank. Further, the government of Austria agreed to accept in Austria a commissioner general, appointed by the Council of the League, who was to be responsible for monitoring the fulfillment of Austria's commitments. The government of Austria also agreed to furnish security to back the reconstruction loan. At the same time, it was understood that the Reparation Commission would give up or modify its claim on the resources of the government of Austria.

The government of Austria and the League both moved swiftly to execute the plan outlined in the protocols. In legislation of 14 November 1922, the Austrian National Bank was formed to replace the old Austrian section of the Austro-Hungarian bank; it was to take over the assets and functions of the Devisenzentrale. The new bank began operations on 1 January 1923 and was specifically forbidden from lending to the government except on the security of an equal amount of gold and foreign assets. The bank was also required to cover its note issues with certain minimal proportions of gold, foreign earning assets, and commercial bills. Further, once the government's debt to the bank had been reduced to 30 million gold crowns, the bank was obligated to resume convertibility into gold.

The government moved to balance its budget by taking concrete steps in several directions. Expenditures were reduced by discharging thousands of government employees. Under the reconstruction scheme, the government promised gradually to discharge a total of 100,000 state employees. Deficits in government enterprises were reduced by raising prices of government-sold goods and services. New taxes and more efficient means of collecting tax and custom revenues were instituted. The results of these measures can be seen by comparing the figures in table A5 with those in table A1. Within two years the government was able to balance the budget.

The stabilization of the Austrian crown was not achieved via a currency reform. At the end of 1924 a new unit of currency was introduced, the schilling, equal to 10,000 paper crowns. The introduction of this new unit

Table A5          The Austrian Budget, 1923–25 (in millions of schillings)

|  | Closed Accounts | | |
| Item | 1923 | 1924 | 1925 |
| --- | --- | --- | --- |
| Total revenue | 697.4 | 900.6 | 908.5 |
| Current expenditures | 779.6 | 810.0 | 741.4 |
| Deficit (−) or surplus (+) | −82.2 | +90.6 | +167.1 |
| Capital expenditures | 76.0 | 103.6 | 90.6 |
| Total balance | −158.2 | −13.0 | +76.5 |

Source: Pasvolsky [25, p. 127].
Note: 1 schilling = 10,000 paper crowns.

of currency occurred long after the exchange rate had been stabilized and was surely an incidental measure.[19]

Table A2 reveals that from August 1922, when the exchange rate suddenly stabilized, to December 1924, the circulating notes of the Austrian central bank increased by a factor of over 6. The phenomenon of the achievement of price stability in the face of a sixfold increase in the stock of "high-powered" money was widely regarded by contemporaries as violating the quantity theory of money, and so it seems to do. However, these observations are not at all paradoxical when interpreted in the light of a view which distinguishes sharply between unbacked, or "outside," money, on the one hand, and backed, or "inside," money, on the other hand. In particular, the balance sheet of the central bank and the nature of its open market operations changed dramatically after the carrying out of the League's protocols, with the consequence that the proper intrepretation of the figures on the total note obligations of the central bank changes substantially. Before the protocols, the liabilities of the central bank were backed mainly by government treasury bills; that is, they were not backed at all, since treasury bills signified no commitment to raise revenues through future tax collections. After the execution of the protocols, the liabilities of the central bank became backed by gold, foreign assets, and commercial paper, and ultimately by the power of the government to collect taxes. At the margin, central bank liabilities were backed 100% by gold, foreign assets, and commercial paper as notes and the deposits were created through open market operations in those assets (see table A6). The value of the crown was backed by the commitment of the government to run a fiscal policy compatible with maintaining the convertibility of its liabilities into dollars. Given such a fiscal regime, to a first approximation, the intermediating activities of the central bank did not affect the value of the crown so long as the assets purchased by the bank were sufficiently valuable. Thus the sixfold increase in the liabilities of the central bank after the protocols ought not to be regarded as inflationary. The willingness of Austrians to convert

**Table A6**          **Austrian National Bank Balance Sheet**
                      **(end of month, in millions of crowns)**

| | Gold | Foreign Exchange and Currency | Loans and Discounts | Treasury Bills | Notes in Circulation | Deposits |
|---|---|---|---|---|---|---|
| **1923:** | | | | | | |
| January | 49,304 | 1,058,244 | 731,046 | 2,556,848 | 4,110,551 | 279,092 |
| February | 83,438 | 1,029,134 | 728,884 | 2,552,682 | 4,207,992 | 178,752 |
| March | 86,097 | 1,336,385 | 821,397 | 2,550,159 | 4,459,117 | 329,109 |
| April | 73,270 | 1,439,999 | 741,858 | 2,550,159 | 4,577,382 | 226,273 |
| May | 73,391 | 1,682,209 | 875,942 | 2,550,159 | 4,837,042 | 343,339 |
| June | 73,391 | 2,532,316 | 730,848 | 2,547,212 | 5,432,619 | 362,237 |
| July | 73,391 | 2,947,216 | 658,966 | 2,539,777 | 5,684,134 | 535,121 |
| August | 73,391 | 3,050,085 | 647,936 | 2,538,719 | 5,894,786 | 413,383 |
| September | 73,391 | 3,126,599 | 863,317 | 2,537,661 | 6,225,109 | 373,673 |
| October | 62,117 | 3,356,232 | 1,069,340 | 2,536,604 | 6,607,839 | 414,882 |
| November | 62,117 | 3,504,652 | 1,094,620 | 2,535,547 | 6,577,616 | 617,321 |
| December | 83,177 | 3,832,132 | 1,325,380 | 2,534,490 | 7,125,755 | 649,424 |
| **1924:** | | | | | | |
| January | 91,274 | 3,811,148 | 1,253,110 | 2,533,434 | 6,735,109 | 536,982 |
| February | 105,536 | 3,921,594 | 1,737,334 | 2,532,379 | 7,364,441 | 558,800 |
| March | 106,663 | 3,953,872 | 1,733,400 | 2,295,428 | 7,144,901 | 752,814 |
| April | 107,059 | 3,669,333 | 2,131,984 | 2,294,471 | 7,315,471 | 696,141 |
| May | 107,443 | 3,344,337 | 2,660,449 | 2,259,839 | 7,554,620 | 641,001 |
| June | 107,762 | 3,178,339 | 3,092,470 | 2,237,794 | 7,774,958 | 741,400 |
| July | 108,342 | 3,254,477 | 3,304,876 | 2,231,173 | 7,995,647 | 896,032 |
| August | 108,256 | 3,453,177 | 3,226,962 | 2,219,459 | 8,002,142 | 997,677 |
| September | 108,950 | 3,724,916 | 2,852,688 | 2,210,527 | 7,998,509 | 890,537 |
| October | 109,327 | 4,032,485 | 2,379,700 | 2,202,106 | 8,213,003 | 502,579 |
| November | 110,643 | 4,312,355 | 1,945,627 | 2,196,181 | 8,072,021 | 484,750 |
| December | 110,890 | 4,770,548 | 1,881,593 | 2,178,185 | 8,387,767 | 533,450 |
| **1925:** | | | | | | |
| January | 111,314 | 3,337,911 | 1,545,295 | 2,172,491 | 7,902,217 | 438,390 |
| February | 111,474 | 3,310,032 | 1,285,158 | 2,150,151 | 7,957,242 | 315,771 |
| March | 111,649 | 3,202,802 | 1,047,719 | 2,107,949 | 7,897,792 | 295,498 |
| April | 112,168 | 3,474,672 | 1,059,069 | 2,088,777 | 7,976,420 | 236,957 |

Source: Young [36, vol. 2, p. 291].

hoards of foreign exchange into crowns which is reflected in table A6 is not surprising since the stabilization of the crown made it a much more desirable asset to hold relative to foreign exchange.[20]

The available figures on unemployment indicate that the stabilization of the crown was attended by a substantial increase in the unemployment rate, though unemployment had begun to climb well before stabilization was achieved (see table A7). The number of recipients of state unemploy-

Table A7            Number of Austrian Unemployed
                    in Receipt of Relief (in thousands)

| Beginning of | 1922 | 1923 | 1924 | 1925 | 1926 |
|---|---|---|---|---|---|
| January | 17 | 117 | 98 | 154 | 208 |
| April | 42 | 153 | 107 | 176 | 202 |
| July | 33 | 93 | 64 | 118 | 151 |
| October | 38 | 79 | 78 | 119 | 148 |

Source: League of Nations [14, p. 87].

ment benefits gradually climbed from a low of 8,700 in December 1921 to 83,000 in December 1922. It climbed to 167,000 by March 1923, and then receded to 76,000 in November 1923.[21] How much of this unemployment was due to the achievement of currency stabilization and how much was due to the real dislocations affecting the Austrian economy cannot be determined. However, it is true that currency stabilization was achieved in Austria very suddenly, and with a cost in increased unemployment and foregone output that was minor compared with the $220 billion GNP that some current analysts estimate would be lost in the United States per one percentage point inflation reduction.

## 2.4  Hungary

Like its old partner in the Hapsburg monarchy, Hungary emerged from World War I as a country much reduced in land, population, and power. It retained only 25% of its territory (down from 325,000 square kilometers to 92,000) and only 37% of its population (down from 21 million to about 8 million). Its financial and economic life was disrupted by the newly drawn national borders separating it from peoples and economic institutions formerly within the domain of the Hapsburg monarchy.

At the end of the war, Hungary experienced political turmoil as the Hapsburg King Charles was replaced by the government of Prince Karolyi. In March 1919, the Karolyi government was overthrown by the Bolsheviks under Bela Kun. The regime of Bela Kun lasted only four months, as Romania invaded Hungary, occupied it for a few weeks, and then withdrew. A new repressive right wing regime under Admiral Horthy then took power. The "white terror" against leftists carried out by supporters of Horthy took even more lives than the "red terror" that had occurred under Bela Kun.

At the end of the war, the currency of Hungary consisted of the notes of the Austro-Hungarian bank. By the provisions of the peace treaties of Trianon and St. Germain, the successor states to the Austro-Hungarian empire were required to stamp the notes of the Austro-Hungarian bank that were held by their residents, in effect, thereby recognizing those notes as debts of the respective new states. Before Hungary executed this provision of the Treaty of Trianon, the currency situation grew more complicated, for the Bolshevik regime had access to the plates for printing one- and two-crown Austro-Hungarian bank notes and it used them to print more notes. The Bolshevik government also issued new so-called white notes. Each of these Bolshevik-issued currencies was honored by the subsequent government.

The Austro-Hungarian bank was liquidated at the end of 1919, and it was replaced by an Austrian section and a Hungarian section. The functions of the Hungarian section of the old bank were assumed in August 1921 by a State Note Institute, which was under the control of the minister of finance. In August 1921, the Note Institute issued its own notes, the Hungarian krone, in exchange for Hungarian stamped notes of the Austro-Hungarian bank and several other classes of notes, including those that had been issued by the Bolshevik regime.

As a loser of the war, Hungary owed reparations according to the Treaty of Trianon. The Reparation Commission had a lien on the resources of the government of Hungary. However, neither the total amount owed nor a schedule of payments was fixed for many years after the war. This circumstance alone created serious obstacles in terms of achieving a stable value for Hungary's currency and other debts, since the unclear reparations obligations made uncertain the nature of the resources which backed those debts.

From 1919 until 1924 the government of Hungary ran substantial budget deficits. The government's budget estimates in table H1 are reported by Pasvolsky substantially to understate the size of the deficits.[22] These deficits were financed by borrowing from the State Note Institute, and were a major cause of a rapid increase in the note and deposit liabilities of the institute. An additional cause of the increase in liabilities of the institute was the increasing volume of loans and discounts that it made to private agents (see table H2). These loans were made at a very

**Table H1**        **Hungarian Budget Estimates, 1920–24**
                    **(in millions of paper crowns)**

|         | Revenue | Expen-ditures | Deficit | Percentage of Expenditures Covered by Issues of Paper Money |
|---------|---------|---------------|---------|-------------------------------------------------------------|
| 1920–21 | 10,520  | 20,210        | 9,690   | 47.9 |
| 1921–22 | 20,296  | 26,764        | 6,468   | 24.1 |
| 1922–23 | 152,802 | 193,455       | 40,653  | 21.0 |
| 1923–24 | 2,168,140 | 3,307,099   | 1,138,959 | 34.4 |

Source: Pasvolsky [25, p. 299].

**Table H2**  Balance Sheet of Hungarian Central Bank or State Note Institute (millions of kronen)

| | Gold Coin and Bullion | Silver Coin | Foreign Currency and Exchange | Bills Discounted | Advances on Securities | Advances to Treasury | Notes in Circulation | Current Accounts and Deposits |
|---|---|---|---|---|---|---|---|---|
| 1921: | | | | | | | | |
| January | — | — | — | 10,924 | 195 | — | 15,206 | 3,851 |
| February | — | — | — | 13,202 | 162 | — | 15,571 | 5,531 |
| March | — | — | — | 12,862 | 160 | — | 15,650 | 5,246 |
| April | — | — | — | 12,178 | 110 | — | 13,114 | 6,802 |
| May | — | — | — | 11,847 | 111 | — | 13,686 | 5,760 |
| June | — | — | — | 11,693 | 108 | — | 18,096 | 1,162 |
| July | — | — | — | 11,787 | 107 | — | 15,799 | 3,532 |
| August | 4 | 1 | — | 17,799 | 1,199 | — | 17,326 | 2,975 |
| September | 5 | 1 | — | 20,994 | 1,194 | — | 20,845 | 2,407 |
| October | 12 | 1 | — | 22,403 | 1,185 | 900 | 23,643 | 2,154 |
| November | 12 | 1 | — | 23,650 | 1,176 | 1,000 | 24,742 | 2,353 |
| December | 12 | 1 | — | 23,859 | 1,158 | 900 | 25,175 | 2,240 |
| 1922: | | | | | | | | |
| January | 13 | 1 | — | 24,195 | 1,147 | 1,300 | 25,680 | 2,488 |
| February | 13 | 1 | — | 23,952 | 1,504 | 1,900 | 26,758 | 2,354 |
| March | 13 | 1 | — | 24,574 | 1,565 | 3,000 | 29,327 | 2,224 |
| April | 13 | 1 | — | 25,120 | 1,565 | 4,100 | 30,580 | 2,901 |
| May | 13 | 1 | — | 25,326 | 1,560 | 5,500 | 31,930 | 3,289 |
| June | 13 | 1 | — | 25,445 | 1,556 | 6,900 | 33,600 | 3,741 |
| July | 13 | 1 | — | 28,783 | 1,546 | 7,200 | 38,357 | 3,929 |
| August | 13 | 1 | — | 37,617 | 1,773 | 7,600 | 46,242 | 5,417 |
| September | 14 | 1 | — | 46,963 | 1,848 | 8,900 | 58,458 | 5,929 |

| | | | | | | | | |
|---|---|---|---|---|---|---|---|---|
| October | 14 | 1 | — | 51,631 | 1,728 | 12,000 | 70,005 | 5,189 |
| November | 15 | 1 | — | 49,246 | 1,861 | 12,500 | 72,016 | 6,408 |
| December | 16 | 1 | — | 50,702 | 2,016 | 16,500 | 75,887 | 4,761 |
| 1923: | | | | | | | | |
| January | 14 | 1 | — | 54,516 | 2,007 | 20,000 | 73,717 | 5,888 |
| February | 23 | 1 | — | 58,358 | 2,013 | 24,000 | 75,135 | 6,600 |
| March | 23 | 1 | — | 71,284 | 2,584 | 29,000 | 82,205 | 11,152 |
| April | 23 | 1 | — | 83,800 | 2,817 | 37,000 | 100,101 | 9,793 |
| May | 23 | 1 | — | 93,396 | 1,763 | 47,200 | 119,285 | 10,609 |
| June | 23 | 1 | — | 120,608 | 2,490 | 59,700 | 154,996 | 12,742 |
| July | 22 | 1 | — | 165,927 | 1,762 | 79,700 | 226,285 | 21,977 |
| August | 22 | 1 | — | 273,605 | 1,789 | 143,000 | 399,487 | 23,629 |
| September | 22 | 1 | — | 380,454 | 1,776 | 243,000 | 588,810 | 60,246 |
| October | 23 | 1 | — | 494,501 | 1,663 | 269,000 | 744,926 | 60,176 |
| November | 23 | 1 | — | 531,403 | 1,047 | 306,000 | 853,989 | 74,970 |
| December | 23 | 1 | — | 582,117 | 935 | 401,000 | 931,337 | 84,791 |
| 1924: | | | | | | | | |
| January | 24 | 1 | — | 654,294 | 9,346 | 526,000 | 1,084,677 | 105,481 |
| February | 23 | 1 | — | 746,471 | 34,023 | 699,000 | 1,278,437 | 164,838 |
| March | 24 | 1 | — | 802,756 | 4,598 | 824,000 | 1,606,875 | 253,935 |
| April | 24 | 1 | — | 1,125,898 | 12,456 | 944,000 | 2,098,091 | 308,121 |
| May | 24 | 1 | — | 1,420,385 | 13,437 | 1,054,000 | 2,486,257 | 527,137 |
| June[1] | 246,947 | 9,823 | 681,268 | 1,192,517 | 17,566 | 1,980,000 | 2,893,719 | 1,135,710 |
| July | 441,832 | 13,545 | 1,110,926 | 1,257,597 | — | 1,980,000 | 3,277,943 | 1,424,578 |
| August | 449,945 | 13,558 | 1,382,885 | 1,438,454 | — | 1,978,130 | 3,659,757 | 1,473,231 |
| September | 540,425 | 13,560 | 1,385,880 | 1,756,636 | — | 1,977,306 | 4,115,925 | 1,416,400 |
| October | 503,377 | 13,301 | 1,658,674 | 1,872,385 | — | 1,976,455 | 4,635,090 | 1,465,356 |
| November | 508,411 | 13,301 | 1,816,102 | 1,984,540 | — | 1,975,631 | 4,442,644 | 1,929,754 |
| December | 532,842 | 13,299 | 1,933,356 | 1,976,888 | — | 1,974,781 | 4,513,990 | 2,069,468 |

**Table H2** (continued)

| | Gold Coin and Bullion | Silver Coin | Foreign Currency and Exchange | Bills Dis-counted | Advances on Securities | Advances to Treasury | Notes in Circu-lation | Current Accounts and Deposits |
|---|---|---|---|---|---|---|---|---|
| 1925: | | | | | | | | |
| January | 509,848 | 12,373 | 1,967,314 | 1,848,620 | — | 1,973,930 | 4,449,650 | 2,138,629 |
| February | 596,334 | 12,374 | 1,989,096 | 1,676,594 | — | 1,973,163 | 4,237,985 | 2,542,262 |
| March | 669,107 | 12,374 | 1,984,006 | 1,514,532 | — | 1,969,809 | 4,270,096 | 2,552,762 |
| April | 653,534 | 12,136 | 2,081,998 | 1,485,898 | — | 1,968,987 | 4,526,216 | 2,470,507 |

Source: Young [36, vol. 2, p. 321].

Note: Figures prior to June 1924 are those of the State Note Institute. The Hungarian National Bank opened 24 June 1924 and took over the affairs of the institute.

[1]After this date gold and silver holdings are shown in terms of paper crowns. Other changes were also made in the presentation of accounts after the opening of the new Hungarian National Bank in June.

low interest rate, in view of the rapid rate of price appreciation, and to a large extent amounted to simple gifts from the Note Institute to those lucky enough to receive loans on such generous terms. These private loans account for a much larger increase in high-powered money in the Hungarian than in the other three hyperinflations we shall study.

As table H3 shows, the Hungarian krone depreciated rapidly on foreign exchange markets, and domestic prices rose rapidly. Between January 1922 and April 1924, the price index increased by a factor of 263. In the same period, the total notes and deposit liabilities of the Note Institute increased by a factor of 85, so that the real value of its liabilities decreased substantially. As in the case of Austria, this decrease was symptomatic of a "flight from the krone," as residents of Hungary attempted to economize on their holdings of krones and instead to hold assets denominated in more stable currencies. As in the case of Austria, the government of Hungary resisted this trend by establishing in August 1922 a Hungarian Devisenzentrale within the State Note Institute.

Table H3 indicates that in March 1924, the rise in prices and the depreciation of the krone internationally both abruptly halted. The stabilization occurred in the face of continued expansion in the liabilities of the central bank, which increased by a factor of 3.15 between March 1924 and January 1925 (see table H2). This pattern parallels what occurred in Austria and has a similar explanation.

As in Austria, the financial reconstruction of Hungary was accomplished with the intervention of the League of Nations. Together with the Reparation Commission and the government of Hungary, the League devised a plan which reduced and clarified the reparations commitment of Hungary, arranged for an international loan that would help finance government expenditures, and committed Hungary to establish a balanced budget and a central bank legally bound to refuse any government demand for unbacked credit. On 21 February 1924, the Reparation Commission agreed to give up its lien on Hungary's resources so that these could be used to secure a reconstruction loan. A variety of Western nations also agreed to give up their liens on Hungary so that the new loan could successfully be floated.

The League's reconstruction plan was embodied in two protocols. The first was signed by Great Britain, France, Italy, Czechoslovakia, Rumania, and Hungary, and guaranteed the "political independence, territorial integrity, and sovereignty of Hungary." The second protocol outlined the terms of the reconstruction plan, and committed Hungary to balance its budget and form a central bank truly independent of the Finance Ministry. The government was also obligated to accept in Hungary a commissioner general, responsible to the League, to monitor and supervise the government's fulfillment of its commitment to fiscal and monetary reform.

**Table H3**           **Hungarian Price and Exchange Rate**

|  | Hungarian Index of Prices[1] | Cents per Crown in New York |
|---|---|---|
| 1921: | | |
| July | 4,200 | 0.3323 |
| August | 5,400 | .2629 |
| September | 6,250 | .1944 |
| October | 6,750 | .1432 |
| November | 8,300 | .1078 |
| December | 8,250 | .1512 |
| 1922: | | |
| January | 8,100 | .1525 |
| February | 8,500 | .1497 |
| March | 9,900 | .1256 |
| April | 10,750 | .1258 |
| May | 11,000 | .1261 |
| June | 12,900 | .1079 |
| July | 17,400 | .0760 |
| August | 21,400 | .0595 |
| September | 26,600 | .0423 |
| October | 32,900 | .0402 |
| November | 32,600 | .0413 |
| December | 33,400 | .0430 |
| 1923: | | |
| January | 38,500 | .0392 |
| February | 41,800 | .0395 |
| March | 66,000 | .0289 |
| April | 83,500 | .0217 |
| May | 94,000 | .0191 |
| June | 144,500 | .0140 |
| July | 286,000 | .0097 |
| August | 462,500 | .0056 |
| September | 554,000 | .0055 |
| October | 587,000 | .0054 |
| November | 635,000 | .0054 |
| December | 714,000 | .0052 |
| 1924: | | |
| January | 1,026,000 | .0039 |
| February | 1,839,100 | .0033 |
| March | 2,076,700 | .0015 |
| April | 2,134,600 | .0014 |
| May | 2,269,600 | .0012 |
| June | 2,207,800 | .0011 |
| July | 2,294,500 | .0012 |
| August | 2,242,000 | .0013 |
| September | 2,236,600 | .0013 |

**Table H3** (continued)

|           | Hungarian<br>Index<br>of Prices[1] | Cents<br>per Crown<br>in New York |
|-----------|-----------------|-----------|
| October   | 2,285,200       | .0013     |
| November  | 2,309,500       | .0013     |
| December  | 2,346,600       | .0013     |
| 1925:     |                 |           |
| January   | 2,307,500       | .0014     |
| February  | 2,218,700       | .0014     |
| March     | 2,117,800       | .0014     |

Source: Young [36, vol. 2, p. 323].

[1]From July 1921 through November 1923, the index numbers represent retail prices and are based on 60 commodities with July 1914 = 100. From December 1923 through March 1925, the figures are based on wholesale prices computed by the Hungarian Central Statistical Office. They refer to the prices of 52 commodities on the last day of the month with 1913 = 100.

A reconstruction loan of 250 million gold krones was successfully placed abroad in July 1924. The loan was secured by receipts from customs duties and sugar taxes, and revenues from the salt and tobacco monopolies. The purpose of the loan was to give the government a concrete means of converting future promises to tax into current resources while avoiding the need to place its debt domestically.

By a law of 26 April 1924, the Hungarian National Bank was established, and it began operations on 24 June. The bank assumed the assets and liabilities of the State Note Institute and took over the functions of the foreign exchange control office, the Devisenzentrale. The bank was prohibited from making any additional loans or advances to the government, except upon full security of gold or foreign bills. The bank was also required to hold gold reserves of certain specified percentages behind its liabilities.

The government of Hungary also tried to establish a balanced budget. Both by cutting expenditures and raising tax collections, the government was successful in moving quickly to a balanced budget (see table H4). Indeed, the proceeds of the reconstruction loan were used perceptibly more slowly than had been anticipated in the reconstruction plan.

As table H2 confirms, the stabilization of the krone was accompanied by a substantial *increase* in the total liabilities of the central bank. But as with Austria, the drastic shift in the fiscal policy regime that occasioned the stabilization also changed the appropriate interpretation of these figures. As table H2 indicates and as the regulations governing the bank required, after the League's intervention the note and deposit liabilities

**Table H4**          **Hungarian Budget, 1924–25 (in millions of crowns)**

| Period | Preliminary Treasury Accounts | | | Reconstruction Scheme | | |
|---|---|---|---|---|---|---|
| | Re-ceipts | Expen-ditures | Surplus (+) or Deficit (−) | Re-ceipts | Expen-ditures | Surplus (+) or Deficit (−) |
| Jul.–Dec. 1924 | 208.0 | 205.9 | +2.1 | 143.8 | 186.3 | −42.5 |
| Jan.–Jun. 1925 | 245.1 | 216.9 | +28.2 | 150.0 | 207.6 | −57.6 |
| Fiscal year 1924–25 | 453.1 | 422.8 | +30.3 | 293.8 | 393.9 | −100.1 |

Source: Pasvolsky [25, p. 322].

of the central bank became backed, 100% at the margin, by holdings of gold, foreign exchange, and commercial paper. In effect, the central bank's liabilities represented "fiat money" before the League's plan was in effect; after that plan was in effect, they represented more or less backed claims on British sterling,[23] the foreign currency to which Hungary pegged its exchange as a condition for British participation in the reconstruction loan.

Figures on unemployment in Hungary are reported in table H5, and unfortunately begin only immediately after the price stabilization had already occurred. All that can be inferred from these figures is that immediately after the stabilization, unemployment was not any higher than it was one or two years later. This is consistent either with the hypothesis that the stabilization process had little adverse effect on

**Table H5**          **Number of Unemployed in Hungary (figures relate only to members of Union of Socialist Workers, in thousands of workers)**

| End of | 1924 | 1925 | 1926 |
|---|---|---|---|
| January | — | 37 | 28 |
| February | — | 37 | 29 |
| March | — | 37 | 29 |
| April | 22 | 36 | 26 |
| May | 23 | 30 | 28 |
| June | 25 | 34 | 26 |
| July | 31 | 32 | |
| August | 30 | 27 | |
| September | 20 | 25 | |
| October | 30 | 23 | |
| November | 31 | 26 | |
| December | 33 | 27 | |

Source: League of Nations [15, p. 50].

unemployment or with the hypothesis that the adverse effect was so long-lasting that no recovery occurred within the time span of the figures recorded. The former hypothesis seems more plausible to me.

## 2.5 Poland

The new nation of Poland came into existence at the end of World War I, and was formed from territories formerly belonging to Germany, Austro-Hungary, and Russia. At the time of its formation, Poland possessed a varied currency consisting of Russian rubles, crowns of the Austro-Hungarian bank, German marks, and Polish marks issued by the Polish State Loan Bank, which had been established by Germany to control the currency in the part of Poland occupied by Germany during the war. For Poland, the armistice of 1918 did not bring peace, a costly war with Soviet Russia being waged until the fall of 1920. Poland was devastated by the fighting and by Germany's practice of stripping it of its machinery and materials during World War I.[24]

The new government of Poland ran very large deficits up to 1924 (see table P1). These deficits were financed by government borrowing from the Polish State Loan Bank, which the new government had taken over from the Germans. From January 1922 to December 1923, the outstanding notes of the Polish State Loan Bureau increased by a factor of 523 (table P2). Over the same period, the price index increased by a factor of

**Table P1**    **Polish Receipts and Expenditures (in thousands of zloty)**

|                   | 1921    | 1922    | 1923      | 1924      | 1925      |
|-------------------|---------|---------|-----------|-----------|-----------|
| Receipts:         |         |         |           |           |           |
| Administration    | 261,676 | 467,979 | —         | —         | 1,491,743 |
| State Enterprises | 11,413  | 14,556  | —         | —         | 133,530   |
| Monopolies        | 72,222  | 47,893  | —         | —         | 356,611   |
| Total             | 345,311 | 530,428 | 426,000   | 1,703,000 | 1,981,884 |
| Expenditures:     |         |         |           |           |           |
| Administration    | 765,263 | 734,310 | —         | —         | 1,830,231 |
| State Enterprises | 115,589 | 145,003 | —         | —         | 106,343   |
| Monopolies        | —       | —       | —         | —         | 45,019    |
| Total             | 880,852 | 879,313 | 1,119,800 | 1,629,000 | 1,981,593 |
| Deficit           | 535,541 | 348,885 | 692,000   | —         | —         |
| Surplus           | —       | —       | —         | 74,000    | 251       |

Source: Young [36, vol. 2, p. 183].
Note: Conversion from marks to zloty was made on the following basis: 1921, 1 zloty = 303.75 marks. First quarter 1922, 1 zloty = 513.52 marks; second quarter, 691.49 marks; third quarter, 1,024.97 marks; and fourth quarter, 1,933.87 marks.

**Table P2**  Balance Sheet of Bank of Poland, 1918–25 (end of month figures)

| Month | Gold[1] | Silver[1] (in-cluding base coin) | Balances with Foreign Banks | Dis-counts | Advances Com-mercial | Advances Govern-ment | Note Circula-tion |
|---|---|---|---|---|---|---|---|
| | | | Polish State Loan Bank figures (prior to May 1924) in millions of marks | | | | |
| 1918: | | | | | | | |
| October | — | — | — | 7.0 | 180.8 | — | 880.2 |
| November | — | — | — | 7.0 | 184.0 | 13.9 | 930.5 |
| December | — | — | — | 6.4 | 183.7 | 117.8 | 1,023.8 |
| 1919: | | | | | | | |
| January | — | — | — | 5.0 | 194.7 | 209.9 | 1,098.1 |
| February | — | — | — | 4.2 | 196.4 | 315.0 | 1,160.0 |
| March | 3.7 | 4.2 | 3.9 | 3.5 | 189.7 | 400.0 | 1,223.2 |
| April | 3.7 | 4.4 | 9.4 | 2.5 | 192.8 | 575.0 | 1,346.0 |
| May | 3.7 | 8.9 | 5.8 | 1.8 | 193.2 | 925.0 | 1,548.3 |
| June | 4.9 | 14.8 | 14.6 | 1.3 | 185.9 | 1,125.0 | 1,784.6 |
| July | 5.7 | 20.1 | 13.3 | 1.1 | 193.9 | 1,925.0 | 2,087.9 |
| August | 6.1 | 20.5 | 20.3 | .7 | 107.4 | 2,525.0 | 2,466.6 |
| September | 6.3 | 21.6 | 69.8 | .1 | 218.9 | 3,225.0 | 2,964.7 |
| October | 6.5 | 24.3 | 91.0 | .3 | 242.4 | 4,375.0 | 3,723.6 |
| November | 6.6 | 24.6 | 151.6 | 3.4 | 270.2 | 5,375.0 | 4,236.2 |
| December | 6.6 | 25.5 | 344.6 | 3.9 | 243.8 | 6,825.0 | 5,316.3 |

**1920:**

| | | | | | | |
|---|---|---|---|---|---|---|
| January | 6.6 | 25.5 | 244.1 | 3.7 | 278.5 | 8,275.0 | 6,719.9 |
| February | 6.8 | 25.9 | 565.7 | 6.4 | 303.0 | 10,775.0 | 8,300.3 |
| March | 6.8 | 25.9 | 685.4 | 8.2 | 319.1 | 14,775.0 | 10,690.6 |
| April | 6.8 | 25.9 | 685.5 | 14.8 | 316.7 | 19,375.0 | 16,027.9 |
| May | 6.8 | 25.9 | 565.7 | 47.2 | 320.9 | 22,375.0 | 17,934.7 |
| June | 6.8 | 25.9 | 894.7 | 161.4 | 488.2 | 27,625.0 | 21,730.1 |
| July | 6.8 | 25.9 | 1,130.9 | 325.9 | 847.5 | 33,375.0 | 26,311.4 |
| August | 9.0 | 33.8 | 1,273.4 | 465.8 | 1,466.1 | 39,625.0 | 31,085.8 |
| September | 9.1 | 34.1 | 174.9 | 333.9 | 1,862.9 | 40,625.0 | 33,203.5 |
| October | 9.5 | 34.4 | 236.7 | 259.1 | 2,527.0 | 46,925.0 | 38,456.8 |
| November | 10.1 | 35.4 | 203.8 | 396.0 | 3,278.4 | 49,625.0 | 43,236.2 |
| December | 12.4 | 37.6 | 80.7 | 611.6 | 3,999.2 | 59,625.0 | 43,236.2 |
| December | 12.4 | 37.6 | 80.7 | 611.6 | 3,999.2 | 59,625.0 | 49,361.5 |

**1921:**

| | | | | | | |
|---|---|---|---|---|---|---|
| January | 12.7 | 39.2 | 205.8 | 1,040.2 | 4,100.2 | 65,625.0 | 55,079.5 |
| February | 12.8 | 39.2 | 476.0 | 955.1 | 4,143.5 | 77,125.0 | 62,560.4 |
| March | 13.1 | 39.8 | 908.5 | 781.0 | 4,745.7 | 93,625.0 | 74,087.4 |
| April | 13.4 | 40.3 | 870.7 | 927.0 | 4,994.4 | 106,625.0 | 86,755.3 |
| May | 13.5 | 40.1 | 536.5 | 1,395.2 | 4,979.0 | 117,625.0 | 94,575.8 |
| June | 14.3 | 41.1 | 49.36 | 1,557.3 | 5,306.5 | 130,625.0 | 102,697.3 |
| July | 19.1 | 41.5 | 601.3 | 2,504.2 | 6,291.5 | 140,625.0 | 115,242.3 |
| August | 19.2 | 42.0 | 368.7 | 3,885.4 | 7,776.9 | 158,000.0 | 133,734.2 |
| September | 19.4 | 42.5 | 1,217.5 | 6,237.3 | 9,878.6 | 178,000.0 | 152,792.1 |
| October | 20.2 | 42.9 | 2,341.3 | 9,529.5 | 12,022.3 | 198,500.0 | 182,777.3 |
| November | 22.6 | 43.5 | 7,040.1 | 14,347.2 | 15,144.3 | 214,000.0 | 207,029.0 |
| December | 24.9 | 43.9 | 12,707.9 | 15,324.4 | 19,300.0 | 221,000.0 | 229,537.6 |

**Table P2** (continued)

| Month | Gold[1] | Silver[1] (including base coin) | Balances with Foreign Banks | Discounts | Advances | | Note Circulation |
|---|---|---|---|---|---|---|---|
| | | | | | Commercial | Government | |
| 1922: | | | | | | | |
| January | 26.3 | 44.2 | 13,614.2 | 15,951.6 | 21,776.9 | 227,350.0 | 239,615.3 |
| February | 28.3 | 44.4 | 14,207.7 | 19,555.0 | 22,327.7 | 230,600.0 | 247,209.5 |
| March | 29.0 | 44.7 | 1,156.4 | 25,451.1 | 25,473.3 | 232,100.0 | 250,665.5 |
| April | 29.5 | 45.2 | 7,388.0 | 28,688.8 | 29,063.7 | 220,000.0 | 260,553.8 |
| May | 30.1 | 45.3 | 23,073.4 | 34,555.0 | 26,067.0 | 217,000.0 | 276,001.1 |
| June | 30.9 | 45.3 | 20,521.4 | 46,629.8 | 24,499.5 | 235,000.0 | 300,101.1 |
| July | 31.5 | 45.4 | 21,741.0 | 47,661.2 | 24,054.4 | 260,000.0 | 335,426.6 |
| August | 31.6 | 45.4 | 51,747.2 | 56,366.6 | 21,079.9 | 285,000.0 | 385,787.5 |
| September | 32.4 | 45.4 | 67,384.1 | 64,093.0 | 22,239.4 | 342,000.0 | 463,706.0 |
| October | 33.5 | 45.4 | 64,060.9 | 81,781.9 | 26,576.5 | 453,500.0 | 579,972.7 |
| November | 33.8 | 45.4 | 78,959.0 | 107,320.1 | 41,278.1 | 519,500.0 | 661,092.4 |
| December | 41.0 | 45.4 | 48,580.4 | 133,400.8 | 47,904.1 | 675,600.0 | 793,437.5 |
| 1923: | | | | | | | |
| January | 41.1 | 44.1 | 34,721.8 | 174,950.1 | 51,899.9 | 799,500.0 | 909,160.3 |
| February | 41.4 | 44.1 | 71,883.7 | 219,610.7 | 61,037.1 | 1,085,000.0 | 1,177,300.8 |
| March | 41.7 | 44.2 | 29,868.7 | 274,657.8 | 85,323.2 | 1,752,000.0 | 1,841,205.6 |
| April | 41.9 | 44.2 | 50,851.9 | 304,725.4 | 156,815.4 | 2,161,500.0 | 2,332,396.8 |
| May | 41.9 | 44.3 | 43,900.7 | 449,440.7 | 217,162.3 | 2,377,000.0 | 2,733,794.1 |
| June | 43.9 | 39.8 | 276,506.3 | 627,339.5 | 310,862.7 | 2,996,500.0 | 3,566,649.1 |
| July | 46.9 | 34.8 | 384,375.1 | 758,112.8 | 390,850.9 | 4,190,500.0 | 4,478,709.0 |
| August | 48.0 | 32.9 | 340,354.4 | 1,372,150.9 | 637,268.2 | 6,473,000.0 | 6,871,776.5 |

| | | | | | | |
|---|---|---|---|---|---|---|
| September | 53.2 | 857,084.5 | 2,077,128.6 | 670,019.6 | 10,265,500.0 | 11,197,737.8 |
| October | 54.2 | 1,510,794.3 | 3,540,434.4 | 1,836,712.7 | 19,080,500.0 | 23,080,402.2 |
| November | 54.3 | 6,499,791.5 | 8,467,033.7 | 3,951,781.9 | 42,854,000.0 | 53,217,494.6 |
| December | 54.9 | 57,499,741.7 | 20,588,037.9 | 28,065,396.8 | 111,332,000.0 | 125,371,955.3 |
| 1924: | | | | | | |
| January | 66.2 | 91,533,085.2 | 43,916,802.8 | 54,181,445.2 | 238,200,000.0 | 313,659,830.0 |
| February | 66.7 | 172,626,128.8 | 67,216,289.7 | 83,829,440.5 | 291,700,000.0 | 528,913,418.7 |
| March | 68.0 | 220,658,210.7 | 138,649,934.8 | 81,231,988.5 | 291,700,000.0 | 596,244,205.6 |
| April | 55.7 | 277,340,925.7 | 199,248,956.4 | 60,589,081.0 | 291,700,000.0 | 570,697,550.5 |
| After conversion of State Loan Bank into Bank of Poland, figures in gold zlotys; no ciphers omitted; 1 zloty = 19.3 cents | | | | | | |
| May | 11,684,963[2] | 214,191,336 | 126,522,906 | 1,801,936 | — | 244,977,010 |
| June | 83,392,914[2] | 256,972,386 | 138,862,243 | 5,826,971 | — | 334,405,730 |
| July | 93,683,430[2] | 272,137,898 | 166,713,469 | 8,236,693 | — | 394,262,550 |
| August | 98,288,324[2] | 266,390,583 | 199,710,736 | 8,224,610 | — | 430,263,045 |
| September | 99,900,015[2] | 233,646,562 | 233,788,177 | 9,230,850 | — | 460,383,770 |
| October | 100,686,634 | 241,894,738 | 245,054,984 | 12,374,342 | — | 503,701,830 |
| November | 102,809,285 | 247,034,974 | 249,560,999 | 12,371,166 | — | 497,600,470 |
| December | 103,362,870 | 269,045,551 | 256,954,853 | 23,897,766 | — | 550,873,960 |
| 1925: | | | | | | |
| January | 104,249,258 | 242,115,258 | 270,423,615 | 23,468,829 | — | 553,174,980 |
| February | 107,032,735 | 206,317,320 | 286,229,180 | 28,467,930 | 18,222,212 | 549,637,420 |
| March | 116,619,825 | 259,392,902 | 306,562,690 | 25,477,638 | 403,354 | 563,171,945 |
| April | 117,428,697 | 216,114,621 | 294,632,508 | 27,319,944 | 35,977,630 | 567,178,830 |

Source: Young [36, vol. 2, p. 348].

[1]Gold at par; silver coin at face value.

[2]Gold and silver.

2,402 while the dollar exchange rate decreased by a factor of 1,397 (see tables P3 and P4). As in the other inflations we have studied, the real value of the note circulation decreased as people engaged in a "flight from the mark." Extensive government exchange controls were imposed to resist this trend.

Tables P2 and P3 indicate that the rapid inflation and exchange depreciation both suddenly stopped in January 1924. Unlike the cases of Austria and Hungary, in Poland the initial stabilization was achieved without foreign loans or intervention, although later in 1927, after currency depreciation threatened to renew, a substantial foreign loan was arranged.[25] But in terms of the substantial fiscal and monetary regime changes that accompanied the end of the inflation, there is much similarity to the Austrian and Hungarian experiences. The two interrelated

Table P3            Polish Index Numbers of Wholesale Prices, 1921–25

| Year | Month | Wholesale Price Index[1] | Year | Month | Wholesale Price Index[1] |
|------|-------|-------------------------|------|-------|-------------------------|
| 1921 | January | 25,139 | 1923 | April | 1,058,920 |
|      | February | 31,827 |      | May | 1,125,350 |
|      | March | 32,882 |      | June | 1,881,410 |
|      | April | 31,710 |      | July | 3,069,970 |
|      | May | 32,639 |      | August | 5,294,680 |
|      | June | 35,392 |      | September | 7,302,200 |
|      | July | 45,654 |      | October | 27,380,680 |
|      | August | 53,100 |      | November | 67,943,700 |
|      | September | 60,203 |      | December | 142,300,700 |
|      | October | 65,539 | 1924 | January | 242,167,700 |
|      | November | 58,583 |      | February | 248,429,600 |
|      | December | 57,046 |      | March | 245,277,900 |
| 1922 | January | 59,231 |      | April | 242,321,800 |
|      | February | 63,445 |      | May | |
|      | March | 73,465 |      | June | |
|      | April | 75,106 |      | July | |
|      | May | 78,634 |      | August | |
|      | June | 87,694 |      | September | |
|      | July | 101,587 |      | October | |
|      | August | 135,786 |      | November | |
|      | September | 152,365 |      | December | |
|      | October | 201,326 | 1925 | January | |
|      | November | 275,647 |      | February | |
|      | December | 346,353 |      | March | |
| 1923 | January | 544,690 |      | April | |
|      | February | 859,110 |      | May | |
|      | March | 988,500 |      |  | |

Source: Young [36, vol. 2, p. 349].
[1]1914 = 100.

Table P4          Polish Exchange Rates, 1919–25

| Year | Month | Cents per Polish Mark | Year | Month | Cents per Polish Mark |
|------|-------|------------------------|------|-------|------------------------|
| 1919 | July | 6.88 | 1922 | September | .0127 |
| | August | 5.63 | | October | .0095 |
| | September | 3.88 | | November | .0065 |
| | October | 3.08 | | December | .0057 |
| | November | 1.88 | 1923 | January | .0043 |
| | December | 1.29 | | February | .0025 |
| 1920 | January | .70 | | March | .0024 |
| | February | .68 | | April | .0023 |
| | March | .67 | | May | .0021 |
| | April | .60 | | June | .0013 |
| | May | .51 | | July | .0007 |
| | June | .59 | | August | .0004 |
| | July | .61 | | September | .00035 |
| | August | .47 | | October | .0001113 |
| | September | .45 | | November | .0000502 |
| | October | .37 | | December | .0000234 |
| | November | .26 | 1924 | January | .0000116 |
| | December | .16 | | February | .0000109 |
| 1921 | January | .145 | | March | .0000113 |
| | February | .130 | | April | .0000114 |
| | March | .132 | | May | — |

| | | | | | Cents per Zloty |
|------|-------|------|------|-------|------|
| | April | .130 | | | |
| | May | .124 | | June | 10.29 |
| | June | .082 | | July | 19.25 |
| | July | .0516 | | August | 19.23 |
| | August | .0489 | | September | 19.22 |
| | September | .0256 | | October | 19.22 |
| | October | .0212 | | November | 19.21 |
| | November | .0290 | | December | 19.20 |
| | December | .0313 | 1925 | January | 19.18 |
| 1922 | January | .0327 | | February | 19.18 |
| | February | .0286 | | March | 19.18 |
| | March | .0236 | | April | 19.18 |
| | April | .0262 | | May | 19.18 |
| | May | .0249 | | June | 19.18 |
| | June | .0237 | | | |
| | July | .0185 | | | |
| | August | 0.0135 | | | |

Source: Young [36, vol. 2, p. 350].

changes were a dramatic move toward a balanced government budget and the establishment of an independent central bank that was prohibited from making additional unsecured loans to the government. In January 1924, the minister of finance was granted broad powers to effect monetary and fiscal reform. The minister immediately initiated the establishment of the Bank of Poland, which was to assume the functions of the Polish State Loan Bank. The eventual goal was to restore convertibility with gold. The bank was required to hold a 30% reserve behind its notes, to consist of gold and foreign paper assets denominated in stable currencies. Beyond this reserve, the bank's notes had to be secured by private bills of exchange and silver. A maximum credit to the government of 50 million zlotys was permitted. The government also moved swiftly to balance the budget (see table P1).

In January 1924, a new currency unit became effective, the gold zloty, worth 1.8 million paper marks. The zloty was equal in gold content to 19.29 cents.

Table P2 reveals that, from January 1924 to December 1924, the note circulation of the central bank increased by a factor of 3.2, in the face of relative stability of the price level and the exchange rate (see tables P3 and P4). This phenomenon matches what occurred in Austria and Hun-

**Table P5          Polish Unemployed**

| 1921: | | 1923: | |
|---|---|---|---|
| January | 74,000 | January | 81,184 |
| February | 90,000 | February | 106,729 |
| March | 80,000 | March | 114,576 |
| April | 88,000 | April | 112,755 |
| May | 130,000 | May | 93,731 |
| June | 115,000 | June | 76,397 |
| July | 95,000 | July | 64,563 |
| August | 65,000 | August | 56,515 |
| September | 70,000 | September | — |
| October | 78,000 | October | — |
| November | 120,000 | November | — |
| December | 173,000 | December | 67,581 |
| 1922: | | 1924: | |
| January | 221,444 | January | 100,580 |
| February | 206,442 | February | 110,737 |
| March | 170,125 | March | 112,583 |
| April | 148,625 | April | 109,000 |
| May | 128,916 | May | 84,000 |
| June | 98,581 | June | 97,870 |
| July | 85,240 | July | 149,097 |
| August | 69,692 | August | 159,820 |
| September | 68,000 | September | 155,245 |
| October | 61,000 | October | 147,065 |
| November | 62,000 | November | 150,180 |
| December | 75,000 | December | 159,060 |

Source: *Statistiches Jahrbuch fur das Deutsche Reich* [33].

gary and has a similar explanation. As table P2 reveals, the increased note circulation during this period was effectively backed 100% by gold, foreign exchange, and private paper.

The available figures on unemployment are summarized in table P5. The stabilization of the price level in January 1924 is accompanied by an abrupt rise in the number of unemployed. Another rise occurs in July of 1924. While the figures indicate substantial unemployment in late 1924, unemployment is not an order of magnitude worse than before the stabilization, and certainly not anywhere nearly as bad as would be predicted by application of the same method of analysis that was used to fabricate the prediction for the contemporary United States that each percentage point reduction in inflation would require a reduction of $220 billion in real GNP.

The Polish zloty depreciated internationally from late 1925 onward but stabilized in autumn of 1926 at around 72% of its level of January 1924. At the same time, the domestic price level stabilized at about 50% above its level of January 1924. The threatened renewal of inflation has been attributed to the government's premature relaxation of exchange controls and the tendency of the central bank to make private loans at insufficient interest rates.[26]

## 2.6 Germany

After World War I, Germany owed staggering reparations to the Allied countries. This fact dominated Germany's public finance from 1919 until 1923 and was a most important force for hyperinflation.

At the conclusion of the war, Germany experienced a political revolution and established a republican government. The early postwar governments were dominated by moderate Socialists, who for a variety of reasons reached accommodations with centers of military and industrial power of the prewar regime.[27] These accommodations in effect undermined the willingness and capability of the government to meet its admittedly staggering revenue needs through explicit taxation.

Of the four episodes that we have studied, Germany's hyperinflation was the most spectacular, as the figures on wholesale prices and exchange rates in tables G1 and G2 reveal. The inflation became most severe after the military occupation of the Ruhr by the French in January 1923. The German government was determined to fight the French occupation by a policy of passive resistance, making direct payments to striking workers which were financed by discounting treasury bills with the Reichsbank.

Table G3 estimates the budget of Germany for 1920 to 1923.[28] The table reveals that, except for 1923, the budget would not have been badly out of balance except for the massive reparations payments made. The disruption caused to Germany's finances by the reparations situation is

**Table G1          German Wholesale Prices, 1914–24**

| Year | Month | Price Index | Year | Month | Price Index |
|------|-------|------------:|------|-------|------------:|
| 1914 | January | 96 | 1918 | January | 204 |
|      | February | 96 |      | February | 198 |
|      | March | 96 |      | March | 198 |
|      | April | 95 |      | April | 204 |
|      | May | 97 |      | May | 203 |
|      | June | 99 |      | June | 209 |
|      | July | 99 |      | July | 208 |
|      | August | 109 |      | August | 235 |
|      | September | 111 |      | September | 230 |
|      | October | 118 |      | October | 234 |
|      | November | 123 |      | November | 234 |
|      | December | 125 |      | December | 245 |
| 1915 | January | 126 | 1919 | January | 262 |
|      | February | 133 |      | February | 270 |
|      | March | 139 |      | March | 274 |
|      | April | 142 |      | April | 286 |
|      | May | 139 |      | May | 297 |
|      | June | 139 |      | June | 308 |
|      | July | 150 |      | July | 339 |
|      | August | 146 |      | August | 422 |
|      | September | 145 |      | September | 493 |
|      | October | 147 |      | October | 562 |
|      | November | 147 |      | November | 678 |
|      | December | 148 |      | December | 803 |
| 1916 | January | 150 | 1920 | January | 1,260 |
|      | February | 151 |      | February | 1,690 |
|      | March | 148 |      | March | 1,710 |
|      | April | 149 |      | April | 1,570 |
|      | May | 151 |      | May | 1,510 |
|      | June | 152 |      | June | 1,380 |
|      | July | 161 |      | July | 1,370 |
|      | August | 159 |      | August | 1,450 |
|      | September | 154 |      | September | 1,500 |
|      | October | 153 |      | October | 1,470 |
|      | November | 151 |      | November | 1,510 |
|      | December | 151 |      | December | 1,440 |
| 1917 | January | 156 | 1921 | January | 1,440 |
|      | February | 158 |      | February | 1,380 |
|      | March | 159 |      | March | 1,340 |
|      | April | 163 |      | April | 1,330 |
|      | May | 163 |      | May | 1,310 |
|      | June | 165 |      | June | 1,370 |
|      | July | 172 |      | July | 1,430 |
|      | August | 203 |      | August | 1,920 |
|      | September | 199 |      | September | 2,070 |
|      | October | 201 |      | October | 2,460 |
|      | November | 203 |      | November | 3,420 |
|      | December | 203 |      | December | 3,490 |

**Table G1** (continued)

| Year | Month | Price Index | Year | Month | Price Index |
|------|-------|------------:|------|-------|------------:|
| 1922 | January | 3,670 | 1923 | July | 7,478,700 |
|      | February | 4,100 |      | August | 94,404,100 |
|      | March | 5,430 |      | September | 2,394,889,300 |
|      | April | 6,360 |      | October | 709,480,000,000 |
|      | May | 6,460 |      | November | 72,570,000,000,000 |
|      | June | 7,030 |      | December | 126,160,000,000,000 |
|      | July | 10,160 | 1924 | January | 117,320,000,000,000 |
|      | August | 19,200 |      | February | 116,170,000,000,000 |
|      | September | 28,700 |      | March | 120,670,000,000,000 |
|      | October | 56,600 |      | April | 124,050,000,000,000 |
|      | November | 115,100 |      | May | 122,460,000,000,000 |
|      | December | 147,480 |      | June | 115,900,000,000,000 |
| 1923 | January | 278,500 |      | July | 115[1] |
|      | February | 588,500 |      | August | 120[1] |
|      | March | 488,800 |      | September | 127[1] |
|      | April | 521,200 |      | October | 131[1] |
|      | May | 817,000 |      | November | 129[1] |
|      | June | 1,938,500 |      | December | 131[1] |

Source: Young [36, vol. 1, p. 530].
[1]On basis of prices in reichsmarks. (1 reichsmark = 1 trillion [$10^{12}$] former marks.)

surely understated by the reparations figures given in table G3. For one thing, considerably larger sums were initially expected of Germany than it ever was eventually able to pay. For another thing, the extent of Germany's total obligation and the required schedule of payments was for a long time uncertain and under negotiation. From the viewpoint that the value of a state's currency and other debt depends intimately on the fiscal policy it intends to run, the uncertainty about the reparations owed by the German government necessarily cast a long shadow over its prospects for a stable currency.

As table G4 reveals, the note circulation of the Reichsbank increased dramatically from 1921 to 1923, especially in the several months before November 1923. As pointed out by Young [36], at the end of October 1923, over 99% of outstanding Reichsbank notes had been placed in circulation within the previous 30 days.[29] Table G4 reveals the extent to which the Reichsbank note circulation was backed by discounted treasury bills. During 1923, the Reichsbank also began discounting large volumes of commercial bills. Since these loans were made at nominal rates of interest far below the rate of inflation, they amounted virtually to government transfer payments to the recipients of the loans.

Especially during the great inflation of 1923, a force came into play which was also present in the other hyperinflations we have studied.

**Table G2**               **German Exchange Rates, 1914–25**

| Year | Month | Cents per Mark | Year | Month | Cents per Mark |
|---|---|---|---|---|---|
| 1920 | January | 1.69 | 1922 | August | .10 |
| | February | 1.05 | | September | .07 |
| | March | 1.26 | | October | .03 |
| | April | 1.67 | | November | .01 |
| | May | 2.19 | | December | .01 |
| | June | 2.56 | 1923 | January | .007 |
| | July | 2.53 | | February | .004 |
| | August | 2.10 | | March | .005 |
| | September | 1.72 | | April | .004 |
| | October | 1.48 | | May | .002 |
| | November | 1.32 | | June | .001 |
| | December | 1.37 | | July | .000,3 |
| 1921 | January | 1.60 | | August | .000,033,9 |
| | February | 1.64 | | September | .000,001,88 |
| | March | 1.60 | | October | .000,000,068 |
| | April | 1.57 | | November | .000,000,000,043 |
| | May | 1.63 | | December | .000,000,000,022,7 |
| | June | 1.44 | 1924 | January | 22.6 |
| | July | 1.30 | | February | 21.8 |
| | August | 1.19 | | March | 22.0 |
| | September | .96 | | April | 22.0 |
| | October | .68 | | May | 22.3 |
| | November | .39 | | June | 23.4 |
| | December | .53 | | July | 23.9 |
| 1922 | January | .52 | | August | 23.8 |
| | February | .48 | | September | 23.8 |
| | March | .36 | | October | 23.8 |
| | April | .35 | | November | 23.8 |
| | May | .34 | | December | 23.8 |
| | June | .32 | 1925[1] | January | 23.8 |
| | July | .20 | | | |

Source: Young [36, vol. 1, p. 532].

[1]Cents per rentenmark and (after October 1924) per reichsmark. 1 rentenmark is equivalent to 1 reichsmark or 1 billion former paper marks. The reichsmark is the equivalent of the gold mark worth 23.82 cents.

**Table G3**  Real German Revenues and Expenditures, Calculated on the Basis of the Cost-of-Living Index (in millions of gold marks)

| | Revenue | | | | Expenditures | | | | | |
|---|---|---|---|---|---|---|---|---|---|---|
| | Taxes | Sundries | Deficit Covered by Loan Transactions | Total | Repayment of Floating Debt | Interest on Floating Debt | Subsidies to Railroads | Execution of Versailles Treaty | Sundries | Total |
| 1920–21 | 4,090.8 | 132.9 | 7,041.9 | 11,265.6 | 821.7 | — | — | — | — | 11,265.6 |
| 1921–22 | 5,235.7 | 100.5 | 6,627.4 | 11,963.6 | 1,039.5 | 811.6 | 1,114.4 | 5,110.6 | 5,738.4 | 11,963.4 |
| 1922–23 | 3,529.1 | 51.4 | 6,384.5 | 9,965.0 | 81.0 | 344.4 | 1,685.5 | 3,600.0 | 4,254.1 | 9,965.0 |
| 1923–24 (first 9 months) | 1,496.1 | 180.6 | 11,836.5 | 13,513.2 | — | 931.0 | 3,725.0 | — | — | 13,513.2 |

Source: Young [36, vol. 2, p. 393].

Table G4    Balance Sheet of German Reichsbank, 1914–24

| | Discounted Bills | | Total Discounted Treasury and Commercial Bills | Advances | Securities |
|---|---|---|---|---|---|
| | Treasury Bills | Commercial Bills | | | |
| **1921:** | | | | | |
| January | 50,594,540 | 2,742,406 | 53,336,946 | 8,881 | 147,126 |
| February | 53,690,412 | 2,760,927 | 56,451,339 | 11,522 | 185,788 |
| March | 64,533,894 | 2,268,745 | 66,802,639 | 2,805 | 217,044 |
| April | 58,841,630 | 2,052,099 | 60,803,729 | 9,238 | 225,777 |
| May | 62,953,604 | 1,809,936 | 64,763,540 | 16,624 | 258,664 |
| June | 79,607,790 | 1,565,406 | 81,172,196 | 6,079 | 282,716 |
| July | 79,981,967 | 1,135,529 | 81,117,496 | 10,686 | 283,381 |
| August | 84,043,891 | 1,002,497 | 85,046,388 | 7,704 | 258,319 |
| September | 98,422,137 | 1,142,218 | 99,564,355 | 3,289 | 277,977 |
| October | 98,704,768 | 881,474 | 99,586,242 | 47,775 | 282,179 |
| November | 114,023,417 | 1,445,667 | 115,469,084 | 90,370 | 247,699 |
| December | 132,380,906 | 1,061,754 | 133,392,660 | 8,476 | 195,912 |
| **1922:** | | | | | |
| January | 126,160,402 | 1,592,416 | 127,752,818 | 20,548 | 198,725 |
| February | 134,251,808 | 1,856,936 | 136,108,744 | 62,305 | 215,362 |
| March | 146,531,247 | 2,151,677 | 148,682,924 | 20,688 | 205,936 |
| April | 155,617,524 | 2,403,044 | 158,020,568 | 134,314 | 229,242 |
| May | 167,793,922 | 3,376,599 | 171,170,521 | 54,361 | 199,314 |
| June | 186,125,747 | 4,751,748 | 190,877,495 | 58,994 | 307,564 |
| July | 207,858,232 | 8,122,066 | 215,980,298 | 141,276 | 313,488 |
| August | 249,765,773 | 21,704,341 | 271,470,114 | 172,966 | 241,162 |
| September | 349,169,650 | 50,234,414 | 400,004,064 | 61,516 | 416,193 |

| | | | | | |
|---|---|---|---|---|---|
| October | 477,201,494 | 101,155,267 | 578,356,761 | 624,368 | 502,348 |
| November | 672,222,197 | 246,948,596 | 919,170,793 | 51,425,030¹ | 381,068 |
| December | 1,184,464,359 | 422,235,296 | 1,606,699,655 | 773,974 | 469,972 |
| 1923: | | | | | |
| January | 1,609,081,121 | 697,216,424 | 2,306,297,545 | 95,316,552 | 483,318 |
| February | 2,947,363,994 | 1,829,341,080 | 4,776,705,074 | 27,422,282 | 1,209,935 |
| March | 4,552,011,661 | 2,372,101,757 | 6,924,113,418 | 2,132,906 | 1,690,011 |
| April | 6,224,899,348 | 2,986,116,724 | 9,211,016,072 | 20,466,948 | 1,207,105 |
| May | 8,021,904,840 | 4,014,693,720 | 12,036,598,560 | 61,030,322 | 697,611 |
| June | 18,338² | 6,914,198,630 | 25,252,198,630 | 188,548,574 | 344,819 |
| July | 53,752² | 18,314² | 72,066² | 2,553,177,597 | 1,422,291 |
| August | 987,219² | 164,644² | 1,151,863² | 25,261² | 15,539,853 |
| September | 45,216,224² | 3,660,094² | 48,876,318² | 98,522² | 1,801,579,570 |
| October | 6,578,650,939² | 1,058,129,855² | 7,636,780,794² | 41,787,532² | 9,536,953² |
| 15 November | 189,801,468,187² | 39,529,577,254² | 229,331,045,441² | 535,714,637² | 8,901,495² |
| 30 November | 96,874,330,250² | 347,301,037,776² | 444,175,368,026² | 7,742,665,263² | 336,495,629² |
| December | (3) | 322,724,948,986² | 322,724,948,986² | 268,325,819,530² | 65,791,385² |
| 1924:[4] | | | | | |
| January | — | — | 755,866 | 336,520 | 12 |
| February | — | — | 1,165,649 | 306,618 | 25 |
| March | — | — | 1,767,443 | 143,102 | 533 |
| April | — | — | 1,916,969 | 156,362 | 91,984 |
| May | — | — | 1,954,930 | 128,597 | 80,011 |
| June | — | — | 1,897,959 | 108,789 | 76,378 |
| July | — | — | 1,798,097 | 62,489 | 76,509 |
| August | — | — | 1,860,843 | 59,983 | 76,331 |
| September | — | — | 2,169,684 | 54,424 | 78,305 |
| 15 October[5] | — | — | 2,153,943 | 15,947 | 77,517 |
| 31 October | — | — | 2,339,616 | 33,443 | 77,699 |
| November | — | — | 2,290,166 | 18,628 | 77,808 |
| December | — | — | 2,064,094 | 16,960 | 77,999 |

(Footnotes appear on p. 82)

**Table G4** (continued)

|  | Notes in Circulation | Demand Deposits | | | |
|---|---|---|---|---|---|
|  |  | Public | Other | Total Demand Deposits | Due to the Rentenbank |
| **1921:** | | | | | |
| January | 66,620,804 | 4,055,904 | 11,778,060 | 15,833,964 | |
| February | 67,426,959 | 7,291,052 | 10,066,036 | 17,357,088 | |
| March | 69,417,228 | 15,206,381 | 12,836,292 | 28,042,673 | |
| April | 70,839,725 | 11,595,618 | 9,260,271 | 20,855,889 | |
| May | 71,838,866 | 3,548,492 | 10,545,201 | 14,093,693 | |
| June | 75,321,095 | 5,647,805 | 14,744,903 | 20,392,708 | |
| July | 77,390,853 | 4,810,026 | 11,014,130 | 15,824,156 | |
| August | 80,072,721 | 4,850,843 | 8,798,756 | 13,649,599 | |
| September | 86,384,286 | 4,618,087 | 15,362,208 | 19,980,295 | |
| October | 91,527,679 | 5,239,628 | 13,063,035 | 18,302,663 | |
| November | 100,943,632 | 5,144,615 | 20,168,499 | 25,313,114 | |
| December | 113,639,464 | 7,591,343 | 25,314,330 | 32,905,673 | |
| **1922:** | | | | | |
| January | 115,375,766 | 5,286,950 | 18,125,502 | 23,421,452 | |
| February | 120,026,387 | 5,806,922 | 20,719,150 | 26,526,072 | |
| March | 130,671,352 | 7,743,735 | 25,614,597 | 33,358,332 | |
| April | 140,420,057 | 7,577,862 | 24,038,306 | 31,616,168 | |
| May | 151,949,179 | 7,711,279 | 25,416,711 | 33,127,990 | |
| June | 169,211,792 | 10,125,837 | 27,047,908 | 37,173,745 | |
| July | 189,794,722 | 9,197,727 | 30,778,489 | 39,976,216 | |
| August | 238,147,160 | 13,708,213 | 42,416,241 | 56,124,454 | |
| September | 316,869,799 | 30,034,309 | 79,978,068 | 110,012,377 | |

| | | | | | |
|---|---:|---:|---:|---:|---:|
| October | 469,456,818 | 34,270,926 | 106,508,333 | 140,779,259 | |
| November | 754,086,109 | 50,353,945 | 190,615,514 | 240,969,459 | |
| December | 1,280,094,831 | 153,190,991 | 377,335,296 | 530,526,287 | |
| **1923:** | | | | | |
| January | 1,984,496,369 | 157,058,537 | 605,205,692 | 763,264,229 | |
| February | 3,512,787,777 | 253,915,266 | 1,329,065,770 | 1,582,981,036 | |
| March | 5,517,919,651 | 368,550,293 | 1,903,533,291 | 2,272,083,584 | |
| April | 6,545,984,355 | 454,403,079 | 3,399,871,714 | 3,854,274,793 | |
| May | 8,563,749,470 | 652,575,366 | 4,410,494,865 | 5,063,070,231 | |
| June | 17,291[2] | 1,648,114,327 | 8,304,602,339 | 9,952,716,666 | |
| July | 43,595[2] | 3,779,235,298 | 24,078[2] | 27,857[2] | |
| August | 663,200[2] | 206,168[2] | 384,912[2] | 591,080[2] | |
| Setember | 28,228,815[2] | 8,186,467[2] | 8,781,150[2] | 16,966,617[2] | |
| October | 2,496,822,909[2] | 606,660,673[2] | 3,261,424,030[2] | 3,868,085,703[2] | |
| 15 November | 92,844,720,743[2] | 72,457,230,513[2] | 57,095,366,904[2] | 129,552,597,417[2] | |
| 30 November | 400,267,640,302[2] | 120,478,936,906[2] | 253,497,803,653[2] | 373,976,740,559[2] | |
| December | 496,507,424,772[2] | 303,114,560,004[2] | 244,906,637,001[2] | 548,024,197,005[2] | |
| **1924:[4]** | | | | | |
| January | 483,675 | 492,985 | 281,320 | 281,305 | 200,000 |
| February | 587,875 | 367,551 | 282,958 | 650,509 | 400,000 |
| March | 689,864 | 352,360 | 352,334 | 704,694 | 800,000 |
| April | 776,949 | 474,411 | 330,561 | 804,972 | 800,000 |
| May | 926,874 | 545,252 | 259,203 | 804,455 | 800,000 |
| June | 1,097,309 | 493,043 | 280,884 | 773,927 | 800,000 |
| July | 1,211,038 | 452,597 | 290,390 | 742,987 | 800,000 |
| August | 1,391,895 | 264,064 | 297,791 | 561,855 | 800,000 |
| September | 1,520,511 | 307,515 | 362,581 | 670,096 | 800,000 |
| 15 October[5] | 1,396,748 | — | — | 828,511 | 800,000 |
| 31 October | 1,780,930 | — | — | 708,728 | 800,000 |
| November | 1,863,200 | — | — | 703,938 | 684,664 |
| December | 1,941,440 | — | — | 820,865 | 456,508 |

(Footnotes appear on p. 82)

Given the method of assessing taxes in nominal terms, lags between the time when taxes were levied and the time when they were collected led to reduced revenues as the government evidently repeatedly underestimated the prospective rate of inflation and as the rapid inflation gave people a large incentive to delay paying their taxes. This effect probably partially accounts for the reduced tax revenues collected during the first nine months of 1923. The French occupation of the Ruhr also helps explain it.

In response to the inflationary public finance and despite the efforts of the government to impose exchange controls, there occurred a "flight from the German mark" in which the real value of Reichsmark notes decreased dramatically. The figures in table G1 indicate that between January 1922 and July 1923, wholesale prices increased by a factor of 2,038 while Reichsbank notes increased by a factor of 378. Between January 1922 and August 1923, wholesale prices increased by a factor of 25,723 while Reichsbank notes circulating increased by a factor of 5,748. The fact that prices increased proportionately many times more than did the Reichsbank note circulation is symptomatic of the efforts of Germans to economize on their holdings of rapidly depreciating German marks. Toward the end of the hyperinflation, Germans made every effort to avoid holding marks and held large quantities of foreign exchange for purposes of conducting transaction. By October 1923, it has been roughly estimated, the real value of foreign currencies circulating in Germany was at least equal to and perhaps several times the real value of Reichsbank notes circulating.[30]

The figures in tables G1 and G2 show that prices suddenly stopped rising and the mark stopped depreciating in late November 1923. The event of stabilization was attended by a "monetary reform," in which on 15 October 1923 a new currency unit called the Rentenmark was declared equivalent to 1 trillion ($10^{12}$) paper marks. While great psychological

---

Footnotes to Table G4

Source: Young [36, vol. 1, pp. 528–29].

Note: End of month figures, in thousands of current marks; from January 1924 in thousands of rentenmarks or reichsmarks. 1 rentenmark is equivalent to 1 reichsmark or 1 trillion ($10^{12}$) former paper marks. The reichsmark is the equivalent of the gold mark worth 23.82 cents.

[1]The large increase of advances at the close of November 1922 occurred because the Reichsbank had to take over temporarily the financing of food supplies from the loan bureaus (Darlehuskassen), as the latter were unable to extend the needed accommodation, their outstanding notes having reached the maximum amount permitted by law.

[2]In billions.

[3]A decree of 15 November 1923 discontinued the discounting of treasury bills by the Reichsbank.

[4]See note above.

[5]Date of first statement of reorganized Reichsbank.

significance has sometimes been assigned to this unit change, it is difficult to attribute any substantial effects to what was in itself only a cosmetic measure.[31] The substantive aspect of the decree of 15 October was the establishing of a Rentenbank to take over the note issue functions of the Reichbank. The decree put binding limits upon both the total volume of Rentenmarks that could be issued, 3.2 billion marks, and the maximum amount that could be issued to the government, 1.2 billion marks. This limitation on the amount of credit that could be extended to the government was announced at a time when the government was financing virtually 100% of its expenditures by means of note issue.[32] In December 1923, the management of the Rentenbank was tested by the government and effectively made clear its intent to meet its obligation to limit government borrowing to within the amount decreed.

Simultaneously and abruptly three things happened: additional government borrowing from the central bank stopped, the government budget swung into balance, and inflation stopped. Table G5 shows the dramatic progress toward a balanced budget that was made in the months after the Rentenbank decree.

The government moved to balance the budget by taking a series of deliberate, permanent actions to raise taxes and eliminate expenditures.

**Table G5**    **Ordinary Revenues and Expenditures of the German Federal Government (from Wirtschift and Statistik, issued by the Statistisches Reichsamt, in millions of gold marks)**

|  | Ordinary Revenue | | Ordinary Expenditures | Excess of Revenue (+) or Expenditure (−) |
|---|---|---|---|---|
|  | Total | Of Which Taxes Yielded | | |
| **1923:** | | | | |
| November | 68.1 | 63.2 | — | — |
| December | 333.9 | 312.3 | 668.7 | − 334.8 |
| **1924:** | | | | |
| January | 520.6 | 503.5 | 396.5 | + 124.1 |
| February | 445.0 | 418.0 | 462.8 | − 17.8 |
| March | 632.4 | 595.3 | 498.6 | 133.8 |
| April | 579.5 | 523.8 | 523.5 | + 56.0 |
| May | 566.7 | 518.7 | 459.1 | + 107.6 |
| June | 529.7 | 472.3 | 504.5 | + 25.2 |
| July | 622.2 | 583.1 | 535.1 | + 86.9 |
| August | 618.2 | 592.0 | 597.6 | + 20.6 |
| September | 665.6 | 609.2 | 581.6 | + 84.0 |
| October | 714.3 | 686.7 | 693.0 | + 21.3 |

Source: Young [36, vol. 1, p. 422].

Young reports that "by the personnel decree of October 27, 1923, the number of government employees was cut by 25 percent; all temporary employees were to be discharged; all above the age of 65 years were to be retired. An additional 10 percent of the civil servants were to be discharged by January 1924. The railways, overstaffed as a result of post-war demobilization, discharged 120,000 men during 1923 and 60,000 more during 1924. The postal administration reduced its staff by 65,000 men; the Reichsbank itself which had increased the number of its employees from 13,316 at the close of 1922 to 22,909 at the close of 1923, began the discharge of its superfluous force in December, as soon as the effects of stabilization became manifest."[33]

Substantially aiding the fiscal situation, Germany also obtained relief from her reparation obligations. Reparations payments were temporarily suspended, and the Dawes plan assigned Germany a much more manageable schedule of payments.

Table G4 documents a pattern that we have seen in the three other hyperinflations: the substantial growth of central bank note and demand deposit liabilities in the months *after* the currency was stabilized. As in the other cases that we have studied, the best explanation for this is that at the margin the postinflation increase in notes was no longer backed by government debt. Instead, in the German case, it was largely backed by discounted commercial bills. The nature of the system of promises and claims behind the central bank's liabilities changed when after the Rentenbank decree the central bank no longer offered additional credit to the government. So once again the interpretation of the time series on central bank notes and deposits must undergo a very substantial change.

By all available measures, the stabilization of the German mark was accompanied by increases in output and employment and decreases in unemployment.[34] While 1924 was not a good year for German business, it was much better than 1923. Table G6 is representative of the figures assembled by Graham, and shows that 1924 suffers in comparison with 1922 but that 1925 was a good year. In these figures one cannot find much convincing evidence of a favorable trade-off between inflation and out-

Table G6    **Index of Physical Volume
of Production per Capita in Germany**

| Year | Index of Production | Year | Index of Production |
|------|---------------------|------|---------------------|
| 1920 | 61 | 1924 | 77 |
| 1921 | 77 | 1925 | 90 |
| 1922 | 86 | 1926 | 86 |
| 1923 | 54 | 1927 | 111 |

Source: Graham [7, p. 287].

put, since the year of spectacular inflation, 1923 was a very bad year for employment and physical production. Certainly a large part of the poor performance of 1923 was due to the French occupation of the Ruhr and the policy of passive resistance.

Despite the evident absence of a "Phillips curve" trade-off between inflation and real output in the figures in tables G1 and G6, there is ample evidence that the German inflation was far from "neutral" and that there were important "real effects." Graham [7] gives evidence that the inflation and the associated reduction in real rates of return to "high-powered" money and other government debt were accompanied by real overinvestment in many kinds of capital goods.[35] There is little doubt that the "irrational" structure of capital characterizing Germany after stabilization led to subsequent problems of adjustment in labor and other markets.

### 2.7  Czechoslovakia

After World War I, the new nation of Czechoslovakia was formed out of territories formerly belonging to Austria and Hungary. Under the leadership of a distinguished minister of finance, Dr. Alois Rasin, immediately after the war Czechoslovakia adopted the conservative fiscal and monetary policies its neighbors adopted only after their currencies had depreciated radically. As a result, Czechoslovakia avoided the hyperinflation experienced by its neighbors.

Under Rasin's leadership, Czechoslovakia early on showed that it was serious about attaining a stable currency. Even before the peace treaties required it, Czechoslovakia stamped the Austro-Hungarian notes then circulating within its border with the Czechoslovakian stamp, thereby recognizing them as its own debt. There was considerable drama associated with this event, as the National Assembly passed the plans for stamping in secret sessions on 25 February 1919. From 26 February to 9 March, the frontiers of the country were unexpectedly closed and foreign mail service was closed. Only Austro-Hungarian notes circulating within the country could be presented for stamping. As part of the stamping process, the government retained part of the notes in the form of a forced loan.[36] About 8 billion crowns were stamped.

A banking office in the Ministry of Finance took over the affairs of the old Austro-Hungarian bank. Czechoslovakia moved quickly to limit by statute the total government note circulation and to prevent inflationary government finance. A law of 10 April 1919 strictly limited the fiduciary or unbacked note circulation of the banking office to about 7 billion crowns. This law was obeyed, and forced the government to finance its expenditures by levying taxes or else issuing debt, which, because of the statutory restriction on government note issues, were interpreted as promises to tax in the future.

From 1920 on, Czechoslovakia ran only modest deficits on current account (see table C1). Among other taxes, Czechoslovakia imposed a progressive capital levy on property, which raised a cumulative amount of about 11 billion crowns by 1925. It also imposed an increment tax on the increased wealth individuals had obtained during the war.

Table C2 shows the note and deposit liabilities of the banking office. The government's abstention from inflationary finance shows up in these figures.

Table C1    **Czechoslovakia, Receipts and Expenditures, 1919–25 (exclusive of expenditures for capital improvements covered by loans)**

|  | 1919 | | 1920 | | 1922 | | 1922 | |
|---|---|---|---|---|---|---|---|---|
|  | Esti-mated | Ac-tual | Esti-mated | Ac-tual | Esti-mated | Ac-tual | Esti-mated | Ac-tual |
| Revenue: | | | | | | | | |
| Ordinary | 2,614 | — | 7,950 | — | 15,923 | — | 17,291 | — |
| Extraordinary | 1,096 | — | 2,477 | — | 1,376 | — | 1,593 | — |
| Total | 3,710 | — | 10,427 | 13,455 | 17,299 | 21,894 | 18,884 | 17,733 |
| Expenditure: | | | | | | | | |
| Ordinary | 2,610 | — | 7,175 | — | 10,672 | — | 13,289 | — |
| Extraordinary | 6,005 | — | 8,103 | — | 7,354 | — | 6,524 | — |
| Total | 8,615 | 7,450 | 15,278 | 13,931 | 18,026 | 18,558 | 19,813 | 18,663 |
| Deficit | 4,905 | — | 4,851 | 476 | 727 | — | 929 | 930 |
| Surplus | — | — | — | — | — | 3,336 | — | — |

|  | 1923 | | 1924 | | 1925 | |
|---|---|---|---|---|---|---|
|  | Esti-mated | Ac-tual | Esti-mated | Ac-tual | Esti-mated | Ac-tual |
| Revenue: | | | | | | |
| Ordinary | 17,961 | — | 15,987 | — | — | — |
| Extraordinary | 851 | — | 404 | — | — | — |
| Total | 18,812 | 15,664 | 16,391 | — | 15,702 | — |
| Expenditure: | | | | | | |
| Ordinary | 13,605 | — | 12,200 | — | — | — |
| Extraordinary | 5,773 | — | 4,703 | — | — | — |
| Total | 19,378 | 16,540 | 16,993 | — | 15,974 | — |
| Deficit | 565 | 876 | 603 | — | 272 | — |
| Surplus | — | — | — | — | — | — |

Source: Young [36, vol. 2, p. 71].

Table C3 shows the path of exchange rates and how, after declining until November 1921, the Czechoslovakian crown rapidly gained to about 3 United States cents.

Table C4 shows the price levels. From 1922 to 1923, Czechoslovakia actually experienced a deflation. Indeed, Rasin's initial plan had been to

**Table C2**    Note Issue of Banking Office of Czechoslovakia, 1919–24
(in thousands of Czech crowns)

| Year | Month | State Notes in Circulation | Year | Month | State Notes in Circulation |
|------|-------|---------------------------|------|-------|---------------------------|
| 1919 | April | — | | May | 9,717,750 |
| | May | — | | June | 9,838,205 |
| | June | — | | July | 9,916,077 |
| | July | 161,106 | | August | 10,171,383 |
| | August | 664,997 | | September | 10,196,880 |
| | September | 1,443,570 | | October | 10,139,366 |
| | October | 2,512,199 | | November | 9,996,550 |
| | November | 3,513,405 | | December | 10,064,049 |
| | December | 4,723,303 | 1923 | January | 9,222,434 |
| 1920 | January | 5,574,688 | | February | 8,947,988 |
| | February | 6,462,825 | | March | 9,157,407 |
| | March | 7,216,438 | | April | 9,567,369 |
| | April | 7,216,438 | | May | 9,327,676 |
| | May | 8,268,695 | | June | 9,375,991 |
| | June | 9,729,233 | | July | 9,448,086 |
| | July | 9,267,874 | | August | 9,218,475 |
| | August | 9,814,920 | | September | 9,311,378 |
| | September | 10,310,228 | | October | 9,278,999 |
| | October | 10,920,514 | | November | 9,250,688 |
| | November | 10,946,653 | | December | 9,598,903 |
| | December | 11,288,512 | 1924 | January | 8,820,093 |
| 1921 | January | 10,888,319 | | February | 8,506,467 |
| | February | 10,914,786 | | March | 8,280,390 |
| | March | 10,921,956 | | April | 8,198,653 |
| | April | 10,928,560 | | May | 9,078,418 |
| | May | 10,851,403 | | June | 8,081,106 |
| | June | 11,167,515 | | July | 8,090,034 |
| | July | 11,134,327 | | August | 9,139,792 |
| | August | 11,455,175 | | September | 8,222,658 |
| | September | 11,570,881 | | October | 8,585,847 |
| | October | 12,327,159 | | November | 8,500,942 |
| | November | 11,871,647 | | December | 8,810,357 |
| | December | 12,129,573 | 1925 | January | 7,916,540 |
| 1922 | January | 11,230,065 | | February | 7,727,880 |
| | February | 10,743,958 | | March | 7,680,867 |
| | March | 10,323,069 | | April | 7,525,934 |
| | April | 10,075,757 | | | |

Source: Young [36, vol. 2, pp. 305–6].

**Table C3**  Czechoslovakian Exchange Rates, 1919–24

| Year | Month | Cents per Crown | Year | Month | Cents per Crown |
|------|-------|-----------------|------|-------|-----------------|
| 1919 | January | — | 1922 | April | 1.960 |
| | February | — | | May | 1.921 |
| | March | — | | June | 1.924 |
| | April | 6.135 | | July | 2.185 |
| | May | — | | August | 2.902 |
| | June | — | | September | 3.231 |
| | July | 5.625 | | October | 3.285 |
| | August | 4.575 | | November | 3.176 |
| | September | 4.575 | | December | 3.097 |
| | October | 3.100 | 1923 | January | 2.856 |
| | November | 1.950 | | February | 2.958 |
| | December | 1.900 | | March | 2.969 |
| 1920 | January | 1.425 | | April | 2.978 |
| | February | .975 | | May | 2.979 |
| | March | 1.275 | | June | 2.993 |
| | April | 1.530 | | July | 2.997 |
| | May | 2.195 | | August | 2.934 |
| | June | 2.335 | | September | 2.995 |
| | July | 2.195 | | October | 2.971 |
| | August | 1.810 | | November | 2.906 |
| | September | 1.535 | | December | 2.925 |
| | October | 1.245 | 1924 | January | 2.898 |
| | November | 1.165 | | February | 2.902 |
| | December | 1.190 | | March | 2.902 |
| 1921 | January | 1.300 | | April | 2.957 |
| | February | 1.290 | | May | 2.939 |
| | March | 1.307 | | June | 2.936 |
| | April | 1.365 | | July | 2.953 |
| | May | 1.460 | | August | 2.979 |
| | June | 1.420 | | September | 2.993 |
| | July | 1.312 | | October | 2.981 |
| | August | 1.225 | | November | 2.989 |
| | September | 1.160 | | December | 3.018 |
| | October | 1.049 | 1925 | January | 3.00 |
| | November | 1.038 | | February | 2.96 |
| | December | 1.249 | | March | 2.97 |
| 1922 | January | 1.732 | | April | 2.96 |
| | February | 1.855 | | May | 2.96 |
| | March | 1.733 | | June | 2.96 |

Source: Young [36, vol. 2, p. 307].

Table C4                Czechoslovakian Wholesale Prices, 1922–24

| Year | Month | Wholesale Price Index | Year | Month | Wholesale Price Index |
|------|-------|----------------------|------|-------|----------------------|
| 1922 | January | 1,675 | | October | 973 |
| | February | 1,520 | | November | 965 |
| | March | 1,552 | | December | 984 |
| | April | 1,491 | 1924 | January | 974 |
| | May | 1,471 | | February | 999 |
| | June | 1,471 | | March | 1,021 |
| | July | 1,464 | | April | 1,008 |
| | August | 1,386 | | May | 1,015 |
| | September | 1,155 | | June | 981 |
| | October | 1,059 | | July | 953 |
| | November | 1,017 | | August | 986 |
| | December | 999 | | September | 982 |
| 1923 | January | 1,003 | | October | 999 |
| | February | 1,019 | | November | 1,013 |
| | March | 1,028 | | December | 1,024 |
| | April | 1,031 | 1925 | January | 1,045 |
| | May | 1,030 | | February | 1,048 |
| | June | 1,001 | | March | 1,034 |
| | July | 968 | | April | 1,019 |
| | August | 958 | | May | 1,006 |
| | September | 957 | | | |

Source: Young [36, vol. 2, p. 307].
Note: July 1914 = 100.

restore the Czechoslovakia crown to the prewar gold par value of the old Austro-Hungarian crown. Following Rasin's assassination, this plan was abandoned and the crown was stabilized at about 2.96 cents.

## 2.8  Conclusion

The essential measures that ended hyperinflation in each of Germany, Austria, Hungary, and Poland were, first, the creation of an independent central bank that was legally committed to refuse the government's demand for additional unsecured credit and, second, a simultaneous alteration in the fiscal policy regime.[37] These measures were interrelated and coordinated. They had the effect of binding the government to place its debt with private parties and foreign governments which would value that debt according to whether it was backed by sufficiently large prospective taxes relative to public expenditures. In each case that we have studied, once it became widely understood that the government would not rely on the central bank for its finances, the inflation terminated and the exchanges stabilized. We have further seen that it was not simply the increasing quantity of central bank notes that caused the hyperinflation, since in each case the note circulation continued to grow rapidly after the exchange rate and price level had been stabilized. Rather, it was the growth of fiat currency which was unbacked, or backed only by government bills, which there never was a prospect to retire through taxation.

The changes that ended the hyperinflations were not isolated restrictive actions within a given set of rules of the game or general policy. Earlier attempts to stabilize the exchanges in Hungary under Hegedus,[38] and also in Germany, failed precisely because they did not change the rules of the game under which fiscal policy had to be conducted.[39]

In discussing this subject with various people, I have encountered the view that the events described here are so extreme and bizarre that they do not bear on the subject of inflation in the contemporary United States. On the contrary, it is precisely because the events were so extreme that they are relevant. The four incidents we have studied are akin to laboratory experiments in which the elemental forces that cause and can be used to stop inflation are easiest to spot. I believe that these incidents are full of lessons about our own, less drastic predicament with inflation, if only we interpret them correctly.

# Notes

1. "Most economists believe that the underlying inflation rate—roughly defined as wage costs less productivity gains—now stands at 9 to 10 percent, and that only a long period of restraint can reduce that rate significantly" (*Newsweek*, 19 May 1980, p. 59).

2. Paul Samuelson has aptly summarized the rational expectations view: "I should report that there is a new school, the so-called 'rational expectationists.' They are optimistic that inflation can be wiped out with little pain if only the government makes *credible* its determination to do so. But neither history nor reason tempt one to bet their way" (*Newsweek*, 28 April 1980). The second sentence of this quote is probably as shrewd a summary of the rational expectations view as can be made in a single sentence. However, it is difficult to agree with the third sentence: as for "reason," no one denies that logically coherent and well-reasoned models underlie the claims of the "rational expectationists"; as for history, the evidence summarized in this paper is surely relevant.

3. There is actually no such thing as a "rational expectations school" in the sense of a collection of economists with an agreed upon model of the economy and view about optimal monetary and fiscal policy. In fact, among economists who use the assumption of rational expectations there is wide disagreement about these matters. What characterizes adherents of the notion of rational expectations is their intention to build models by assuming that private agents understand the dynamic environment in which they operate approximately as well as do government policymakers. Adherence to this notion leaves ample room for substantial diversity about the many other details of a model. For some examples of rational expectations models with diverse implications, see Lucas [21], Barro [2], Wallace [35], Townsend [34], and Sargent and Wallace [31]. Despite their diversity, it is true that all of these models impel us to think about optimal government policy in substantially different ways than were standard in macroeconomics before the advent of the doctrine of rational expectations in the early 1970s.

4. Bresciani-Turroni wrote: "Whoever studies the recent economic history of Europe is struck by a most surprising fact: the rapid monetary restoration of some countries where for several years paper money had continually depreciated. In some cases the stabilization of the exchange was not obtained by a continuous effort, prolonged over a period of years, whose effects would show themselves slowly in the progressive economic and financial restoration of the country, as occurred before the War in several well-known cases of monetary reform. Instead, the passing from a period of tempestuous depreciation of the currency to an almost complete stability of the exchange was very sudden" [3, p. 334]. Compare these remarks with the opinion of Samuelson cited in note 2 above.

5. The notes were "backed" mainly by treasury bills which, in those times, could not be expected to be paid off by levying taxes, but only by printing more notes or treasury bills.

6. League of Nations [13, p. 101].

7. Keynes wrote: "It is not lack of gold but the absence of other internal adjustments which prevents the leading European countries from returning to a pre-war gold standard. Most of them have plenty of gold for the purpose as soon as the other conditions favorable to the restoration of a gold standard have returned" (Keynes [11, p. 132]). Writing about Germany in 1923, Keynes said: "The government cannot introduce a sound money, because, in the absence of other revenue, the printing of an unsound money is the only way by which it can live" (Keynes [10, p. 67]).

8. This view can be expressed more precisely by referring to the technical literature of optimum economic growth. I am recommending that a good first model of the gold standard or other commodity money is a real equilibrium growth model in which a government issues debt, makes expenditures, and collects taxes. Examples of these models were studied by Arrow and Kurz [1]. In such models, government debt is valued according to the same economic considerations that give private debt value, namely, the prospective net revenue stream of the institution issuing the debt. A real equilibrium growth model of this kind can also be used to provide a formal rationalization of my claim below that open market operations in private securities, foreign exchange, and gold should have no effect on the price level, i.e. the value of government demand debt.

9. It is relatively straightforward to produce a variety of workable theoretical models of a commodity money or gold standard, along the lines of note 8. It is considerably more difficult to produce a model of a fiat money, which is costless to produce, inconvertible, and of no utility except in exchange. Kareken and Wallace [9], Wallace [35], and Townsend [34] describe some of the ramifications of this observation. The workable models of fiat money that we do have—for example, those of Townsend [34] and Wallace [35]—immediately raise the question of whether voluntarily held fiat money can continue to be valued at all in the face of substantial budget deficits of the order of magnitude studied in this paper. Such models lead one to assign an important role to government restrictions, particularly on foreign exchange transactions, in maintaining a valued, if involuntarily held, fiat money. Keynes [10] and Nichols [24] also emphasized the role of such restrictions.

10. The sweeping implications of this principle for standard ways of formulating and using econometric models were first described by Lucas [19]. The principle itself has emerged in a variety of contexts involving economic dynamics. For some examples, see Lucas [20] and Sargent and Wallace [30].

11. Sargent and Wallace [32] describe a sense in which it might be difficult to imagine that a regime change can occur. As they discovered, thinking about regime changes in the context of rational expectations models soon leads one to issues of free will.

12. The Treaty of St. Germain, signed in September of 1919, required the successor states of the Austro-Hungarian empire to stamp their share of the notes of the Austro-Hungarian bank. The stamp converted those notes to the currency, i.e. debt, of the new states. The Austrian section of the old Austro-Hungarian bank functioned as the central bank of Austria for several years after the war.

13. Needless to say, the central bank encountered a strong demand for loans at this rate and had to ration credit.

14. At the time, some commentators argued that since the real value of currency had decreased and so in a sense currency was scarce, the increased note issue of the central bank was not the prime cause of the inflation. Some even argued that money was "tight" and that the central bank was valiantly struggling to meet the shortage of currency by adding printing presses and employees. This argument is now widely regarded as fallacious by macroeconomists. Disturbingly, however, one hears the very same argument in the contemporary United States.

15. "In Vienna, during the period of collapse, mushroom exchange banks sprang up at every street corner, where you could change your krone into Zurich francs within a few minutes of receiving them, and so avoid the risk of loss during the time it would take you to reach your usual bank. It became a reasonable criticism to allege that a prudent man at a cafe ordering a bock of beer should order a second bock at the same time, even at the expense of drinking it tepid, lest the price should rise meanwhile" (Keynes [10, p. 51]).

16. See Young [36, vol. 2, p. 16]. That a government might want to adopt such measures if it were using inflationary finance was pointed out by Nichols [24].

17. Pasvolsky [25, p. 116].

18. The content of this protocol is highly sensible when it is remembered that the value of a state's currency and other debt, at least under the gold standard, is determined by its ability to back that debt with an appropriate fiscal policy. In this respect, its situation is no different from that of a firm. In 1922, there was widespread concern within and without Austria that its sovereignty was at risk. (See the desperate note delivered by the Austrian minister to the Supreme Council of the Allied governments quoted by Pasvolsky [25, p. 115]). The first protocol aimed to clarify the extent to which Austria remained a political and economic entity capable of backing its debts. A similar protocol was signed at the inception of Hungary's financial reconstruction.

19. It should be noted that for two years the new bank vigorously exercised its authority to control transactions in foreign currency. Only after March 1925 were restrictions on trading foreign exchange removed.

20. This explanation is consistent with the argument advanced by Fama [6]. There is an alternative explanation of these observations that neglects the distinction between inside and outside money, and that interprets the observations in terms of a demand function for the total quantity of "money." For instance, Cagan [4] posited the demand schedule for money to take the form

$$(1) \qquad M_t - P_t = \alpha(E_t P_{t+1} - P_t), \qquad \alpha < 0,$$

where $P_t$ is the logarithm of the price level, $M_t$ is the logarithm of the money supply, and $E_t P_{t+1}$ is people's expectation of the log of price next period. There is always a problem in defining an empirical counterpart to $M_t$, but it is often taken to be the note and deposit liabilities of the central bank or "high-powered" money. The money demand schedule or "portfolio balance" schedule incorporates the idea that people want to hold less wealth in the form of real balances the faster the currency is expected to depreciate. Equation (1) can be solved to give an expression for the equilibrium price level of the form

$$(2) \qquad P_t = \frac{1}{1 - \alpha} \sum_{i=0}^{\infty} \left( \frac{\alpha}{\alpha - 1} \right)^i E_t M_{t+i},$$

where $E_t M_{t+i}$ is what at time $t$ people expect the money supply to be at time $t + i$.

Consider the following two experiments. First, suppose that the government engages in a policy, *which everyone knows in advance*, of making the money supply grow at the constant high rate $\mu > 0$ from time 0 to time $T - 1$, and then at the rate zero from time $T$ onward. In this case, the inflation rate would follow the path depicted in figure 2.N.1.

For the second experiment, suppose that initially everyone expected the money supply to increase at the constant rate $\mu$ forever but that at time $T$ it becomes known that henceforth the money supply will increase at the rate 0 forever. In this case, the inflation rate takes a

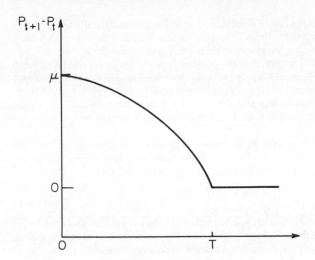

**Fig. 2.N.1**     Inflation path with an expected decrease in money supply growth from $\mu$ to 0 at time $T$.

sudden drop at time $T$, as shown by the path in figure 2.N.2. Now since the inflation and the expected inflation rate experience a sudden drop at $T$ in this case, it follows from equation (1) that real balances must increase at $T$. This will require a sudden once and for all *drop* in the price level at $T$.

This second example of a previously unexpected decrease in the inflation rate provides the material for an explanation of the growth of the money supplies after currency stabilization. In the face of a previously unexpected, sudden, and permanent drop in the rate of money creation, the only way to avoid a sudden drop in the price level would be to

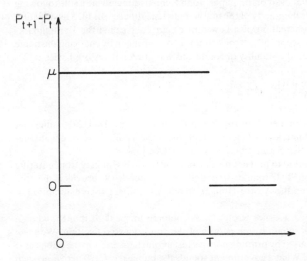

**Fig. 2.N.2**     Inflation path with a previously unexpected decrease in money supply growth from $\mu$ to 0 at time $T$.

accompany the *decrease* in the rate of money creation with a once and for all *increase* in the money supply. In order to *stabilize* the price level in the face of a decreased rate of change of money, the level of the money supply must jump upward once and for all.

What actually occurred in the four countries studied here was not a once and for all jump but a gradual increase in the money supply over many months. This could be reconciled with the observations within the model (1) if people were assumed only gradually to catch on to the fact of stabilization and to decrease the rate of inflation that they expected as the currency stabilization continued to hold. I find this explanation hard to accept, but it is a possibility.

An alternative way to reconcile the preceding explanation with the gradual upward movement of "high-powered" money after the stabilizations is to add adjustment lags to the portfolio balance schedule (1). For example, consider replacing (1) with

$$(1')\qquad (M_t - P_t) = \alpha(E_t P_{t+1} - P_t) + \lambda(M_{t-1} - P_{t-1})$$

$$\alpha < 0,\ 0 < \lambda < 1.$$

In this case, an abrupt stabilization of expected inflation induces only a gradual adjustment of real balances upward at the rate of $1 - \lambda$ per period. My own preference at this point is for an explanation that stresses the distinction between backed and unbacked money.

21. See Pasvolsky [25, p. 161].

22. See Pasvolsky [25, p. 298].

23. Within a year and a half, these became a claim on gold as Britain returned to the gold standard.

24. Unlike Austria, Hungary, and Germany, Poland did not owe war reparations.

25. *League of Nations* [13, p. 111].

26. *Ibid.*, p. 108.

27. See the account in Paxton [26, pp. 146–50].

28. Also see Graham [7, pp. 40–41].

29. Keynes wrote: "A government can live for a long time, even the German government or the Russian government, by printing paper money . . . A government can live by this means when it can live by no other" (Keynes [10, p. 47]).

30. See Young [36, vol. 1, p. 402] and Bresciani-Turroni [3, p. 345].

31. After reading an earlier draft of this paper, John Kennan directed me to the following passage in Constance Reid's biography of the mathematician Hilbert: "In 1923 the inflation ended abruptly through the creation of a new unit of currency called the Rentenmark. Although Hilbert remarked sceptically, 'One cannot solve a problem by changing the name of the independent variable,' the stability of conditions was gradually restored" (Reid [27, pp. 162–63]).

32. Young [36, vol. 1, p. 421].

33. Young [36, vol. 1, p. 422].

34. See Graham [7, chapter 12].

35. Theoretical models of money along the lines proposed by Samuelson [29] predict that too much capital will be accumulated when the government fiscal policy is so profligate that money becomes valueless. See Samuelson [29] and Wallace [35].

36. The frontiers were closed to prevent notes from Austria and Hungary from entering the country. The Treaty of St. Germain, signed 10 September 1919, provided that the successor states should stamp the Austro-Hungarian notes, signifying their assumption of the debt.

37. Of inflationary finance, Keynes wrote: "It is common to speak as though, when a government pays its way by inflation, the people of the country avoid taxation. We have seen this is not so. What is raised by printing notes is just as much taken from the public as is beer-duty or an income-tax. What a government spends the public pay for. There is no such thing as an uncovered deficit. But in some countries it seems possible to please and content the public, for a time at least, by giving them, in return for the taxes they pay, finely

engraved acknowledgments on water-marked paper. The income tax receipts, which we in England receive from the surveyor, we throw into the wastepaper basket; in Germany they call them bank-notes and put them into their pocketbooks; in France they are termed Rentes and are locked up in the family safe" (Keynes [10, pp. 68–69]).

38. See Pasvolsky [25, pp. 304–7].

39. A deep objection to the interpretation in this paragraph can be constructed along the lines of Sargent and Wallace [30], who argue that for a single economy it is impossible to conceive of a rational expectations model in which there can occur a change in regime. In particular, the substantial changes in ways of formulating monetary and fiscal policy associated with the ends of the four inflations studied here can themselves be considered to have been caused by the economic events preceding them. On this interpretation, what we have interpreted as changes in the regime were really only the realization of events and human responses under a single, more complicated regime. This more complicated regime would have to be described in a considerably more involved and "state contingent" way than the simple regimes we have described. I believe that the data of this paper could be described using this view, but that it would substantially complicate the language and require extensive qualifications without altering the main practical implications.

# References

1. Arrow, K. J., and Mordecai, K. 1970. *Public investment, the rate of return, and optimal fiscal policy*. Baltimore and London: John Hopkins University Press.
2. Barro, R. J. 1974. Are government bonds net wealth? *Journal of Political Economy* 82, no. 6 (November/December): 1095–1118.
3. Bresciani-Turroni, C. 1937. *The economics of inflation*. London: George Allen & Unwin.
4. Cagan, P. 1956. The monetary dynamics of hyperinflation. In M. Friedman, ed., *Studies in the quantity of money*. Chicago: University of Chicago Press.
5. de Bordes, J. v. W. 1924. *The Austrian crown*. London: P. S. King & Son.
6. Fama, E. F. 1980. Banking in the theory of finance. *Journal of Monetary Economics* 6, no. 1 (January): 39–58.
7. Graham, F. D. 1930. *Exchange, prices, and production in hyperinflation: Germany, 1920–23*. New York: Russell & Russell.
8. Kareken, J. H., and Wallace, N. 1980. *Models of monetary economics*. Minneapolis: Federal Reserve Bank of Minneapolis.
9. Kareken, J. H., and Wallace, N. 1980. Introduction to *Kareken and Wallace* [8].
10. Keynes, J. M. 1924. *Monetary reform*. New York: Harcourt, Brace & Co.
11. Keynes, J. M. 1925. The United States and gold. In Young [36, vol. 1, pp. 131–33].

12. Layton, W. T., and Rist, C. 1925. *The economic situation of Austria*. Report presented to the Council of the League of Nations, Geneva, 19 August.

13. League of Nations. 1946. *The course and control of inflation*. Geneva.

14. League of Nations. 1926. *The financial reconstruction of Austria*. General Survey and Principal Documents, Geneva.

15. League of Nations. 1926. *The financial reconstruction of Hungary*. General Survey and Principal Documents. Geneva.

16. League of Nations. 1926. *Memorandum on currency and central banks, 1913–1925*, vol. 1. Geneva.

17. League of Nations. 1927. *Memorandum on public finance (1922–1926)*. Geneva.

18. League of Nations. 1925. *Memorandum on currency and central banks, 1913–1924*, vol. 1. Geneva.

19. Lucas, R. E., Jr. 1976. Econometric policy evaluation: A critique. In K. Brunner and A. H. Meltzer, eds., *The Phillips curve and labor markets*, pp. 19–46. Carnegie-Rochester Conference Series on Public Policy, Vol. 1. Amsterdam: North-Holland.

20. Lucas, R. E., Jr. 1972. Econometric testing of the natural rate hypothesis. In O. Eckstein, ed., *The Econometrics of Price Determination Conference*. Washington: Board of Governors, Federal Reserve System.

21. Lucas, R. E., Jr. 1980. Equilibrium in a pure currency economy. In Kareken and Wallace [8].

22. Lucas, R. E., Jr., and Sargent, T. J. 1979. After Keynesian economics. Federal Reserve Bank of Minneapolis, *Quarterly Review*, spring.

23. Lucas, R. E., Jr., and Sargent, T. J. 1981. Rational expectations and econometric practice. Introductory essay to R. E. Lucas, Jr., and T. J. Sargent, eds., *Rational expectations and econometric practice*. Minneapolis: University of Minnesota Press.

24. Nichols, D. 1974. Some principles of inflationary finance. *Journal of Political Economy* 82, no. 2, part 1 (March/April): 423–30.

25. Pasvolsky, L. 1928. *Economic nationalism of the Danubian states*. New York: Macmillan.

26. Paxton, R. O. 1975. *Europe in the twentieth century*. New York: Harcourt Brace Jovanovich.

27. Reid, C. 1979. *Hilbert*. New York: Springer-Verlag.

28. Salemi, M. K. 1976. Hyperinflation, exchange depreciation, and the demand for money in post World War I Germany. Ph.D. thesis, University of Minnesota.

29. Samuelson, P. A. 1958. An exact consumption-loan model of interest with or without the social contrivance of money. *Journal of Political Economy* 66 (December): 467–82.

30. Sargent, T. J. 1980. Rational expectations and the reconstruction of macroeconomics. Federal Reserve Bank of Minneapolis, *Quarterly Review*, summer.
31. Sargent, T. J., and Wallace, N. 1975. Rational expectations, the optimal monetary instrument, and the optimal money supply rule. *Journal of Political Economy* 83, no. 2 (April).
32. Sargent, T. J., and Wallace, N. 1976. Rational expectations and the theory of economic policy. *Journal of Monetary Economics* 2, no. 2 (April): 169–83.
33. *Statistiches Jahrbuch fur das Deutsche Reich.* 1924/25.
34. Townsend, R. M. 1980. Models of money with spatially separated agents. In Kareken and Wallace [8].
35. Wallace, N. 1980. The overlapping generations model of fiat money. In Kareken and Wallace [8].
36. Young, J. P. 1925. *European currency and finance.* vols. 1 and 2. (Commission of Gold and Silver Inquiry, United States Senate, serial 9.) Washington: Government Printing Office.

# 3 United States Inflation and the Choice of Monetary Standard

Robert J. Barro

## 3.1 The Association among Money, Prices, and Nominal Interest Rates

In analyzing recent United States inflation it is natural—at least for me—to begin with Milton Friedman's famous statement, "Inflation is always and everywhere a monetary phenomenon."[1] This proposition receives a lot of support from evidence across countries, over long periods of time within a variety of individual countries, and from some extreme inflationary experiences. As examples, one can note the rapid inflations in several Latin American countries—all of which were accompanied by excessive monetary growth—the long-period association between money and prices in the United States under differing monetary environments, and the parallel between monetary and price movements during extreme hyperinflations, such as that in post–World War I Germany. At present I want to focus on the accuracy of Friedman's proposition for the United States experience since World War II and, especially, for developments in recent years. As will be seen, it is important particularly at the present time to recognize that the phrase "monetary phenomenon" refers not only to movements in the quantity of money but also to factors that influence the public's willingness to hold money—that is, the demand for money.

The association between inflation and growth of monetary aggregates seems to be a close one over periods of more than a few years. For example, for the 1948 to 1979 period in the United States, the average inflation rate—as measured by changes in the deflator for the gross national product, which is a broad index with desirable properties—was

Robert J. Barro is with the Department of Economics, University of Chicago, and the National Bureau of Economic Research.

3.7% per year. The corresponding average growth rate of the M1 definition of the money stock, which comprises currency and checkable deposits, was 3.8% per year. The overall relation divides conveniently into two subperiods. For the first interval, from 1948 to 1965, the average inflation rate was 2.0% per year and the average monetary growth rate was 2.3% per year. (These rates appear now to constitute little inflation and money growth, although the amounts were sufficient at the time to generate the experiment with wage-price guideposts in the 1960s.) For the second subperiod, from 1965 to 1979, the average inflation rate was 5.7% per year and the average monetary growth rate was also 5.7% per year. The advance in the average inflation rate from the first period to the second was, in fact, paralleled by an increase in the average monetary growth rate. However, this precise a linkage would not have appeared if we had looked at year-to-year relations rather than the association over several years.

The correspondence between the numbers for average inflation and rate of monetary expansion over the two long subperiods is misleading in any case, because it obscures two major phenomena whose effects on inflation happened to be roughly offsetting. First, economic growth would allow for some absorption of money without provoking inflation. My estimate of the magnitude of this effect—the net result of an offsetting trend during the post-World War II period away from the real demand for money as defined by M1 and toward the demand for other assets—is that a growth rate of the money stock equal to about 1½% per year would be consistent with zero inflation. On this count the average inflation rate over the 1948–79 period should have been 2.3% per year— 1½% per year below the average rate of monetary expansion—rather than the actual value of 3.7% per year.

An opposing, positive effect on prices arose since 1948 because the increases in average rates of price change, which became anticipated, were then reflected in higher nominal interest rates. That is, lenders required this rise in interest rates to compensate for inflation and— because they would be repaying with deflated dollars—borrowers were correspondingly willing to pay the higher nominal rates. For present purposes, the important effect is the inverse influence of these higher interest rates on the public's willingness to hold non-interest-bearing money. Like an increase in the supply of money for a given level of real demand—as determined by real income and others factors—a reduction in the demand for money generates a higher level of prices. That is, the general price level must rise in order for individuals to be satisfied to hold the existing stock of money rather than spend it on commodities or interest-bearing assets.

Over the 1965–79 period, the interest rate on Aaa rated (long-term) corporate bonds rose from 4.5% to 9.6%; my estimate is that the negative effect of this change on the demand for money raised the average inflation rate from 1965 to 1979 by almost 2% per year. It is often said that these types of shifts in the demand for money—also referred to as increases in the velocity or frequency of monetary circulation—represent one-time influences on the level of prices rather than continuing influences that appear as a higher average rate of inflation. However, the "one-time" price level effect was sufficient in this case to contribute a substantial amount to the average inflation rate over the years 1965–79.

Over the entire 1948 to 1979 period, the interest rate on Aaa corporate bonds advanced from 2.8% to 9.6%, which I estimate pushed up the average rate of inflation over the full thirty-one years by about 1.1% per year—still a substantial effect on average inflation from the channel of higher velocity.

The mechanism by which higher expected inflation is embedded in higher nominal interest rates, which reduce the demand for money and thereby push up the price level, is significant in interpreting some longer-term aspects of the inflationary experience over the years 1948–79, but it is far more important in accounting for the lack of a close year-to-year association between changes in money and changes in prices. Up to 1965, the year-to-year movements in long-term interest rates were relatively small: the largest one-year changes were the increases by about one-half a percentage point for 1957 and 1959. Therefore, although the shifts in demand for money that were provoked by interest rate changes or other factors could have weakened the year-to-year correlation between inflation and monetary growth substantially, the channel of shifting interest rates did not generate the volatility of prices that has recently become familiar.

The moderate fluctuations in long-term interest rates before 1965 can, in turn, be related to the relative stability of long-term inflationary expectations. These anticipations would be justified under our earlier type of monetary system, which provided some constraints on the long-run expansion of monetary aggregates. I will return to this theme shortly.

The behavior of long-term interest rates has been far more volatile since 1965: year-to-year movements by one-half a percentage point or more have become typical, and increases in the neighborhood of one full percentage point occurred in 1969, 1970, 1974, and 1979. For 1980 the rise in long-term rates was on the order of two percentage points. (Incidentally, the largest negative change was −0.6 percentage points in 1971.) Quantitatively, I estimate that each one percentage point move in these interest rates is associated positively—through the channel of higher velocity that was described above—with about a four percentage point shift in the one-year inflation rate. Therefore the recent volatility of interest rates, induced by volatility of inflationary expectations, corresponds to magnified fluctuations in short-run inflation rates.

There are some unsettled issues concerning the timing among interest rate shifts, velocity changes, and price level movements. In the case of money supply shocks (though apparently not for fully perceived changes in money), there appear to be positive output effects in the United States out to a lag of one to two years. The full positive response of the general price level to a monetary surprise seems to take as long as four years. On the other hand, the velocity shifts that are associated with interest rate changes have no noticeable counterpart in the form of positive output movements. (There is an indication of a minor negative effect.) A full positive response of the price level within one year is consistent with preliminary econometric evidence, although some lagged effect for an additional year cannot be decisively ruled out. While the detailed findings are tentative and subject to some estimation problems, they suggest that the common practice of lumping money supply shocks and velocity shifts together as disturbances to "nominal aggregate demand" may be seriously misleading. Unlike for the case of monetary shocks, shifts in inflationary expectations—which are reflected in interest rate movements and in consequent changes in velocity—seem capable of producing dramatic movements in the general price level within a one-year period.

The interplay between inflationary expectations, interest rates, and current actual inflation applies as much in the negative direction as it does in the positive one that has been prevalent in recent years. Long-term interest rates declined precipitously from around 13% in March 1980 to about 11% in July. If interest rates had stayed at this reduced level for the remainder of 1980, my estimate for overall 1980 inflation (based on the deflator for the gross national product) would have been about 12% rather than the roughly 18% value that would have been associated with the March level of interest rates. (The actual rate of inflation for the GNP deflator for 1980 was 9.3%.)

The sensitivity of short-run price level movements to shifts in inflationary expectations has implications for the forecastability of inflation. Suppose that movements in long-term bond yields are unpredictable, which holds as a close approximation because participants in the efficient security markets would react strongly to perceived future changes in bond prices. In this case the volatility of bond yields—which currently seems understated at plus or minus one percentage point per year—combined with a fourfold association between long-term interest rate movements and price level changes over a year suggests a minimal forecast error for one-year-ahead inflation rates of plus or minus 4% per year. (This conclusion obtains if no other price-determining variables are strongly correlated with long-term interest rate movements). For the present economic environment, this analysis indicates that no econometric model could ever reduce the average error in one-year-ahead inflation rate predictions below this amount.

This analysis of inflation has focused on money supply and demand influences rather than on numerous special factors that primarily influence relative prices. The general price level is not found by simple addition of the relative prices for food, oil, medical care, housing, and so on. In fact, any absolute level of prices and any overall rate of inflation are consistent with any specified configuration of levels or changes in relative prices. This observation leaves open the possibility that a particular allocative disturbance could raise the general price level and simultaneously increase some specified relative prices. For example, a harvest failure in the United States, which raises the relative price of food, also has some downward impact on United States aggregate output and thereby a positive effect on the absolute price level for a given behavior of the money stock. Similarly, a rise in the relative costs of (imported) oil tends to depress United States real income and thereby raise the overall level of prices. Any positive monetary response to this type of disturbance would reinforce the inflationary impact, although the limited evidence on money supply behavior does not support this hypothesis. In any event these possibilities for short-term interplays between inflation and relative price changes should not obscure the point that the principal movements in United States inflation cannot be explained along these lines.

## 3.2  The Role of a Monetary Standard

A key issue is the reason for the changes in the behavior of interest rates and the relation of these changes to developments in the monetary process. My conjectured scenario is as follows. In earlier periods before roughly 1965, the monetary regime guaranteed some long-run stability in monetary growth and therefore in long-term inflation, which in turn restricted the effects of shifting inflationary expectations on movements of long-term interest rates. Elements of the monetary regime that worked in this direction were fixed exchange rates and some remnants of the classical gold standard, as reflected in the maintenance of a fixed value for the dollar price of gold (although gold was subject at most times to some exchange restrictions). The pegging of some nominal prices—that is, the willingness of the central bank to buy or sell a specific commodity for a fixed number of dollars—and the related balance-of-payments mechanism—whereby a country that inflated unduly lost international reserves such as gold or some paper alternatives that became popular in the post–World War II period—provided at least some restraint on long-run world monetary expansion. The international economy has been moving gradually away from this type of monetary setup since World War I and especially since the 1930s, although some remnants of the gold standard and fixed exchange rates in the form of the post–World War II Bretton Woods arrangements were in operation as recently as 1971.

Although there were earlier periods when the United States did not adhere to a gold or silver standard, these episodes typically occurred in times of war and could reasonably be perceived as temporary. For example, the United States was on a system of flexible exchange rates following the Civil War until the resumption of the gold standard in 1879. In fact, the drop by about 50% in the price level from 1866 to 1879 can be viewed as a prerequisite for returning to the prewar gold price. It seems reasonable to view this period as substantially influenced by the prospects for eventual return to the gold standard at the earlier parity. The period since 1971 seems to be the first time that we have completely severed, both currently and prospectively, the link between our money and a commodity base. Perhaps the most interesting aspect of this policy move was its casual nature—after all, most people thought that the important economic action in 1971 was the institution of the Nixon price controls.

An earlier manifestation of the trend away from a commodity standard was the removal of silver from most United States coins minted after 1964. I have often (only partly in jest) referred to this action as one of President Johnson's most significant policy moves. The Johnson decision on silver and Nixon's 1971 attempt to demonetize gold were typically viewed at the time as aspects of the modern trend away from the special monetary role of the precious metals. But they seem more appropriately regarded as a continuation of the well-established tendency of all unrestrained monarchs to secure revenue by debasing the currency. In fact, a principal point of the gold standard was to control governments, and we have not become sufficiently modern to come up with a statisfactory substitute (although governments have perhaps become more adept at eliminating these constraints).

There were some good economic reasons for shifting to a flexible exchange rate system. Under the Bretton Woods regime where exchange rates were pegged within relatively narrow bounds, individual countries often resorted to restrictions on trade in commodities and capital in order to prevent balance-of-payments deficits, which would have led naturally to lower rates of domestic monetary growth and inflation. These trade restrictions tended in general to retard economic efficiency. Further, with countries unwilling to tie domestic monetary policies fully to the dictates of the fixed exchange rate/gold standard setup, there were recurring financial crises that led occasionally to large devaluations (or, less frequently, to upward adjustments in the form of revaluations) of individual currencies. (Of course, this process had the indirect benefit of providing high levels of employment for central bankers and financial crisis managers more generally. But presumably, these people have experienced no trouble finding work in the present, calm financial climate.) There were some real benefits along the above lines from switching to flexible exchange rates, although the tendency toward adopting trade restrictions seems to be again on the rise.

What is certainly clear is that before 1971 most economists underestimated the extent to which the international system of fixed exchange rates with some role for gold served, although imperfectly, to restrain growth in the world money supply and thereby the world price level. Since the move in 1971 toward flexible exchange rates and the complete divorce of United States monetary management from the objective of a pegged gold price, it is clear that the nominal anchor for the monetary system—weak as it was earlier—is now entirely absent. Future monetary growth and long-run inflation appear now to depend entirely on the year-to-year "discretion" of the monetary authority, that is, the Federal Reserve. Not surprisingly, inflationary expectations and their reflection in nominal interest rates and hence in short-run inflation rates have all become more volatile.

The current high long-term nominal interest rates seem principally to represent the financial markets' prediction of an increase in future monetary growth and long-term inflation, a possibility that arises because of the shift to a paper money regime that possesses no nominal anchor. Further, the expectation of future monetary expansion and inflation is sufficient, as discussed earlier, to account for a leap in the short-run actual rate of inflation without a contemporaneous acceleration of monetary aggregates. However, it remains true even under our present monetary arrangements (one cannot really call it a monetary "standard") that the realization of higher long-term inflation is contingent on faster growth of the actual money supply. This magnitude of acceleration of money cannot, in fact, be discerned from the observed monetary data. Following average annual rates of monetary growth of 7–8% for 1977–79 (for the new M1-B concept of money, which includes NOW accounts and similar types of interest-bearing, checkable deposits), there was a sharp deceleration of money from February through May 1980. This monetary contraction was apparently reversed for June–July: my estimate was that money growth for all of 1980 would be at roughly a 5–6% rate. Even a return to the previous monetary growth rate of 8% per year would lead in the long run to annual inflation rates of only about 6–7%, which are well below both the actual inflation rate for 1980 and the forecasts of future average inflation that were implicit in nominal interest rates during 1980. The inflation predictions that were implicit in security market yields for 1980 were on the order of 10–11% for a long-term average. These projections corresponded, in turn, to forecasted long-run monetary growth of about 12% per year, as contrasted with the actual values for 1980 of less than 8% (which itself represented an acceleration from the 2% rate that prevailed earlier in the post–World War II period). I surely do not claim to have inflation and monetary growth predictions that are superior to those revealed by the financial markets; after all, much more than me, their livelihood depends on making reasonable forecasts.

### 3.3 Possibilities for Monetary Reform

If the above scenario is correct, the inflation problem must be analyzed in terms of changes to the basic monetary structure. It would make a major difference if institutional changes were made that once again provided a nominal anchor for the monetary system. The important constrast is between mechanisms that precommit the long-run path of nominal aggregates and those, like the present procedure, which allow nominal values to evolve in the long run as the accumulation of short-run monetary decisions that are subject at each date to policymaker "discretion." A system that ensures long-run price stability would also sharply dampen the volatility of interest rates, which are a major factor in the variability of short-term inflation rates.

### 3.4 Commodity Standards

As mentioned before, our previous systems with nominal anchors have involved fixed exchange rates with some role for a pegged price of a reserve commodity such as gold. One possibility would be to return to this type of system, possibly with an expanded commodity base substituting for the special position of gold or silver. Some detailed proposals of this type were advanced many years ago under the title of commodity-reserve currency. The history of this idea goes back almost a hundred years to Alfred Marshall's proposal for using gold and silver together in the form of a stable bimetallism, which is usually called "symmetallism." The basic idea is for the central bank to vary the money supply and its corresponding commodity reserve as dictated by pegging the price of a reserve bundle that includes so many ounces of gold, so many ounces of silver, a few bricks, a certain amount of wheat, and so on. That is, the central bank would stand ready to buy or sell units of this reserve bundle at a fixed dollar price. It has been argued that considerations of storability and homogeneity severely limit the feasible scope for this type of commodity reserve.

One general drawback of this type of setup is the resource cost for maintaining the commodity base, which seems now to be a trivial price if it would actually buy a satisfactory remedy for inflation. The biggest problem may be that the "saving" in these resource costs typically takes the form of additions to government revenue via direct or indirect debasement of the currency. Another problem with commodity standards involves fluctuations in the pegged price of the reserve bundle relative to prices in general—which are the ultimate objects of interest. This problem is likely to arise when the commodity reserve is not representative of consumer market baskets, as seems surely to be the case. In this context it is, however, doubtful that the extreme recent fluctuations in the real prices of gold and silver would have arisen if the international economy had remained on the gold standard.

It is in any case clear from history that even a reasonably serious gold standard—such as that operating in the pre–World War I period—may have ruled out chronic inflation, but did not prevent sharp short-run changes in domestic monetary aggregates, which were associated under our fractional-reserve banking system with financial panics and economic contractions. For example, the sharp downturn from 1893 to 1897— which seems second in severity over the last century only to the Great Depression of the 1930s—occurred during the peak operation of the gold standard. Of course, the elimination of fractional-reserve banking may have prevented these problems.

### 3.5  A Monetary Constitution

More realistic possibilities seem to involve the establishment of some type of monetary constitution,[2] which would involve precise legal restrictions (hence, precommitments) on the long-term path of nominal aggregates. The well-known constant-growth-rate rule for the money supply, long advocated by Milton Friedman, is a monetary system of this general type. The important aspect of Friedman's proposal is neither the constancy of the growth rate nor the choice of a particular number for the rate nor the precise definition of the monetary aggregate, but rather the firm commitment to and hence anchor on some future nominal values. This type of system would also avoid a number of difficulties and costs that characterize commodity standards. However, while this type of monetary constitution seems attractive in theory, it should be emphasized that our historical experience provides evidence only about the workings of regimes with nominal anchors that are of the gold standard type, not about environments where the behavior of paper money is backed by explicit legal commitments. Clearly, the form of these commitments is an important matter that warrants extensive discussion. Notably, the law or constitutional provision would have to be written so as to provide proper inducements to ensure that government officials behaved in accordance with the rules. I certainly do not wish to exaggerate the probability of achieving satisfactory governmental compliance.

Although the most important consideration is the capacity of a monetary constitution to peg some future nominal values, there is also some significance to the choice of concept for the target monetary aggregate. This decision is analogous to the selection of a specific reserve bundle under a commodity-reserve-currency scheme. Stabilization of the monetary base—currency plus bank reserves held at the Federal Reserve—has the advantage of applying to a magnitude that is under reasonably close control of the monetary authority. On the other hand, some earlier experiences, most notably the Great Depression, indicate that control of the base does not guarantee stability of broader monetary aggregates or the general price level. From 1929 to 1933 the monetary base advanced at an average annual rate of 3.4% at the same time that M1 declined at an average rate of 7.3% and the price level fell by an average of 6.3% per year. Similar, but less dramatic, behavior for the monetary aggregates applies to the 1937 recession. The Great Depression experience involved sharp increases in the public's demand for currency and in banks' demand for reserves, both of which were spurred by widespread bank failures. The 1937 recession involved a startling rise in required reserves by the Fed. Conceivably, these large variations in the relation of the money supply to the monetary base could no longer occur; in particular, the institution of federal deposit insurance seems to have eliminated bank failures as a major element in money supply determination. However, particularly with the Federal Reserve's moves in the spring of 1980 to extend reserve requirements to a variety of institutions, one cannot confidently rule out the type of dramatic shift in required reserves that occurred in 1937.

At the other end of the spectrum, one could instruct the Fed to stabilize the general price level. However, because this proposal applies to a variable that is only indirectly influenced by Fed instruments, it would invite volatility in the monetary aggregates. A compromise between stabilization of the monetary base and stabilization of the price level would be a rule expressed in terms of the most familiar monetary aggregate, M1, which includes currency and checkable deposits—that is, media of exchange. Empirical evidence indicates that, first, this aggregate can be reasonably well controlled by the Fed at least on a quarter-to-quarter basis and, second, stabilization of this concept of money goes a long way toward ensuring stability of overall economic activity.

Another issue that arises is whether, say, quarterly errors in achieving money growth targets should be compensated or forgotten in subsequent quarters. For example, suppose that the monetary rule dictates expansions in seasonally adjusted M1-B at a 2% annual rate. If the actual growth for one quarter is excessive by an annual rate of 1%, should the next quarter's target be 2% or 1% (or some value in between)? In a regime where past mistakes are ignored in formulating future growth rate targets, the level of nominal aggregates (and the price level) at future dates involves the summation of all these random errors. The levels of money and prices therefore become increasingly unpredictable as the horizon increases. Further, a system where mistakes are forgotten seems less likely to be well enforced. Therefore there are some arguments for requiring monetary errors to be made up in future periods. The precise timing of this adjustment seems unimportant, although a full correction for the subsequent quarter is one possibility.

## 3.6  Wage and Price Controls

The discussion of monetary structures that anchor expectations about future dollar values should be contrasted with a different approach that also frequently stresses expectations, namely, wage and price controls. The systems I have analyzed constrain fluctuations in expectations about future prices by providing substantive constraints on the future monetary magnitudes that ultimately determine inflation. In this way the limited fluctuations of inflationary expectations feed back into stability of current values of interest rates and prices. However, a key element in this analysis is the reasonableness or rationality of the stable expectations that emerge. The mechanism is internally consistent in the sense that individuals have an objective basis for their beliefs and do not observe patterns for money and prices that deviate dramatically and persistently from their expectations.

Arguments for wage and price controls often stress the important effect of shifting inflationary expectations on current prices and interest rates. However, these proposals neglect the rationality of these expectations in the sense of their consistency with the underlying institutional setup that determines monetary behavior. Expectations cannot be stabilized without stabilizing the variables—in this case long-run money growth and inflation—to which the expectations pertain. The recurring failure of controls reflects their focus on symptoms rather than on the underlying sources of inflation.

## 3.7  The Nature of Policy Advice

I conclude by commenting on a type of policy advice that seems not so useful for economists to offer. Namely, there is a tendency—in which I certainly have shared—to recommend year-by-year values for money growth, deficits, and so on, without questioning the underlying policy structure. Telling the Federal Reserve to select substantially different values—usually lower values—for monetary growth seems similar to urging firms and households to choose different numbers for prices, employment, production, and so on. As in the case of the private sector, it is reasonable to view the Fed's monetary decisions as emerging from a given structure of constraints and rewards, although possibly the nature of this process is less well understood for the case of the monetary authority than it is for businesses and consumers. In particular, I doubt whether it makes much difference whether the Federal Reserve Board chairman's name is Volcker or Miller or Burns or even—almost beyond imagination—Milton Friedman. Recommendations for changed monetary behavior would be most usefully expressed in terms of proposed alterations to the underlying constraint and reward structure. The adoption of a monetary constitution or reinstatement of a gold standard type of regime represents this type of change in the structure of policy. Discussions of the inflation problem would be usefully phrased in terms of the desirable or undesirable operating characteristics of alternative monetary regimes, which include the gold standard and other possibilities.

# Notes

1. Milton Friedman, "Inflation: Causes and Consequences," Council for Economic Education (Bombay: Asia Publishing House, 1963), reprinted in *Dollars and Deficits* (Englewood Cliffs, N.J.: Prentice-Hall, 1968), p. 39.

2. Another possibility, which I have not given attention to in this paper, involves removing the government from the money-issue business. Media of exchange would then be provided entirely by private entities. The workings of a private, noncommodity monetary system are not well understood (at least by me).

# 4 Explorations in the Gold Standard and Related Policies for Stabilizing the Dollar

Robert E. Hall

## 4.1 Introduction

Steadily worsening inflation has brought renewed interest in the gold standard as a way to stabilize the purchasing power of the dollar. Only a few economists openly advocate the return to the gold standard; most regard it as a dangerous anachronism. My purpose in this paper is to explore the good and bad features of the gold standard and its generalization, the commodity standard, without taking a stand for or against the idea. A properly managed commodity standard emerges as a potential competitor to a properly managed fiat money system as a way to achieve price stability. Both systems require good management. Simply switching from our existing badly managed fiat money to a badly managed commodity standard might well be a step backward.

The basic findings of the paper are:

1. During the years of the gold standard in the United States (1879–1914), inflation was kept to reasonable levels but cumulated over decades so that the long-run purchasing power of the dollar declined by 40%. The gold standard does not meet the requirement of long-run stabilization of the real value of the dollar. Moreover, recent instability in the world gold market would have brought alternating periods of severe inflation and deflation had the United States been on the gold standard.

2. An acceptable commodity standard could be based on a package of several commodities, chosen so that the historical association of the price

Robert E. Hall is professor in the Department of Economics and Senior Fellow of the Hoover Institution, Stanford University. He also serves as director of the Research Program on Economic Fluctuations and the Project on Inflation of the National Bureau of Economic Research and as chairman of the NBER's Business Cycle Dating Group.

The author thanks Robert Barro for helpful comments and the National Science Foundation for research support. All opinions are his own.

of the package and the cost of living has been close. An example of such a package contains ammonium nitrate, copper, aluminum, and plywood.

3.  Even with the best choice of a commodity standard, it is necessary to redefine the standard periodically. Monthly changes in the commodity content of the dollar should be used according to a fixed rule. Such a rule can promise almost exact long-run stability in the cost of living.

4.  Whatever type of commodity standard is adopted, the government should not hold reserves of the commodity. Manipulation of reserves and intervention in commodity markets defeat the anti-inflationary purpose of the commodity standard.

5.  Though a good commodity standard would have been far superior to the actual monetary policy of the past two decades, better management of the existing system based on fiat money might have done as well or better. The commodity standard is not inherently superior to fiat money as a way to stabilize the cost of living. The commodity standard is just as subject to abuse as is the existing system.

## 4.2    The Nature of a Commodity Standard

Under a commodity standard, the government would establish a precise definition of the dollar as a particular quantity of a commodity or quantities of several commodities. For many years in the United States, the dollar was simply 0.04838 of an ounce of gold, for example. As I will argue later in this paper, it is probably better to define the dollar in terms of a resource unit containing a number of commodities rather than in terms of a single commodity like gold. The resource unit itself would be legal tender and would replace dollar bills and the accounting entries currently serving as legal tender in this country. Of course, the physical resources would not actually circulate as currency. Banks and other services would be free to offer accounts denominated in dollars. The Federal Reserve would no longer maintain reserve accounts; reserve requirements and the whole apparatus limiting bank deposits would be abandoned.

The commodity standard stabilizes prices by providing a definition of the dollar in terms of real economic quantities. In this respect it differs sharply from the current system where the dollar is defined as a piece of paper whose value comes only from a scarcity created by the government. Advocates of commodity standards believe that establishment of the standard will prevent the government from continuing the kind of inflation we have had over the past twenty years. However, a commodity standard has within it a policy instrument whose effects on the economy, inflationary and otherwise, are very similar to the effects of the money stock under today's system: The government can redefine the commodity content of the dollar at any time. The dollar price of the resource unit is closely analogous under a commodity standard to the monetary base under a fiat money system. The government can create inflation under a commodity standard by raising the dollar price of the resource unit just as it has created inflation by raising the number of dollars in the monetary base. Furthermore, there are very good reasons why the government *should* have the power to change the dollar price of the resource unit, just as there are very good reasons for the government to change the monetary base under the current system. There is no substitute for good management in order to achieve satisfactory price stability.

Both a commodity standard and conventional fiat money rest on the legal tender power of the government. Under the power, the government provides the courts with a precise legal definition of what action is required to discharge a dollar debt. In the present system, the currency issued by the Federal Reserve is legal tender. Delivery of currency legally discharges a debt, though in practice most debts are discharged by payment in reserves (through a check on a commercial bank), not currency. The policies of the Federal Reserve keep currency and reserves trading at exact par, except occasionally for small coins, which may sell at a premium. Because legal tender is just an arbitrary paper liability of the Fed, the legal tender definition of the monetary unit makes no promise about the purchasing power of the dollar. People writing contracts involving future payments in dollars take their chances on the government's success in ensuring the future meaning of the dollar. Though the needs of the courts are perfectly well met by the current system, the public suffers because of the instability of the real value of the dollar. Even so, a great many contracts—bonds, mortgages, annuities, installment borrowing, and even some forward purchases of goods and services—continue to be written in terms of the United States dollar. And in nations whose monetary units are even less stable than the dollar, future obligations are frequently stated in terms of the dollar.

## 4.3  The Gold Standard

The definition of legal tender exclusively in terms of a paper liability of the United States government dates from the creation of the Federal Reserve in 1914. Before then, legal tender was gold or its equivalent in gold-backed certificates of the federal government. In effect, the dollar was defined as 0.04838 of an ounce of gold. If there arose a question about the settlement of a debt, the courts could ask if the appropriate amount of gold or an asset of the same value had been offered.

Though the United States government continued to issue a paper currency during the era of the gold standard (1879–1914) and to limit the rights of private banks to issue currency, the substantive effect of the policy came from the legal definition of the dollar, not from the government's control of the money stock. Essentially the same control of prices could have been achieved just from the definition of legal tender, without any control of the private creation of money. In any case, there was no serious attempt to control the deposits of banks, which were a growing fraction of the money supply.

The gold standard dramatically limited inflation relative to what happened during the Civil War or the 1970s, but did not completely stabilize the price level by any means. Over the period from 1880 to 1910, annual rates of inflation measured over five-year intervals varied from − 1.3% per year from 1890 to 1895 to 2.1% per year from 1905 to 1910. There was continual mild inflation around 2% per year from 1895 to 1910 because of shifts in the world supply of gold. Though annual rates of inflation never reached troublesome levels, the compounding of inflation year after year meant the gold standard was quite ineffective in stabilizing the long-run purchasing power of the dollar. Between 1895 and 1912, the cost of living rose 40%. Forward economic arrangements made in 1895 were seriously dislocated by the surprising decline in the real value of the dollar over the ensuing two decades.

Recent turbulence in gold markets casts even more serious doubt on the wisdom of a dollar defined in terms of a fixed quantity of gold. Between 1968 and 1970, the purchasing power of an ounce of gold fell by 18%. Then its purchasing power rose by 350% to a peak in 1974, declined by 32% over the next two years, and then rose by 600% to another peak in 1980. Had the United States been on the gold standard over this period, there would have been considerable inflationary pressure in 1968–70, 1974–76, and 1981, and crushing deflation in 1970–74 and 1976–80. Because a United States gold standard might have stabilized the gold market over this period had we been on the gold standard, it is not accurate to say that the changes in the United States price level would have been as large as the actual changes in the purchasing power of gold, but large changes in the price level would certainly have occurred. The fixed gold standard is not the answer for price stability.

### 4.4   Defining the Dollar in Terms of a Resource Unit

The gold standard is one instance of a more general technique for defining the dollar. Any commodity can take the place of gold, as long as the replacement is sufficiently homogeneous and easily measured. Further, the dollar can be defined in terms of a composite of several commodities. There was a serious proposal in the nineteenth century to define the dollar as half gold and half silver, which would have avoided some of the fluctuations of prices under the pure gold standard.

As a general matter, the dollar could be defined in terms of a resource unit containing a number of standardized commodities. Primary industrial and agricultural commodities are the logical candidates. To avoid the instability of the gold standard, it is desirable to choose a resource unit whose value has moved closely with the cost of living historically. Then pegging its value by defining the dollar in terms of the resource unit will come close to stabilizing the cost of living.

After studying the relation between the cost of living and the prices of a long list of suitable commodities, I have selected a resource unit containing just four of them to serve as an example of a possible definition of the dollar. The long list contained wheat, sugar, heating oil, soybean oil, plywood, copper, tin, zinc, nylon, cotton, ammonium nitrate, latex, mercury, and aluminum. The four commodities whose combined price has moved closely with the cost of living are aluminum, copper, plywood, and ammonium nitrate. A resource unit that I will call the ANCAP comprising 33 cents worth of ammonium nitrate, 12 cents worth of copper, 36 cents worth of aluminum, and 19 cents worth of plywood (all in 1967 prices) had a market price very close to the cost of living throughout the postwar era. Its worst instabilities occurred in 1955, when the price of the resource unit rose by nine percentage points more than the cost of living, and in 1974, when the price of the unit rose by ten percentage points more. In 1970, the price of the unit fell relative to the cost of living by almost 9%. In other years, changes in the price of the resource unit have been closer to the changes in the cost of living. In particular, the gyrations of the United States and world economies in 1979 and 1980, with attendant high rates of inflation, brought about no important shifts in the price of the resource unit relative to the cost of living. In other words, had we defined the dollar as the resource unit, the cost of living would have been steady within two or three percentage points instead of rising by 11 and 13% in those two years.

### 4.5  Achieving Price Stability under a Commodity Standard

A fixed commodity standard will bring about fluctuations in the cost of living as the supply and demand for the resource unit ebbs and flows. Whenever the costs of producing the unit decline relative to the cost of living, the cost of living will rise and the public will complain about inflation. Exactly this happened in the first decade of the twentieth century. Under a fixed commodity standard, inflation is not a monetary phenomenon but a real one—it reflects the changing real circumstances of the economy.

A simple answer to the instability of prices under a commodity standard was offered by Irving Fisher in 1920 in his book *Stabilizing the Dollar*. The answer is just as good today as sixty years ago. What is needed is gradual adjustments in the definition of the dollar so that its purchasing power remains constant as time passes. When the commodities in the resource unit are in plentiful supply and inflation is consequently a problem, the number of resource units in the dollar needs to be raised. To put it the other way around, the dollar price of a resource unit needs to be lowered to offset inflation as it occurs. Similarly, when the price level drops below target, the dollar price of the resource unit should be raised.

Readjustments in the dollar price of the resource unit could be the responsibility of the Federal Reserve Board just as the quantity of money is under the board's discretion in the present system. Much the same considerations would underlie the setting of the dollar price as permeate monetary policy today. A higher dollar price of the resource unit stimulates the economy in the short run and brings a higher cost of living in the longer run, just as monetary expansion does in the current system. Probably the major obstacle to ending inflation over the past decade has been the concern about the deep recession that is feared as a consequence of sharply lower money growth rates. Under a commodity standard, exactly the same concern would limit anti-inflation policy. There would be strong pressure for continual increases in the dollar price of the resource unit in order to keep up with the inflationary momentum built into the economy today. It is no more realistic to expect that the dollar price of the resource unit could be held constant under a commodity standard than it is to expect an immediate move to zero growth of the money stock under the present system.

Because discretionary monetary policy gave us the current high rates of inflation and has made almost no progress in reducing money growth so as to lower inflation, it is tempting to eliminate discretion and install a simple policy rule that would guarantee price stability. Within the commodity standard, a simple rule proposed by Irving Fisher seems very suitable: Every month, change the dollar value of the resource unit by a formula. The formula prescribes a 1% decrease in the dollar price for each percent by which the most recent cost of living index exceeds the target level. If the cost of living is below target, raise the dollar price by the same rule.

In the United States, the cost of living is measured by the Consumer Price Index (CPI), which is simply the market price of a rather extensive basket of goods and services. In effect, Fisher's formula defines the dollar as enough resource units to buy the CPI basket at its most recently measured price.

Adaptive redefinition of the dollar through the formula would lead ultimately to a price level very close to the target embedded in the formula. The duration of the adjustment process depends on the flexibility of the prices of the consumer goods in the CPI. Every redefinition of the dollar would bring immediate parallel responses of highly flexible prices in formal and informal auction markets. How soon the changes are transmitted to markets for finished goods and for labor is a matter of controversy among economists. If something like a Phillips curve governs wages and some prices, then the redefinition of the dollar brings unemployment or boom. When some accident pushes the cost of living above the target, the formula calls for a lower dollar price of the resource unit. Sellers who do not adjust their dollar prices downward will be asking for more resources in return for what they are selling. There will be an excess supply of goods in all markets where prices do not fall immediately. On the other hand, there will be excess demand in the market for resource units, where the dollar price of output has declined, unless the dollar costs of inputs including labor also decline. Thus the redefinition of the dollar puts downward pressure on wages and prices throughout the economy. The only upward pressure is on the dollar price of the resource unit, which is fixed by the government's legal tender decree.

If wages and prices do not yield right away to the stabilizing pressure from the redefinition of the dollar, output and employment will fall. Sales of goods and services other than resource units will be constrained by inadequate demand because of their excessive prices. Output of resource units will be limited by supply, because the price has been depressed without an immediate compensating reduction in costs. In the aggregate, output and employment will fall. As prices and wages yield to the pressure of excess supply, full employment will be restored as the cost of living drops back to the target.

The Fisher formula is applied each month, and so intensifies pressure on prices and wages as time passes unless the cost of living returns to its target level. If many successive downward shifts in the dollar price of the resource unit are needed to coax the cost of living back to its target level after a disturbance, the real costs of the disturbance are correspondingly higher.

Aggressive redefinition of the dollar value of the resource unit is virtually a necessity in an economy with sticky prices and wages. Under a fixed commodity standard, all shifts in the purchasing power of the resource unit have to be accommodated by changes in the price level. When the resource unit becomes scarcer, the cost of living must fall. If this requires a prolonged period of excess supply, output and employment may be below potential for an excessively long time. With an adjustable commodity standard, the real consequences are much less severe. As soon as excess supply begins to drive the cost of living below the target, relief is obtained in the form of an upward movement in the dollar price of the resource unit. Monthly redefinitions continue until the new equilibrium is achieved at the target cost of living and a higher dollar price of the resource unit. The cumulative lost output and employment is far less than under the fixed commodity standard.

### 4.6    An Example of the Adjustable Commodity Standard

To give a fuller explanation of how an adjustable standard would work, I will give an extended example. The reader should understand that this is an example, not a detailed proposal. It is still very much an open question whether a commodity standard can be made to perform as well as a conventional monetary system or, if it can, what characteristics it should have.

The first step in creating a workable commodity currency is to issue a detailed physical definition of the resource unit. Under a gold standard this is simply a matter of stating the amount and purity of the gold. For the four-commodity resource unit mentioned earlier in this paper, the ANCAP, much more needs to be said, and probably the Bureau of Standards would be the appropriate agency to provide the exact specifications of the resource unit. For the two metals in the unit, copper and aluminum, weight and purity are again the important characteristics. For plywood, the type of wood, the thickness, the type of adhesive, and the quality of the two outside surfaces have to be specified. For ammonium nitrate, the purity, the permissible levels of contaminants, and the moisture content are important. For all four commodities, quality specifications in great detail are made routinely in commercial contracts for delivery of the commodities, and these specifications would provide a guide for defining the resource unit in adequate detail for the courts.

In addition to the physical characteristics of the resource unit, it is important to prescribe the location. Gold is so valuable that its transport costs are negligible and it is unnecessary to specify where it is located when it is delivered to make a payment. For most other commodities, physical delivery to the creditor is undesirable and impractical. Instead, as in organized commodities markets today, a standard delivery point should be established for each commodity. Again, existing practices provide a guide for the definition of the resource unit.

The next step is to set the dollar price of the resource unit. Market enforcement of the price will be precise and immediate; it is impossible for the sum of the market prices of the amounts of the commodities in the resource unit to depart significantly from the announced dollar price of the unit. The reason is simple. If the sum of the prices exceeded the set price, then sellers would receive more than one resource unit in value every time they sold a unit. Remember that when sellers post a dollar price, they have the right to receive payment in resource units instead of any other form of payment. Sellers could make unlimited profits by selling and reselling, each time coming out ahead in resource units. Naturally, as they attempted to do so, they would bid down the prices of the commodities to the point where their sum was equal to the government's set price. Buyers would do exactly the same thing if the sum of the prices of the commodities fell short of the set price. Whenever the sum of the prices departed from the set price by more than transactions costs, an opportunity for covered arbitrage would become available, and experience in countless markets teaches that experts quickly eliminate all opportunities for covered arbitrage.

The dollar price of the resource unit could be set by the discretion of a government agency, just as the Federal Reserve Board sets the quantity of money today. But discretionary policy is exactly what has given us high rates of inflation for the past two decades, so the move to a commodity standard for the dollar should also involve a move to a fixed policy rule that guarantees the eventual return to a stable dollar. Something like Irving Fisher's rule is appropriate, though his proposal of monthly adjustments by the full amount of the error in the price level is probably much too aggressive. Instead, monthly adjustments one-twelfth as large seem to be about right. Accordingly, an example of a formula is: Each month, depress the dollar price of the resource unit by one-twelfth of the amount by which the most recent CPI exceeds the target level. Over the course of a year in which the CPI is consistently 1% too high, the dollar price will be lowered by a full percent. In other words, apply Fisher's formula monthly at annual rates. The monthly adjustment would rarely exceed a few tenths of a percent.

The final step in putting the economy onto the adjustable ANCAP standard is to decide on the appropriate target path for prices. The standard will keep the cost of living quite close to the path, so it is much more than the wishful thinking of previous government announcements of disinflation targets. Still, the conflict between gradualism and cold turkey policies is just as acute under a commodity standard as under the current monetary approach to price stabilization. Under gradualism, the target price path would eliminate inflation at one or two percentage points per year. In order to limit the adverse effects of disinflation on employment and output, the momentum of inflation is slowed gradually over a period of five to ten years. As public confidence grows in the success of the new approach to price stabilization, the decline in the target inflation rate could be made more aggressive. Sensible specific targets for the CPI are given in table 4.1 Again the target is not just wishful thinking. The dollar price of the resource unit is to be pushed as far as necessary to get the cost of living close to the target.

**Table 4.1**    **Proposed Price Targets**

| Year | Level | Rate of Inflation |
|------|-------|-------------------|
| 1980 (actual) | 247 | |
| 1981 | 271 | 10 |
| 1982 | 296 | 9 |
| 1983 | 320 | 8 |
| 1984 | 339 | 6 |
| 1985 | 352 | 4 |
| 1986 | 359 | 2 |
| 1987 and after | 359 | 0 |

How well would the economy function under the ANCAP standard? At first, the public would react with a healthy skepticism bred by numerous unsuccessful anti-inflationary policies of the past two decades. During this period, depressed employment and output would be a possibility, as the policy struggled against the public's instinct to continue raising wages and prices. As the public became convinced that the price targets were going to be met, the depressive effects would disappear. Whether the process would take six months or three years we do not know. In any case, by the middle of the decade the system would be close to its steady state. From then on, long-term stability of the cost of living would be guaranteed by the commodity standard. Short-run instabilities would remain. In years of plentiful commodity supply, the cost of living would rise a little, which would set in motion the automatic redefinition of the dollar to restore its purchasing power. The economy would experience a few months of mild inflation, followed by a few months of deflation as the redefinition took effect. At the same time, a boom in real activity would occur, possibly followed by a recession.

Periods of worldwide increases in commodity prices, as in 1973–74, would have the opposite effect, triggering a deflation and recession under the commodity standard. Subsequently, the dollar would be redefined to contain fewer resource units, the cost of living would begin to rise, and real activity would recover. However, it is an inherent feature of commodity standards that sharp changes in world commodity markets create fluctuations in an economy relying on the standard.

How would the ANCAP standard change daily economic life? Plainly, its most important effect would be the restoration of long-run stability in the purchasing power of the dollar. The many long-run dollar commitments made by the typical citizen—pensions, mortgages, employment agreements, bonds, and the like—would function again in the way they were originally intended to. To the nonspecialist, the change in the definition of the dollar would not have any other visible manifestations. Daily business would continue to be conducted in familiar ways; the option to take payment in commodities would never be exercised by anyone but an arbitrage specialist. The typical American would be no more aware of the system that enforced the definition of the dollar than is the tourist today who changes money in a foreign country is aware of the apparatus of the foreign-exchange market.

## 4.7   The Government Should Not Hold Commodity Reserves under a Commodity Standard

Under a commodity standard, the government will be tempted to intervene in markets for the commodities used to define the dollar. When some upward pressure on costs occurs, the government will be under pressure to validate them by selling commodities rather than by letting the system push costs back down. In short, commodity sales from a reserve let the government deliberately create inflation, contrary to the intent of the commodity standard.

The postwar history of the United States illustrates this point very well. United States policy continued to peg the dollar price of gold at $35 per ounce for several years after inflation got started. Not until the spring of 1968 was official intervention in the gold market halted. Stabilization of the price of gold was possible in the face of rising prices of almost everything else only because the government had accumulated an enormous gold reserve. Selling out of the reserve and so pegging the dollar price of gold did nothing to limit inflation.

Not only does intervention in commodity markets blunt the price-stabilizing power of the commodity standard, but it introduces an unacceptable instability of its own. If the government is committed to a policy of intervention, it constantly faces the danger of running out of reserves. History has shown repeatedly that governments do not react to exhaustion of reserves by letting the commodity standard work by itself after intervention becomes impossible. Instead, they protect reserves by raising the money price of the commodity, again an inflationary move.

For two reasons—the inflationary potential of government commodity sales and the likelihood of redefinitions of money to protect reserves—it is centrally important to prohibit government intervention in commodity markets. The role of the government should be limited to defining the dollar in terms of commodities, not trying to influence the relative price of commodities. That relative price should be set by private markets.

### 4.8   A Commodity Standard Is Not Clearly Superior to a Well-managed Fiat Money System

The preceding discussion suggests that we would have been much better off under the ANCAP standard starting in 1965 than we were under the blundering monetary policy we actually had. But blunders are just as possible under a commodity standard. The dollar price of the resource unit is a policy instrument similar in many respects to the money stock in our current system. It would have been tempting to raise the dollar price for the same reasons and under the same circumstances as we actually raised the money stock. Holding the line on the dollar price would have been excoriated as excessively restrictive policy just as holding the line on money would have been in the 1960s and early 1970s.

Under proper management, a fiat money system could promise long-run price stability through exactly the same kind of adaptive policy as Irving Fisher proposed for the commodity standard. If the Federal Reserve lowered the money stock whenever the cost of living exceeded the target and raised it whenever the cost of living was too low, using the same rule—one-twelfth of a percent less money each month for each percent of excessively high prices—stability of the cost of living would be assured. Compared to a commodity standard, such a system would insulate the economy more effectively from commodity shocks, but at the cost of making it vulnerable to shifts in the demand for money. We do not know at this stage which type of shock is more destabilizing.

## 4.9  Conclusions

The gold standard is unacceptable as a basis for stabilizing the dollar because variations in the relation between the world price of gold and the United States cost of living are much too large. Under a gold standard, every drop in the demand for gold would bring sharp inflation. Even Irving Fisher's monthly redefinition of the gold content of the dollar could not keep up with the world gold market. A commodity standard based on more prosaic commodities whose prices have moved closely with the cost of living—for example, the ANCAP bundle mentioned in this paper—would do a good job of stabilizing the purchasing power of the dollar. Fisher's systematic redefinition is important to offset long-run changes in the relative price of the resource unit and the cost of living. A well-designed commodity standard would be a good way, but not the only way, to restore stability to the dollar.

# Reference

Fisher, I. 1920. *Stabilizing the dollar*. New York: Macmillan.

# 5 The Effect of Inflation on the Private Pension System

Jeremy I. Bulow

## 5.1 Introduction

One clear consequence of the increased inflationary expectations of recent years has been a sharp increase in nominal interest rates. Additionally, nominal interest rates including long-term rates have become much more volatile in recent years. Because the liabilities of defined benefit pension plans are primarily nominal in form, changes in interest rates can greatly affect the value of these liabilities.

Increases in long-term interest rates have provided windfall transfers of tens of billions of dollars from employees to employers. Even workers in plans with benefits linked to final salary have virtually no protection against the effect of an increase in nominal interest rates. The reason is that at any given time the worker holds a fixed nominal claim on the firm. The value of that claim is eroded if inflation rates (and thus interest rates) rise. This loss in benefit value will not in general be compensated for by future salary increases.

The structure of this paper is as follows: In section 5.2 the effect of inflation on the value of individual workers' benefits is discussed. A major point is that even if a plan provides benefits based on final salary, the worker still owns a nominal pension claim and is not hedged against inflation. Next, the section 5.3, the effect of inflation on aggregate benefits is discussed, including the distribution of inflation risk among workers, firms, and the federal government. In section 5.4 some empirical evidence is presented as to how inflation has affected large pension plans. Section 5.5 contains speculation on the likely effect of high inflation rates on the form of the pension contract and on the competing

Jeremy I. Bulow is with the Graduate School of Business, Stanford University.

interests of different groups of employees (young versus old) given the current status of pension plans. Last, Section 5.6 concludes the paper.

## 5.2   How Inflation Affects Individual's Pension Benefits

Consider a pension plan which gives a worker a benefit based on final average salary. There are several ways in which the real value of such a worker's benefits are reduced by unexpected changes in the inflation and interest rates:

1. Benefits are generally not indexed for inflation after retirement. Thus an increase in the inflation rate would reduce the worker's real benefits in the years after retirement, below what was expected.

2. If benefits are integrated with social security and social security benefits are tied to inflation, an increase in the price level can mean a decline in private pension benefits received.

3. Often benefits are related to an average of the last several years' salary rates of the employee. Increases in the inflation rate matched by equal increases in salary will reduce the ratio of benefits (based on an average salary) to final pay, below what was expected. For example, if benefits are based on an average of the last five years' pay, this base will likely be close to the actual final salary in a period of no inflation, where it may be significantly below final salary in a period of high inflation.

Such effects are not trivial—Winklevoss (1977) has estimated that a five percentage point increase in both salary growth rates and interest rates would reduce the present value of the benefits of a typical worker by about 13%. However, these "mechanical" effects (derived from assuming that the worker's future real *salary* is unaffected by the inflation rate) represent only a small part of the effect of inflation on the value of workers' benefits.

The most important factor is that the benefits a worker has accumulated at any point in time represent a fixed nominal sum. That is, if a worker left the firm at any particular moment, he would have coming to him some fixed nominal pension benefits. The present value of those nominal benefits can be discounted at the riskless nominal interest rate, assuming that the pension plan is sufficiently well funded so that there is no need to discount benefits any further. An increase in long-term interest rates will thus decrease the value of this nominal claim.

That is, the worker accumulates nominal pension benefits each year. As the worker continues on the payroll, he accumulates more nominal benefits. However, unexpected changes in the inflation rate change the value of previously accumulated pension rights. There is no reason to believe that firms will gratuitously "make up" this loss to employees. Even if benefits are fully indexed for inflation after the employee reaches the normal retirement age, even if there is no plan integration with social security, and even if benefits are based strictly on the worker's final salary, the employee is not hedged against inflation unless his benefits are also indexed for inflation that occurs while he is working.

A simple three-period example can make this important point clear. Assume that workers work for two periods and then receive a pension in the third period of their lives. Imagine that benefits are indexed from the time after the worker receives his second year's paycheck to the time of the pension payoff in year three. Also, imagine that there is a competitive labor market in which the firm currently can hire an employee for $13,000 in total compensation—whether it is in the form of salary or a combination of salary and pension benefits. Now compare the following four scenarios:

*Scenario 1.* There is no inflation and the interest rate is zero. The firm establishes a pension plan granting the workers a benefit equal to 30% of final (second-year) salary times the number of years worked.

Salary each year will be $10,000 under this pension scheme, with pension benefits of $3,000 paid to someone who leaves the firm after one year and $6,000 paid to someone who leaves after two years.

*Scenario 2.* There is a 20% inflation rate, and the interest rate is also 20%. Benefits are indexed from the day the employee leaves the firm until they are actually received. Again the benefit formula is that benefits equal 30% of final salary times the number of years worked.

In this case the first-year salary of the worker will still be $10,000, with a $3,000 pension benefit being accumulated. If the worker left the firm after one year, the actual nominal benefit received in year three would be $4,320, or $3,000 × 1.20 × 1.20 allowing for two years of inflation. If the employee stayed a second year, his salary would rise to $12,000. The eventual pension received would be 60% of $12,000 or $7,200, times 1.20 for one year of inflation. The net pension benefit would be $8,640, or twice the benefit received by the worker who left after one year.

*Scenario 3.* Now consider the same situation as scenario 2, except that the pension plan only begins indexing benefits after the employee reaches retirement age.

In this situation the worker will receive a salary of $10,400 in the first year of employment. Should the worker leave, he or she would have accumulated a pension worth 30% of that amount, or $3,120. Allowing for a year of indexing between the worker reaching retirement age at year two and receiving a benefit in year three, the net benefit received would be 1.20 × $3,120, or $3,744. The present value of that amount in year one is $2,600, which added to the $10,400 in salary provides the worker with a total compensation of $13,000.

In year two the worker will have to be paid a salary of $11,700. With such a salary, final pension benefits would amount to 0.6 × 11,700 × 1.2 = $8,424. The incremental benefit received from working that second year would be $8,424 − $3,744 = $4,680. Discounting for a year's interest, the present value of the increase in the worker's benefits from an extra year of service would amount to $4,680/1.20 = $3,900. Added to the $11,700 salary, this would give the worker a total second-year compensation of $15,600, or $13,000 in year one dollars.

An important point here is that even with fully anticipated inflation the nonindexation of benefits in the preretirement period leads to higher salaries (and less valuable pension accruals) for young workers relative to older workers. For example, in both scenarios 1 and 2 real salaries and real pension accruals were the same in both working periods. In scenario 3 first-period real salary was higher and second-period real salary was lower than in the other situations. Of course, the corollary of salary being tilted toward the younger worker is that pension benefits are tilted toward the older worker. With inflation the last period of employment provides a disproportionate share of pension benefits because, in addition to increasing years of service, the last year's salary raises the base for which benefits based on prior service is determined.

For a pension plan of the type described above (benefits based on a constant times final salary times years worked) the present value of accrued benefits rises from one year to the next by roughly $[(1/T + g + i]B$, where $T$ is the number of years of prior service, $g$ is the growth rate in salary, $i$ is the interest rate, and $B$ is the beginning value of accrued benefits. This formula would be exact were (1) this analysis done in a continuous rather than discrete form (i.e. looking at the rate of benefit accrual at a moment in time rather than from one year to the next) and (2) the fact that the older worker has a higher chance of surviving to retirement considered.

Of the three reasons that benefits grow, the interest factor $i$ is due to benefits being a year closer to receipt. Benefits would grow by this amount even if the employee did not stay with the firm. This part of growth can rightfully be thought of as interest on previously accrued benefits and is thus not part of the benefits attributable to the latest year's service. The factor $1/T$ accounts for the fact that if the employee has worked, say, twenty-one years instead of twenty his benefits are 1/20 higher. The factor $g$ allows that benefits are based on a final salary $100g\%$ higher. With inflation, the $g$ factor becomes more prominent and a higher fraction of total benefit accumulation occurs in the final years of employment.

Table 5.1 shows the percentage of final pension benefits accrued after ten, twenty, thirty, and forty years of service for a worker whose salary is growing at various rates, with benefits proportional to years of service.

While scenario 3 pointed out the effect of anticipated inflation in flattening out wage/age profiles (raising the salaries of younger workers and reducing the salaries of older workers), scenario 4 points out the risk the worker takes with regard to anticipated inflation.

Table 5.1      **Benefits Accrued as a Function
of Salary Growth Rate and Years of Service,
as a Percentage of Final Benefits**

| Years of Service | Salary Growth | | | |
|---|---|---|---|---|
| | 0% | 3% | 5% | 8% |
| 10 | 25.0 | 10.3 | 5.8 | 2.5 |
| 20 | 50.0 | 27.7 | 18.8 | 10.7 |
| 30 | 75.0 | 55.8 | 46.0 | 34.7 |
| 40 | 100.0 | 100.0 | 100.0 | 100.0 |

*Scenario 4.* No inflation is expected, but benefits are indexed for the period after the employee reaches normal retirement age. The pension formula is still that benefits will equal 30% times years of service times final salary.

In the first year the worker is paid $10,000 just as in scenario 1. The value of the worker's pension benefit is $3,000. Now, however, assume that between year one and year two the inflation rate jumps to 20% per year. Since benefits will only be indexed after year two, the employee who leaves after year one will receive a benefit of only $3,600.

At the beginning of year two the present value of that benefit is only 3,000 year two dollars rather than the $3,600 present value of benefits with full indexation (as under scenario 2).

If the worker stays with the firm, his second-year salary will be $11,625. The worker's pension will be 0.60 × $11,625 × 1.20 to allow for postretirement indexation. This works out to a pension of $8,370, which has a present value in year two of $6,975. Subtracting the $3,000 present value of benefits if the employee quits after one year leaves the value in terms of pension benefits from working the second year at $6,975 − $3,000 = $3,975. This added to a salary of $11,625 gives a total second-year compensation of $15,600. The employer will not be willing to pay more than this amount because he can go out in the labor market and hire other workers for $15,600, which is the total cost of this employee at a wage of $11,625.

Relative to scenario 2, scenario 4 shows that lack of protection against first-period inflation causes the worker to receive a salary that is $375 lower and a pension benefit that is lower by $225 in year two dollars ($270 in year three dollars, or $8,640 less $8,370). This total reduction of $600 in year two compensation exactly equals the difference in the value of the worker's pension benefits ($3,600 versus $3,000) because the first-year benefits were not indexed until retirement in the event the worker left the firm.

What scenario 4 shows is this: A worker receives a pension benefit tied to his salary. His total compensation rises with inflation. His pension benefits are indexed to inflation, after retirement. The worker does not terminate his employment prior to the normal retirement age, and the rules under which pension benefits are determined are not changed. Nevertheless the worker ends up paying the price of unanticipated inflation.

Of course, if the inflation rate dropped from 20% to 0, the worker would have had a gain. Assuming no preretirement indexation and an expectation of 20% inflation, the first year's pay would have been $10,400 in salary with a promise of a nominal pension of $3,120 plus postretirement indexation as in scenario 3. If there is no inflation instead of the anticipated 20%, the value of this package is $13,520 instead of $13,000 (the pension having a value of $3,120 instead of $2,600). Thus workers gain if the inflation rate is below expectations and lose if the inflation rate exceeds expectations.

## 5.3   The Effect of Inflation on Aggregate Pension Benefits

The passage of the Employee Retirement Income Security Act of 1974 (ERISA) established the maximum liability of a firm in the event of the termination of its pension plan(s).

The firm's liability beyond the money in the pension fund can be written as

(1) $$FL = \min [A-F, \max [0, \min (G-F, .3E)]],$$

where $FL$ = firm liability, $A$ = accrued pension benefits, $F$ = amount of money in the pension fund, $G$ = benefits guaranteed by the Pension Benefit Guaranty Corporation (PBGC), and $E$ = market value of the firm's equity. $A$ and $G$ are both calculated by discounting benefits at the nominal interest rate.

Guaranteed benefits $G$ differ from accrued benefits primarily in that (1) only vested benefits are guaranteed; (2) there is a limit to the amount of guaranteed benefits any individual can receive; (3) any benefits due to plan amendments made during the last five years are only partially guaranteed; and (4) only pension benefits (not death and miscellaneous benefits) are guaranteed.

The liability of the PBGC in the event of plan termination can be written as

(2) $$PBGCL = \max [0, G-F - .3E],$$

where $PBGCL$ = PBGC liability and the value of the workers' claims in termination can be written as

(3) $$T = FL + PBGCL + F \text{ or}$$

(3') $$T = \max [G, \min (A, F)],$$

where $T$ equals the value of the workers' claims in the event of plan termination.

Of these variables, $A$ and $G$ are directly related to nominal interest rates. The value of pension fund assets, $F$, and the market value of the firm, $E$, are not directly related to interest rates.

When inflation and interest rates change, the value of the claims of the firm, government, and workers in termination are all affected. These termination liabilities are probably the best estimate of the true economic position of the three parties, even though a plan may be unlikely to terminate. The argument is analagous to saying that the value of the worker's individual pension claim can be calculated on the basis of what the worker could receive if the worker immediately terminated employment, even if we are certain that the worker will end up staying on with the firm until the normal retirement age. This argument is made in detail in my NBER Working Paper no. 402 (pp. 23–26).

Increases in interest rates have reduced both $A$ and $G$. On the basis of formulas (1) through (3') we can say who gains and who loses when these changes in interest rates occur.

If $F > A$ (the plan is overfunded), then an increase in interest rates simply reduces accrued liabilities. The value of the workers' claims are reduced, with the benefit going to the firm.

If $A > F > G$ (the plan has enough benefits to cover guaranteed but not all accrued benefits), then a termination leaves the workers with $F$ and the firm with no extra liability. Changes in the values of $A$ and $G$ do not influence the value of aggregate worker benefits (which remain at $F$) though there is a potential transfer of benefits among workers.

If $F + .3E > G > F$, the PBGC still has no liability and the workers have benefits worth $G$. An increase in interest rates will reduce $G$ and thus both worker benefits and firm liability.

If $G > F + .3E$, then the firm is facing a maximum liability of $.3E$ beyond the money in the pension fund. An increase in interest rates which reduces $G$ hurts workers but does not affect the firm. In this case $G - F - .3E$ is the liability of the PBGC, and this liability is reduced when interest rates increase.

The above analysis is in reality only an approximation, in part because of long-term labor contracts. For example, with long-term contracts, just because all benefits are currently funded (i.e. $F > A$) does not mean that a drop in interest rates gives workers an increase in wealth proportional to the increase in $A$. The reason is that the decreased spread between $F$ and $A$ increases the likelihood that the firm will be able to make use of its option to limit its liability to $F$. Essentially the pension debt becomes more risky as it grows in value relative to the amount of money in the pension fund, and this increased risk in benefits is what holds down the gain to workers. In general, workers will lose from interest rate increases while the PBGC and the firm will gain. The exact amount and allocation of gain will vary depending on the relative values of $A$, $F$, $G$, and $E$ with the earlier analysis providing a rough distribution of the burden.

## 5.4   The Effect of Inflation on the Value of Pension Benefits

The purpose of this section is to provide a rough estimate of the aggregate funding status of defined benefit pension plans and an indication of the sensitivity of this liability to changes in nominal interest rates.

In their annual report "Funding Costs and Liabilities of Large Corporate Pension Plans" (1980) the firm of Johnson & Higgins stated that the 432 of the Fortune 500 firms for which they could collect data had vested liabilities of $163.363 billion, of which 80% of the benefits were funded. Of the 200 largest nonfinancial corporations, they were able to collect data on 139, finding 94% of $53.361 billion in vested benefits were funded at the end of 1979. The firm attempts to include only defined benefit plans in their analysis; however, sometimes it is difficult to separate defined contribution and defined benefit assets on the basis of publicly available data.

(Note: "Total vested liabilities . . . were calculated by adding the total unfunded vested liabilities of plans for which a plan asset value was available to the total plan asset figure. The ratio of plan assets to total vested liabilities was then calculated. This overstates aggregate total vested liabilities to some degree and correspondingly understates the ratio of plan assets to total vested liabilities, i.e., the funded percent of total vested liabilities. This is countered in part, however, by the fact that most vested liabilities figures are as of the beginning of the year, while assets—usually not including book accruals—are as of the end of the year" [Johnson & Higgins 1980, p. 40].)

Vested liabilities are often used by actuaries as an approximation for the maximum firm liability in the event of plan termination. The differences are that benefits vested in the last five years are only partially guaranteed, there is a limit to the benefits guaranteed to each individual, firms have a maximum liability equal to 30% of the market value of their equity, and if the plan has enough money to pay all vested benefits it is also liable to pay any other accrued benefits in termination.

Guaranteed benefits can sometimes be significantly less than vested benefits. Every three years the auto companies sign new contracts that greatly increase unfunded vested benefits. Those benefits might rightfully be written off at least over the three years of the labor contract, but instead they are immediately placed on the pension fund balance sheet. Thus, counting all vested benefits as part of the firm's current pension liability may make the firm seem worse off than it really is because the liability is immediately recorded while the corresponding asset (present value of future labor services provided in return for the pension benefits) is only recognized over the life of the contract.

On the other hand, arguments have been made by some authors (including Feldstein and Seligman 1980) that a high fraction of accrued but not vested benefits should be included as part of the firm's pension liability. For the sake of agrument, we will include an estimate of all such liabilities, times their actuarial probability of being vested, as part of the firm's pension liability. Winkelvoss [1977] estimates that for a prototypical plan the additional cost of immediate vesting versus vesting after 10 years is that the plan's accrued liability rises by a little over 2% (p. 178). This is consistent with the actual numbers reported by the few firms (e.g. Esmark, Woolworth, and General Electric) for which I have been able to obtain figures for both vested and accrued benefits. To be conservative, no reductions will be made here for the differences between vested and guaranteed benefits, but 5% will be added to vested benefits to allow for accrued but not vested benefits.

The most important adjustments that must be made are for the interest rate assumptions used by firms. A 1978 survey of 246 large plans by Reporting Research Corporation found an average interest rate assumption (weighted by plan assets) of 6.0%. A May 1977 survey by *Institutional Investor* magazine (unweighted by fund assets) yielded an average assumption of 5.85%. The Bell System, with over $20 billion in pension fund assets (little of which was included in the Reporting Research survey), used an interest rate assumption of 6%. Allowing for the possibility of some recent increases in rate assumptions, this analysis will use an average interest assumption of 6.5%.

Next it is necessary to choose the correct interest rate at which to discount pension liabilities. The minimum rate to use is the long-term riskless rate of interest. Moody's Aaa bonds yielded 8.19% at the end of 1977, 9.94% at the end of 1978, and 12.06% at the end of 1979. Since the end of 1979, long-term rates have gone even higher, while fluctuating substantially. This analysis will include calculations using interest rate assumptions of 8, 10, and 12%.

Finally, it is necessary to estimate the effect of a change in the interest rate assumption. There are some rules of thumb used in the actuarial profession. Basically, an approximation is that a change in the interest rate assumption from 5 to 6% reduces pension costs by 20%. The implication is that the duration of pension debt is slightly longer than the duration of a consol. Furthermore, the timing of pension debt is such that its duration is less sensitive to interest rates than is a consol's duration.

For example, in figure 5.1 we see that vested pension benefits (in dollar terms, not adjusted for interest) owed tend to have a distribution which peaks several years in the future. A consol has constant payments. Now

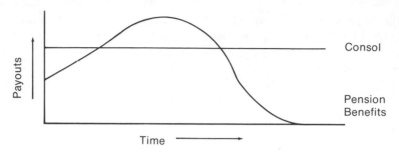

**Fig. 5.1**            Sample distribution of maturity of currently vested pension
                       benefits.

imagine that the consol and the pension benefits had the same duration.
An increase in interest rates will decrease the duration of the pension
debt by less than the consol. That is because with an increase in interest
rates the consol, with more short term and very long term liabilities, will
find the relative weight of its short debt increased relative to the pension
case. For example, in the extreme case where all pension debt is due after
twenty years, a 5% interest rate would give the consol and pension debt
identical durations (and some sensitivities in value to the interest rate).
However, if the interest rate rose to 6%, the duration of the consol would
be 16⅔, while the duration of the pension debt would still be twenty. This
analysis implies that a conservative estimate of the change in value of
pension debt with regard to an interest rate increase is to assume the debt
is proportional to one divided by the interest rate.

Winklevoss estimated (p. 197) that for a typical plan using a 7%
interest rate assumption, changing the assumption to 5% would make the
accrued liability 138.7% as large, while 9% would make benefits 74.9%
as large and 11% would drop the present value of benefits to 57.9% of the
11% rate. These numbers are all consistent with the statement that
assuming the present value of benefits for a plan is inversely proportional
to the interest assumption will slightly understate the impact of an increase in interest rates. The assumption to be used here is more conservative: that for every 5% increase in the interest rate (e.g. from 10 to
10.5%) the present value of benefits would fall by 4%. More precisely the
market value of liabilities were estimated by the formula:

$$\text{market value of liabilities} = \text{book value of liabilities} \times (\text{book interest rate/market interest rate})^{4/5}.$$

Assuming that other relevant (e.g. mortality) actuarial assumptions
are accurate, it is now possible to estimate corrected pension liabilities.
(Remember, the salary growth assumption is irrelevant to valuing

accrued liabilities, so an unrealistically low estimate on that account has no effect.)

The 571 firms cited in the Johnson & Higgins survey have funded benefits of 0.80 × $163 billion plus 0.94 × $53 billion, or $180 billion, and vested benefits of $217 billion. Adding 5% for accrued but not vested liabilities yields total liabilities of $228 billion.

Unfunded liabilities are $228 billion less $180 billion = $48 billion for these firms. This number would have to be projected over the corporate sector as a whole, but the firms surveyed here do represent the bulk of private defined benefit pension plan assets. Now, however, corrections must be made for the interest rate assumption used in calculating these liabilities. Under the assumption that liabilities are inversely proportional to the interest rate, liabilities drop to $193 billion with an 8% interest assumption. Using a 10% assumption drops the present value of the liabilities to $162 billion. At an interest rate of 12% the present value of liabilities falls to $140 billion and at 14% it falls to $123 billion. Comparing these liabilities with $180 billion in pension assets produces net unfunded liabilities of the following amounts.

| Interest Rate | Unfunded Liabilities |
|:---:|:---:|
| 6.5% | $48 billion |
| 8.0% | $13 billion |
| 10.0% | − $18 billion |
| 12.0% | − $40 billion |
| 14.0% | − $57 billion |

Note that as the interest assumption rises pension plans as a whole appear to be better and better funded. Using a rate of roughly 9% or more to discount liabilities is sufficient to put pension plans as a whole in the black.

During 1980 the stock market rose while interest rates also increased. The net effect was that pension assets, consisting of both equities and debt of shorter duration than pension liabilities, on the whole almost surely rose in value while the present value of liabilities was reduced. Therefore taking into account recent developments would make the pension system appear even better funded.

It is important to recognize how sensitive the net liability position is to changes in stock prices and long-term interest rates. A one percentage point change in interest rates affects the present value of liabilities by about $10 billion. To the extent that plans do not hedge all these liabilities with fixed interest assets of similar duration, or nonpension assets negatively correlated in value with interest rates, firms (and the PBGC) bear significant interest rate risk in their pension funds. Workers also bear tremendous interest rate risk. Whether having workers bear this risk is "bad" is not an easy question. It could be that the owners of vested benefits also tend to have mortgages which cancel their pension risk. However, the issue is one that deserves some thought.

## 5.5    The Effect of Inflation on Future Pension Agreements

Increases in interest rates affect the pension system in three main ways. First, higher interest rates make the present value of the same nominal benefits lower. Thus the nominal terms of a pension plan could be uniformly improved without a change in pension costs, should interest rates move to a higher level. Second, high rates reduce the present value of younger workers' benefits more than they reduce the value of older workers' benefits. That is because the younger workers will not receive their benefits for a longer period of time, and thus their benefits are reduced more sharply by higher interest rates. Third, the higher variance in inflation rates increases the pension liability risk discussed in section 5.3. Changes in interest rates cause transfers to and from workers. More variance causes the magnitude of such transfers to be larger.

The obvious consequence of the first effect—higher interest and inflation rates reducing the value of the benefits under any given pension contract—is that the terms of pension plans will be improved if the percentage of total compensation to be paid in pension benefits is to remain constant.

The second effect—any given plan terms giving younger workers a lower share of total pension benefits—should produce several subtle changes in pension compensation arrangements. First, pension plan terms may be changed to tilt benefits slightly more to younger workers in the absence of inflation. As an example, a plan could be changed to provide a worker with a pension equal to final salary times 2% for each year worked up to fifteen, and 1.5% for each additional year rather than for the fraction of final salary to just be directly proportional to years worked. Second, salary/age profiles could be slightly flattened. Pension costs of the Forture 500 have run about 8% of wages in recent years. A shift in how this money is allocated (e.g. from say 6% of wages for the younger half of a payroll and 10% for the older half, to 4% for the younger half and 12% for the older workers) may be correctable by giving younger workers slightly larger wage increases than older workers. Third, with the older workers getting a higher fraction of pension benefits, the younger workers may be able to negotiate a greater percentage of new fringe benefits. For example, in a union bargaining situation the young workers may go along with an increase in pension benefits, which do not help them much, if the older workers will go along with a push for maternity benefits.

A fourth possibility is the increased use of early retirement plan provisions. Such provisions tend to give early retirees a better than actuarially fair deal. Early retirement plans can be shown to essentially flatten out the accrual of pension benefits over a normal working life. At the normal retirement age a worker still has the same accrued benefits, but the early retirement option makes the value of young workers' benefits significantly higher.

Fifth, it is possible that the future will see some integrated defined contribution/defined benefit plans. Under such a plan the firm could contribute a fixed percentage of salary to a defined contribution fund and could provide a deferred annuity equal to some fixed percentage of salary (i.e. a defined benefit) for each year of service. (This could be done in two separate plans: a defined benefit and a "thrift" plan.) Under moderate inflation, defined benefit plans provided a distribution of benefits which gave younger workers a somewhat lower fraction of their compensation in the form of pension benefits than older workers received. With current high inflation rates this effect has been greatly exaggerated. Within the bounds of ERISA it may not be possible to create a defined benefit plan with the same effective "tilt" in pension compensation as was achieved before. A straight defined contribution plan, however, would eliminate the "tilt" entirely. Should older workers prefer to receive a higher fraction of their income in pension benefits than younger workers do, the defined contribution solution may not be entirely satisfactory. A combination plan may be one way of approximating the same tilt in the accrual of benefits as existed under moderate inflation.

Note that little has been mentioned about the indexing or partial indexing of benefits. Indexing is a natural topic to consider as a remedy for all three effects cited at the begining of this section. However, the indexing problem is not simple. Indexing already accrued benefits would sharply raise their value, essentially representing a gift from the firm (and, less voluntarily, the PBGC) to its employees. Such a gift would raise the value of benefits accrued by workers in the past without reducing their future negotiating position for compensation. Under a union plan some indexing is possible if the workers agree to pay for this indexing by taking lower compensation over the life of a new contract. However, the cost of indexing can be so great that such an arrangement is impractical. For example, indexing up to 4 or 5% inflation could easily double the value of a plan's vested benefits (just as reducing the interest rate by that amount would do). A firm like General Motors, which has a present value of vested benefits approaching eleven figures, could only agree to double these benefits if its workers were willing to take billions less in salary each year for the duration of a three-year labor contract. Thus formal indexing of past benefits seems unlikely.

While newly granted benefits could be more easily indexed, employees would still have to adjust to paying a large amount in the nominal terms of a plan for indexing. It is unclear whether workers would wish to pay such a price. For example, a sixty-five-year-old worker may prefer a fixed nominal pension to one that starts at a lower amount but is indexed to the CPI. One reason is that such a person may prefer to get his money out of the pension plan earlier and to consume more at sixty-five than seventy-five. Another reason is that the individual is not constrained to spending the funds when received, and after retirement age may prefer to manage his assets himself rather than have them tied up in a pension plan which no longer is providing large tax benefits. A third reason is that the index used (e.g. CPI) may not be representative of this person's future consumption expenses. Social security is already indexed to the CPI, and in recent years the CPI has seemingly outstripped the inflation of prices in many older people's consumption baskets because of housing prices. Thus the employee may not want to hedge his non–social security income against the CPI. Such a person might prefer to have the cash to hedge against his own future consumption via, say, the purchase of some desired durable assets.

Nevertheless, some partial indexing on a formal or informal basis has appeared in some pension plans. Many firms make ad hoc adjustments to the benefits of already retired employees. A much smaller number of firms have formal, usually limited, indexing plans. Also, some firms allow workers to take as a lump sum the present value of their pension benefits—with their benefits being discounted at low fixed nominal interest rates.

All such provisions tend to raise the present value of worker benefits. To the extent that such options were not fully considered, the numerical estimates of the surplus in the previous section are high. Provisions such as those listed above also mean that the worker is not always fully exposed to the risk inherent in changes in nominal interest rates. For example, if workers have the option of receiving a lump sum discounted at a fixed nominal rate, the present value of their benefits is protected at least against changes in postretirement interest rates. Note, however, that even full postretirement indexing does not protect the worker against changes in interest rates in the years remaining until retirement, the issue emphasized in the first section of the paper.

It is important to remember that the pension plan is not the only way the worker can hedge against inflation. Many younger workers may prefer to hedge by buying a house and taking out a mortgage. Older workers may also prefer to hedge against their personal wants rather than a general index.

The higher variance in inflation rates is likely to make both firms and workers want to reduce the size of transfers that occur when interest rates change. One possible change other than partial indexing could be a move toward determination of benefits more by what happens to the asset side of the pension fund balance sheet than by what happens to the liability side. The most obvious way to do this is by shifting at least partially toward defined contribution plans. Thus it is possible that firms may decide to increase profit sharing and thrift plans relative to pension plans in the coming years.

Finally, firms may also decide to hedge their pension liabilities by placing more fixed interest debt in their pension funds. Such debt will fluctuate in value along with the firm's pension liabilities. Also, some authors have argued that there may be a tax advantage to placing bonds in the firm's pension fund. (This argument has been made most prominently by Fischer Black and Irwin Tepper.) While the tax advantage question is still open to debate, if the Black-Tepper argument holds, the tax effect is directly proportional to interest rates. Thus higher interest rates would provide an incentive for the firm to hold more debt in its pension plan.

### 5.6  Conclusion

Inflation, primarily through the channel of higher interest rates, has caused important changes in the private pension system. Workers have lost out to both firms and the Pension Benefit Guaranty Corporation. Benefits have been skewed toward older workers. The plans' capital gains on their nominal liabilities have made the private pension system extremely solvent.

Indexing private pensions would be extremely expensive and does not appear imminent. However, other changes in plan structure may lead to reducing workers' inflation risk in their pension assets. Finally, both the increased variance and levels of nominal interest rates may actually lead to an increase in the proportion of pension assets held in long-term fixed interest securities.

# References

Bulow, J. 1979. Analysis of pension funding under ERISA. NEBER Working Paper no. 402 (October).

Feldstein, M., and Seligman, S. 1980. Pension funding, share prices, and national saving. NBER Working Paper no. 509 (July).

Johnson & Higgins. 1980. Funding costs and liabilities of large corporate pension plans. 1980 Executive Report.

Winklevoss, H. E. 1977. *Pension mathematics*. Homewood, Ill.: Richard D. Irwin.

# 6  The Disruptive Effect of Inflation on the Organization of Markets

Dennis W. Carlton

This paper argues that a neglected but significant effect of inflation is the disruption of the way firms conduct business. Evidence on actual transaction prices is used to illustrate how far actual market behavior differs from that predicted by simple supply equal to demand models. A theory is presented that accounts for the evidence and links together liquidity of markets, product heterogeneity, price rigidity and quantity rationing, and firm size. The concluding section applies the theory to analyze the effects of inflation and presents data on the effects of inflation. The paper concludes that inflation has forced firms to rely on more liquid markets, to use more standardized products, and to make greater use of prices to allocate goods than they would have without inflation.

## 6.1  Introduction

Inflation has plagued the United States economy since the late 1960s. I use the word "plagued" because there seems to be a unanimous sentiment that inflation is bad. There is much less agreement among economists as to why inflation is bad. This paper discusses what I believe to be a neglected but significant effect of inflation, namely the disruption of well-established methods of transacting business.[1] Because of this effect, inflation can cause dramatic and undesirable changes in the types of goods that get sold and in the structure of markets.

Dennis W. Carlton is with the Law School of the University of Chicago and the National Bureau of Economic Research.

The author thanks P. Diamond, R. Hall, E. Kitch, R. Lucas, F. Mishkin, L. Telser, and R. Topel for helpful comments, and V. France, R. LaLonde, and R. Miller for research assistance. This research was supported by the NSF.

The next section reports on the pattern of transaction prices found in a sample of businesses during a relatively noninflationary period, 1957–66. These data enable us to learn how businessmen like to structure their transactions and emphasize how far actual market behavior deviates from that predicted by a naive textbook model in which price continuously adjusts so as to keep supply equal to demand. Motivated by the empirical findings of section 6.2, section 6.3 sketches the general theory of the close relation between the organization of markets, the size and structure of firms in the industry, and the transactional arrangements used by business. Section 6.4 uses this theory to discuss and present evidence on the impact of inflation on markets and firm structures.

## 6.2 Evidence on How Actual Markets Work

One of the first lessons an economics student learns is that the competitive price of a homogeneous product is determined by the intersection of a supply and demand curve. This very simple model predicts that price should be continuously changing in response to changes in supply and demand. The model also presumes a highly liquid market in the sense that any buyer can buy and any seller can sell at any time at the known market price. Since there is a single market price, all buyers' prices change simultaneously when either demand or supply changes. Price is the sole mechanism used to allocate goods to buyers.

Economists recognize that this simple model may not provide an accurate description of how all markets operate. In fact, markets differ greatly in how well their behavior conforms to that predicted by the simple model. At one extreme are highly liquid markets, like organized exchanges (e.g., New York Stock Exchange), where transactions can take place almost instantaneously at the market price, which is determined at each moment by the interactions of many potential buyers and sellers. At the other extreme are highly illiquid markets where the good that is transacted has attributes customized to the individual transaction between the buyer and seller and where there is no continuously available "market price" quoted because each transaction involves a unique good.

To determine how close the behavior of any market is to that predicted by the simple supply equal to demand model, it is necessary to examine the behavior of transaction prices in that market. We examine transaction prices during the period 1957–66. This period was characterized by relatively low rates of inflation. The data, collected by James Kindahl and George Stigler, report the transaction prices paid by buyers for various goods usually on a monthly basis for the ten-year period 1957–66.[2] The buyers provided practically all the price information. The buyers were composed primarily of large companies, but also included hospitals and federal, state, and local governments.

Table 6.1 lists by product the average duration of price inflexibility in months and the standard deviation of duration. The calculations are based on the total number of spells during which the transaction price between a particular buyer and seller remains unchanged. (For each observed pairing of buyer and seller, there is a price series reflecting the actual transaction prices paid over time. Since a buyer typically continues to do business with the same seller after a price change, each pairing of a buyer and seller produces a price series with several spells during which the transaction price is unchanged.)

Table 6.1 is based on an interpolation of the price series. The main assumptions underlying the interpolation are that when data are missing (most relevant when a series is reported only every three months) then if the price is unchanged between reports it is assumed constant between reports. If the price changes between reports, we assume only one price change. This method creates an upward bias in estimated rigidity, though examination of some complete data series appears to indicate that the bias is not sufficiently important so as to alter the inferences to be made from table 6.1.

Several facts are striking about table 6.1. First, it is evident that for many transactions between individual buyers and sellers, price once set tends to remain unchanged for substantial periods of time (over one year in many cases). This fact suggests that quantity allocations (e.g. rationing) and not price may be the mechanism used to allocate some goods when supply or demand changes. Presumably, the seller's personal knowledge about the demander's needs will influence the allocation.

**Table 6.1**        **Price Rigidity by Product**

| Product | Number of Contracts Observed[a] | Average Duration of Price Rigidity (months) | Standard Deviation of Duration (months) |
|---|---|---|---|
| Steel | 348 | 13.0 | 18.3 |
| Nonferrous metals | 209 | 4.3 | 6.1 |
| Petroleum | 245 | 5.9 | 5.3 |
| Rubber tires | 123 | 8.1 | 12.0 |
| Paper | 128 | 8.7 | 14.0 |
| Chemicals | 658 | 12.8 | 10.7 |
| Cement | 40 | 13.2 | 14.7 |
| Glass | 22 | 10.2 | 12.1 |
| Truck motors | 59 | 5.4 | 6.3 |
| Plywood | 46 | 4.7 | 7.7 |

[a]"Number of contracts" means the number of price series between individual buyers and sellers for a good of specified characteristics.

Second, for any one product, the standard deviation of length of rigidity is quite high. This suggests that for any one product there are a wide variety of contracts with differing price flexibility. In other words, it appears from table 6.1 that there are some contracts that have very flexible prices while others have very inflexible prices for the same broad commodity group. This suggests (and more detailed studies confirm) that the correlation of price movements among different contracts for the same type of commodity need not be very close. We expect that the goods whose prices are flexible are more standardized in their characteristics than the goods whose prices are inflexible. (The more customized the good, the fewer the number of potential buyers and sellers and the less liquid is the market, and hence [as we shall explain more fully in section 6.3] the less flexible the price.) Finally, there are enormous differences across industries in degree of price flexibility.

In table 6.2 evidence is presented on the frequency of price rigidity for two of the many types of transactions represented in table 6.1, annual and monthly. Transactions were classified as monthly or annual according to the buyer's reporting of the duration of the current agreement. "Monthly" means that there is no negotiated understanding beyond the current month, while "annual" means there is a contract that lasts for one year. I will refer to these two types of transactions as monthly contracts and annual contracts. Table 6.2 provides us with more detailed evidence than table 6.1 on the flexibility of prices.

Many interesting facts emerge from an analysis of the data in table 6.2. The contracting structures for each product are obviously different. A curious finding is that there are many "annual" contracts whose prices change well before one year has elapsed while there are many "monthly" contracts whose prices often do not change for one year. The implication seems to be that contract terms are obviously very flexible and adaptations to sudden changes in market conditions are frequent. Ongoing relations between buyer and seller probably account for this type of behavior.

We expect the monthly contracts to represent purchases of less stable buyers and therefore expect less reliance by a seller on his personal knowledge of the buyer's needs to allocate goods and more reliance on the price system. Table 6.2 confirms this view by showing that monthly contract prices move more frequently than those for an annual contract. This also establishes that there are contracts whose prices remain unchanged at the same time that demand and supply forces are changing other contract prices for the same general commodity. This confirms what we had inferred earlier from table 6.1, namely that correlation of different contract prices for the same general commodity need not be high.

It is possible to use the data of tables 6.1 and 6.2 to hazard some guesses as to which markets resemble liquid markets with flexible prices perform-

**Table 6.2**          **Frequency of Duration of Price Rigidity for Annual and Monthly Contracts Based on Spells of Price Rigidity**

| Product | Contract Type | Number of Contracts[a] | 0–3 Months | 3 Months– 1 Year | 1–2 Years | 2–4 Years | Over 4 Years |
|---|---|---|---|---|---|---|---|
| Steel | Annual | 11 | .11 | .41 | .24 | .22 | .03 |
|  | Monthly | 111 | .48 | .27 | .15 | .07 | .04 |
| Nonferrous | Annual | 8 | .16 | .69 | .12 | .03 | 0 |
| metals | Monthly | 87 | .78 | .20 | .02 | .01 | 0 |
| Petroleum | Annual | 66 | .20 | .69 | .07 | .04 | 0 |
|  | Monthly | 16 | .83 | .15 | .02 | 0 | 0 |
| Rubber | Annual | 32 | .19 | .72 | .07 | .01 | .01 |
| tires | Monthly | 24 | .44 | .42 | .07 | .01 | .06 |
| Paper | Annual | 22 | .04 | .69 | .18 | .08 | .01 |
|  | Monthly | 36 | .46 | .36 | .12 | .04 | .02 |
| Chemicals | Annual | 286 | .11 | .58 | .17 | .09 | .06 |
|  | Monthly | 134 | .53 | .27 | .09 | .06 | .04 |
| Cement | Annual | 8 | .04 | .78 | .13 | .04 | 0 |
|  | Monthly | 4 | .64 | .29 | .02 | .04 | .02 |
| Glass | Annual | 8 | 0 | .87 | .10 | .03 | 0 |
|  | Monthly | 9 | .51 | .22 | .18 | .09 | 0 |
| Truck | Annual | 8 | .05 | .86 | .09 | 0 | 0 |
| motors | Monthly | 34 | .69 | .26 | .04 | .01 | 0 |
| Plywood | Annual | 0 |  |  |  |  |  |
|  | Monthly | 2 | .99 | .02 | 0 | 0 | 0 |

Note: The numbers in the rows of the table may not add to one because of rounding.
[a]Note that "Number of Contracts" is not the number of spells of price rigidity in all contracts. See the discussion preceding table 6.1 and footnote a of table 6.1.

ing the allocative role and which markets resemble illiquid markets with fixed prices and quantity allocations performing the allocative role. Nonferrous metals, petroleum, and plywood seem likely to have submarkets that are highly liquid (for these three categories, over 75% of monthly contracts change price within three months), while steel, paper, and chemicals seem likely to have submarkets that are highly illiquid (for these markets, over 25% of the annual contracts change price less than every year). It is very obvious from table 6.2 that for some goods there are likely to be both highly liquid and highly illiquid submarkets. The highly liquid submarket probably involves a more standardized variant of the product than the illiquid submarket. The evidence of table 6.2 suggests that both liquid and illiquid markets were significant factors in United States manufacturing in the period 1957–66.

## 6.3    The Theory of Market Organization and Firm Structure

Every market economy must simultaneously solve the problems of which type of goods to produce, how large and vertically integrated the producing firms should be, and how sellers should transact with buyers. Whether the transactions for a certain good take place in a liquid or illiquid market will turn out to be a key factor in explaining the evidence of the previous section and in understanding how inflation will affect a particular market.[3]

A requirement for a market to be liquid is that there be many potential buyers and sellers at each moment. In order for markets to be liquid it is often necessary for the quality attributes of the good to be very standardized to assure that any two units of the good should be regarded as highly intechangeable from a buyer's or a seller's point of view. This standardization is designed to generate lots of potential buyers and sellers for *the* product. (If goods are not standardized and not regarded as interchangeable, then each transaction is unique and there can be no liquid market for *the* product since there is no one product.) The advantage of a liquid market is that it is easy (i.e. not costly) to transact quickly at the market price. The disadvantage of a liquid market is the standardization of the product. Each buyer will usually want some slightly different attributes in the product. For example, if the buyers are other firms purchasing inputs, the idiosyncratic nature of each buyer's production process might lead each buyer to want a slightly different design of a particular machine. There cannot be a liquid market for every single slightly different variety of good—there would not be enough buyers and sellers to ensure the liquidity of any of the markets.

There will therefore be a very close relation between how liquid markets are and the variety of slightly different models of a product produced. At one extreme, everyone uses a standardized product (e.g. wheat futures) and a liquid market (e.g. Chicago Board of Trade for wheat futures) can exist. (Whether the liquid market is an organized exchange or not is not as important as whether it is highly liquid.) At the other extreme, each buyer wants a uniquely designed product and no liquid market can exist. In general, we expect to see demanders using the liquid market to purchase the standardized goods for some of their needs and using an illiquid market to contract forward to buy highly individualized varieties of the good. As preferences shift from standardized to custom designed products, the liquidity of the market for the standardized good diminishes until eventually no liquid market remains. The observed degree of product heterogeneity and market liquidity will be a result of balancing the benefits from increased liquidity against the costs of reduced product heterogeneity.

Liquid markets which determine *the* market price at which buyers and sellers can always transact serve another valuable purpose in addition to providing liquidity—they reveal the market price to both traders and nontraders.[4] Suppose that the firm purchases a customized input on a forward contract with a seller. Initially, competition among sellers assures the buyer of a competitive price. However, as time progresses, the seller who initially obtained the business may be in a position to exert temporary monopoly power over the buyer, since he is the only seller who can satisfy the buyer's needs quickly. How can a buyer ensure that when the seller changes the price for the customized product the seller is not exercising monopoly power? Alternatively, suppose a firm decides not to use a standardized input product and instead decides to produce the customized product itself—i.e. the firm vertically integrates. How can the firm determine if its production division is producing the customized input efficiently? The answer to both questions is that the firm can use the price movements in the highly liquid market for the standardized product to monitor the cost of either buying or producing the customized product. Using the readily available price movements of the standardized product will be a good way to monitor provided that the costs of producing the standardized and customized products are highly correlated. The presence of a closely related liquid market makes it easier to transact in or internally produce an illiquid good.[5]

Whenever a product is sold in an illiquid market, setting the price requires a negotiation between the buyer and seller. Since negotiations are time-consuming and therefore costly, both the buyer and the seller will not want to be always renegotiating the price.[6] (Even when there is a closely related liquid market whose price can be used to index the contract price in the illiquid market, it will still be the case [as long as the relation between the liquid and illiquid market is not perfect—i.e. the indexing is imperfect] that transacting in the illiquid market is more costly than transacting in the liquid marked.) Therefore it is reasonable to expect and the evidence presented earlier confirms that price (or the price structure if there is [imperfect] indexing), once set, may not change for some period of time. But if the price is unchanged over time, how do goods, or more precisely, how does the sellers' productive capacity, get allocated efficiently to buyers? The answer is that the price system is not the sole mechanism used in the short run to allocate goods in illiquid markets. It is possible to show that in a world of uncertainty with illiquid markets it can be more efficient to use fixed price contracts combined with quantity rationing than to use variable price contracts. The reason is that in a liquid market, *the* market price is readily known while in an illiquid market it is not. Any method of allocation has costs. Using prices may be inefficient if *the* market price can only be guessed with error.

Quantity and price allocation may be preferable to pure price allocation whenever sellers have very good knowledge of the *relative* needs of their customers. (E.g. a supplier may know that two of his customers have identical needs even though the supplier is unable to guess the market clearing price.) In an illiquid market, the more homogeneous are the needs of buyers and the greater is the variability in demand, the more efficient is the price plus quantity allocation likely to be. Roughly speaking, price is used to weed out those who generally want the good from those who do not, while rationing (quantity allocations) is used to get the good to those who need it most at each instant.

We have now outlined the relation between the existence of liquid and illiquid markets, the variety of goods produced, the use of various contractual arrangements, vertical integration, and price and quantity allocation mechanisms. In order to completely link the existence of markets to the structure of firms, it is necessary to discuss firm size. Most economists would agree that explanations of firm size based on production economies cannot convincingly explain the distribution of firm size across industries. We focus on how the failure to have property rights in information plus the nonexistence of futures or spot markets explains the size distribution of firms.[7]

Suppose that an individual has special knowledge that the price of wheat will rise. That individual can take advantage of his information by buying long on the futures market for wheat. Futures markets enable individuals to take advantage of any special information without having to become a wheat dealer. Suppose that a futures market does not exist, but a spot market does. Then, the individual with knowledge of a price rise could become a wheat broker and earn a capital gain on his wheat. The nonexistence of a futures market forces the individual to enter the wheat business to take advantage of his information. (Taking advantage of the information by investing in equity [i.e., common stocks] of wheat firms or in firms that sell products whose price is affected by wheat prices is likely to be less desirable than going into the wheat business because the correlation of the wheat price with other [even closely related] prices is not likely to be perfect.) Moreover, the special information the buyer has about wheat prices may be derived from special knowledge about the prices of specialized (illiquid) inputs used to produce wheat (e.g. specialized labor). In such a case, the efficient way to take advantage of the information is not to become a broker middleman but rather to become a wheat producer who utilizes inputs in the most efficient way.

When either organized futures or spot markets fail to exist, we can expect the most informed firm to be a producer firm in the industry. The firm earns a return on its information not through financial transactions involving pieces of paper but through real transactions involving the good. The firm takes advantage of its information by varying its output, so we expect the best informed firm to have the most flexible production technology of the firms in the industry.[8] Also, because of knowledge about specialized input prices, we expect the most informed firm to be the most vertically integrated firm in the industry.

This completes the sketch of a complicated set of interrelationships between market organization and firm structure. The theory just outlined is capable of explaining the evidence examined earlier and is necessary in order to properly assess the disruptive effect inflation can have.

## 6.4   Effects of Inflation

Inflation is often defined to mean a general increase in all prices. That definition fails to emphasize a key fact—namely that inflation increases uncertainty. During inflation there is greater uncertainty about what future price levels will be. Moreover, during inflation there is greater uncertainty about relative prices (the price of one good relative to that of another good). The view that completely separate forces determine relative prices and the general price level is not valid on either theoretical or empirical grounds. (See e.g. Cukierman 1979 for a theoretical discussion, and Vining and Elwertowski 1976 and Parks 1978 for empirical evidence showing that the variability of relative prices depends on inflationary conditions.)

What effect will this added uncertainty have? First, it will mean that it is more difficult for firms to plan for the future since the added uncertainty makes it more difficult to predict the future. Second, it will change the relative advantages of liquid versus illiquid markets.

Recall from section 6.3 that the advantage of not using a highly liquid market was that the buyer could custom design the product rather than take delivery of a standardized product. The complication was that if a buyer contracted with a seller for a customized product in an illiquid market, it was hard to determine what the market price should be especially after the contract had been entered into. The presence of a liquid market with a market price always readily available for some related product made it easier to transact in the illiquid good by enabling the buyer to monitor the seller when the seller wished to alter price. If inflation injects uncertainty into the price system, then it is likely to become more difficult to use the price of a good sold in a liquid market to estimate the marginal cost of the closely related good sold in the illiquid market. Buyers in illiquid markets therefore will be less able to use the market price of the liquid market to monitor their own contracts. In other words, inflation degrades the information content of price in the liquid market and makes it harder to transact in the illiquid market. (More precisely, inflation causes the error in predicting real marginal cost to rise.) Moreover, we saw earlier that to avoid the problem of continuous, costly renegotiation, buyers and sellers prefer to have a fixed price (or fixed price structure if there is indexing) for some time period. However, sellers will be increasingly reluctant to give fixed price contracts (or contracts in which the price is indexed to a product whose price is not perfectly correlated with its own production costs) as price variability increases. Therefore, since the relative advantage of using an illiquid market decreases during inflation, we expect to see a shift away from specialized goods sold in illiquid markets to more standardized goods sold in liquid markets.

Even neglecting the renegotiation problem and the reluctance of sellers to offer long-term fixed price contracts, we expect the use of illiquid markets to diminish. Recall that in illiquid markets, quantity allocations are based not only on price but on a seller's judgment as to which of his customers needs the good the most. As inflation injects uncertainty into the system, the judgments of the seller about the relative needs of different buyers may become less accurate, so the method of allocating goods by judgment becomes inefficient relative to the use of price alone.

An alternative that avoids the problems of renegotiation and the reluctance of sellers to get locked into a fixed price (structure) is for the buyer to produce the customized good internally. The difficulty with internal production is that without a liquid market for a closely related product, it may be difficult for the firm to easily monitor whether its internal production costs are reasonable. If inflation injects uncertainty into the economic system and lessens the ability to use the price in the liquid market to predict the cost of the illiquid good, then vertical integration becomes less desirable since monitoring becomes more difficult.

In summary, in response to inflationary uncertainty, we expect to see fewer contracts with fixed prices for long time periods, fewer customized goods, greater use of standardized goods sold in a liquid market, a move from outside contracting of customized goods to internal production through vertical integration, and a move from vertical integration to reliance on standard quality goods sold in a liquid market where *the* market price is easy to observe. All of these changes may be undesirable from an efficiency standpoint.[9] Without inflation, the desired combination of liquidity and product diversity was achieved by balancing the (private) benefits of diversity against the (private) costs of illiquidity. Inflation injects uncertainty into the system, alters trade-offs, and causes deviations from the initially desired combinations. It is unfortunately very difficult to document whether the above predictions on the effect of inflation reflect the experience of the United States economy in the 1970s. No data source comparable to the one used to construct tables 6.1 and 6.2 is available. However, there have been reports of abandonment of fixed price contracts in such commodities as paperboard, domestic copper, and coal.

If inflation adds uncertainty to the economic system, we can expect there to be a greater divergence in beliefs about future prices. This will lead to an incentive to create markets for people to act on their beliefs (Grossman 1977); hence we can expect futures markets to become more prevalent. If a futures market already exists, we expect it to be used more during inflationary times.

Table 6.3 shows the number of new futures markets that have been established during the periods 1960–73 and 1974–78 on the major exchanges in the United States. The table supports the theory that the average yearly rate of new contract introduction should be much higher in the more recent inflationary period.

Another measure of the importance of futures contracts is the volume of contracts traded. Table 6.4 presents evidence on futures contracts traded at the Chicago Mercantile Exchange (excluding the International Monetary Market) and on grain futures contracts traded at major grain exchanges.

Table 6.4 indicates a strong positive correlation between volume traded and inflation, just as the theory predicts. Moreover, the recent introduction and growth of financial futures since 1975 and the options market since 1974 provides further support for the theory that the importance of futures markets increases as inflation increases. My own preliminary econometric research suggests that holding crop size constant, an unanticipated 1% change in the rate of inflation raises volume traded on grain futures markets by about 1 to 5%.

The increase in the use of futures markets and liquid spot markets should have a definite effect on the size of firms. Without liquid markets in which it is easy to transact, it is necessary to become a member of the

**Table 6.3**      **Introduction of New Futures Contracts and Inflation**

|  | 1960–73 | 1974–78 |
|---|---|---|
| Number of new futures contracts introduced on the major U.S. futures exchanges[a] | 95 | 50 |
| Average yearly rate of introduction of new futures contracts | 6.8 | 10 |
| Average rate of inflation (measured by Dec. to Dec. changes in the CPI)[b] | 3.3 | 8.0 |

[a]I am grateful to John Labuszewski, formerly staff economist at the Chicago Board of Trade and now director of economic research at the Mid-America Commodity Exchange, for compiling these data using information from the Association of Commodity Exchange Firms and "Ranking of Commodities/Market Share Report, Part I, 1979," an internal CBOT memorandum.

[b]Source: *Economic Report of the President, 1982*, table B-55. Washington: Government Printing Office.

Table 6.4              Volume of Futures Trading and Inflation

|  | Volume of Contracts on CME (thousands)[a] | Volume of Sales in Bushels on Futures Markets, All Grains (billions)[b] | Inflation Rate During the Year (Measured by Dec. to Dec. Changes in CPI)[c] |
| Year | | | |
| --- | --- | --- | --- |
| 1955 | 549.0 | 12.4 | .4 |
| 1960 | 567.3 | 11.2 | 1.5 |
| 1965 | 889.0 | 26.9 | 1.9 |
| 1970 | 3,317.4 | 25.5 | 5.5 |
| 1975 | 5,758.8 | 67.7 | 7.0 |
| 1978 | 10,008.9 | 93.5 | 9.0 |

[a]Source: *Chicago Mercantile Exchange Yearbook*, 1978, p. 6.
[b]Exchanges included are Chicago Board of Trade, Chicago Open Board of Trade, Kansas City Board of Trade, and Minneapolis Grain Exchange. Source: *Chicago Board of Trade Statistical Annual Report*, 1978, p. 9.
[c]Source: *Economic Report of the President, 1982*, table B-55. Washington: Government Printing Office.

industry in order to earn a return on superior information. As discussed earlier, those firms with the best information are likely to be vertically integrated, the most profitable, and the most flexible. However, with well-organized spot and especially futures markets it is possible for someone with superior information to earn a return on that information without physically producing or, in the case of futures markets, storing the good. The individual simply takes a position in the futures market or, lacking a futures market, buys and sells on the spot market. Therefore, in inflation we expect to see a rise in the number of liquid spot markets and futures markets, a rise in the number of brokers (people who just buy and sell) if only a spot market comes into existence, and perhaps a decrease in the concentration of industry (because now a firm does not have to produce to earn a return on its information). Once again, it is difficult to use available data to test these hypotheses about inflation.

Inflation is not a *uniform* general increase in all prices that can be easily handled by indexing all prices. Instead, inflation is a general increase in prices accompanied by much uncertainty that disrupts the methods of conducting business and alters the characteristics of goods that are produced. Inflation forces greater reliance on liquid markets—i.e. it forces greater reliance on the price system to allocate relatively homogeneous goods. What is important to recognize is that this move toward the simple model of supply and demand may be *undersirable*; (see note 9). The greater reliance on the price system may represent a serious cost of inflation. What the theory and the evidence outlined earlier tell us is that it is sometimes better to have illiquid markets with customized products than to have a liquid market with a homogeneous product. The efficiency of an economic system is not measured by the liquidity of its markets, the degree to which it uses price to allocate goods, or how closely the simple supply equal to demand model predicts market behavior, but rather by how well diverse consumer demands are satisfied. By injecting needless uncertainty into the economic system, inflation may interfere with the efficient methods of satisfying consumers and may impose substantial costs on society by forcing consumers and business firms to use markets they would not otherwise have used and to consume more standardized products than they would otherwise have chosen. It is this disruption of transaction, consumption, and production patterns that helps explain why the public dislikes inflation.

# Notes

1. Two noteworthy articles recognizing the effect of inflation on transaction costs are Okun (1975) and Wachter and Williamson (1978). The spirit of my paper and its conclusions are similar in many respects to those of Wachter and Williamson (1978).

2. I thank C. Freidland and G. Stigler for their help in explaining the data to me. See Stigler and Kindahl (1970) for an analysis of these data.

3. See Telser and Higginbotham (1977) for a discussion of liquidity and its relation to future markets.

4. The literature in finance examines this point in detail. See, for example, Grossman and Stiglitz (1980) and the references cited therein. Also, see Kitch (1980).

5. Will the optimal number of liquid and illiquid markets be established by private market forces? The answer appears to be no. Liquidity generates a positive externality for which no compensation is necessarily received.

6. See Wachter and Williamson (1978).

7. See Kitch (1980) for an interesting discussion on this point. See also Carlton (1980).

8. See Carlton (1982).

9. As section 6.2 (see note 5) pointed out, there is an externality associated with the existence of liquid markets. The theory of second best, applied to the problem under study, shows that it will be difficult, theoretically, to make unambigious welfare statements about inflation. Only statements about private (not social) benefits and costs are possible. Because of the second-best problem, the analysis implies that a zero rate of inflation is not likely to be socially optimal. However, it seems clear that as the rate of inflation increases, the increased private costs of inflation identified in this paper can eventually overwhelm second-best considerations. Therefore the effect of inflation on the organization of markets and transactions does represent a potential cost to society and is a cost that analysts should be aware of.

# References

Carlton, D. 1980. Discussion of "The law and economics of rights in valuable information: A comment." *Journal of Legal Studies* 9 (December): 725–26.

————. 1982. Planning and market structure. In J. J. McCall, ed., *The economics of information and uncertainty*. Chicago: University of Chicago Press for the NBER.

Cukierman, A. 1979. Relative price variability, inflation, and the allocative efficiency of the price system. Mimeo, Carnegie-Mellon University.

Grossman, S. 1977. The existence of futures markets, noisy rational expectations, and informational externalities. *Review of Economic Studies* 64 (October): 431–49.

Grossman, S., and Stiglitz, J. 1980. On the impossibility of informationaly efficient markets. *American Economic Review* 70 (June): 393–408.

Kitch, E. 1980. The law and economics of rights in valuable information. *Journal of Legal Studies* 9 (December): 683–724.

Okun, A. 1975. Inflation: Its mechanics and welfare costs. *Brookings Papers on Economic Activity* 2: 351–401.

Parks, R. 1978. Inflation and relative price variability. *Journal of Political Economy* 86 (February): 79–95.

Stigler, G., and Kindahl, J. 1970. *The behavior of industrial prices*. New York: Columbia University Press for the NBER.

Telser, L., and Higginbotham, H. 1977. Organized futures markets: Costs and benefits, *Journal of Political Economy* 85 (October): 969–1000.

Vining, D., and Elwertowski, T. 1976. The relationship between relative prices and the general price level. *American Economic Review* 66 (September): 699–708.

Wachter, M., and Williamson, O. 1978. Obligational markets and the mechanics of inflation. *Bell Journal of Economics* 9 (Autumn): 549–71.

# 7    Inflation, Capital Taxation, and Monetary Policy

Martin Feldstein

The interaction of inflation and existing tax rules has powerful effects on the American economy. Inflation distorts the measurement of profits, of interest payments, and of capital gains. The resulting mismeasurement of capital income has caused a substantial increase in the effective tax rate on the real income from capital employed in the nonfinancial corporate sector. At the same time, the deductibility of nominal interest expenses has encouraged the expansion of consumer debt and stimulated the demand for owner-occupied housing. The net result has been a reduction of capital accumulation.

These effects of the fiscal structure have been largely ignored in the analysis of monetary policy. As I explain in this paper, I believe that the failure of the monetary authorities to recognize the implication of the fiscal structure has caused them over the years to underestimate just how expansionary monetary policy has been. Moreover, because of our fiscal structure, attempts to encourage investment by an easy-money policy have actually had an adverse impact on investment in plant and equipment.

In the first three sections of this paper, I review some of my own research on the impact of inflation on effective tax rates, share prices, and nonresidential fixed investment. The fourth section discusses how ignoring the fiscal structure of the economy caused a misinterpretation of the tightness of monetary policy in the 1960s and 1970s. The paper concludes by commenting on the implications of this analysis for the mix of monetary policy, fiscal policy, and the tax structure.

Martin Feldstein is with Harvard University and the National Bureau of Economic Research.

The views expressed here are the author's and should not be attributed to Harvard University or the NBER.

## 7.1   Inflation, Effective Tax Rates, and Net Rates of Return

Our tax laws were written for an economy with little or no inflation. With an inflation rate of 6% to 8% or more, the tax system functions very badly. The problem is particularly acute for the taxation of income from capital. Despite reductions in statutory rates over the 1960s and 1970s the effective tax rates on the income from savings have actually increased sharply in recent years because inflation creates fictitious income for the government to tax. Savers must pay tax not only on their real income from savings but on their fictitious income as well.

Without legislative action or public debate, effective tax rates on capital income of different types have been raised dramatically in the last decade. This process of raising the effective tax rate on capital income is hard for the public at large to understand or even for most members of Congress. What appear to be relatively low rates of tax on interest income, on capital gains, and on corporate profits as measured under current accounting rules are actually very high tax rates, in some cases more than 100%, because our accounting definitions are not suited to an economy with inflation.

As anyone with a savings account knows, even a 12% interest rate was not enough last year to compensate a saver for the loss in purchasing power of his money that resulted from the 13% inflation. The present tax rules ignore this and tax the individual on the full nominal amount of his interest receipts. An individual with a 30% marginal tax rate would get to keep only an 8.4% return on an account that paid 12%. After adjusting this yield for the 13% inflation in 1979, such an individual was left with a real after-tax return of *minus* 4.6%! The small saver was thus penalized rather than rewarded for attempting to save.

The effect of inflation on the taxation of capital gains is no less dramatic. In a study published in 1978 (Feldstein and Slemrod 1978), Joel Slemrod and I looked first at the experience of a hypothetical investor who bought a broad portfolio of securities like the Standard and Poor's 500 in 1957, held it for twenty years, and sold it in 1977. An investor who did that would have been fortunate enough to have his investment slightly more than double during that time. Unfortunately, the consumer price level also more than doubled during that time. In terms of actual purchasing power, the investor had no gain at all on his investment. And yet of course the tax law would regard him as having doubled his money and would hold him accountable for a tax liability on this nominal gain.

After seeing this experience for a hypothetical investor, we were eager to know what has been happening to actual investors who have realized taxable capital gains and losses. Fortunately, the Internal Revenue Service has produced a very interesting set of data: a computer tape with a sample of more than 30,000 individual tax returns reporting realized capital gains or losses on corporate stock in 1973. While the sample is anonymous, it is the kind of scientific sample that can be used to make accurate estimates of national totals.

The results of this analysis were quite astounding. In 1973, individuals paid tax on $4.6 billion of capital gains on corporate stock. When the costs of those securities are adjusted for the increase in the price level since they were purchased, that $4.6 billion capital gain is seen correctly as a loss of nearly one billion dollars. Thus people were paying tax on $4.6 billion of capital gains when in reality they actually sold stock that represented a loss of nearly a billion dollars. Moreover, although people paid tax on artificial gains at every income level, the problem was most severe for those investors with incomes of less than $100,000.

While the lower capital gains tax rates that were enacted in 1978 reduce the adverse effects of inflation, lowering the tax rate does not alter the fact that people will continue to pay taxes on nominal gains even when there are no real gains. They now pay a lower tax on those gains, but they still pay a tax on what is really a loss.

Although interest recipients and those who realize nominal capital gains are taxed on fictitious inflation gains, by far the most substantial effect of inflation on tax burdens is the extra tax paid because of the overstatement of profits in the corporate sector. In a paper published last year (Feldstein and Summers 1979), Lawrence Summers and I found that the mismeasurement of depreciation and inventories raised the 1977 tax burden on the income of nonfinancial corporations by more than $32 billion. This represents a 50% increase in the total tax paid on corporate source income by corporations, their shareholders, and their creditors.

Some lawyers and economists have argued that inflation does not increase the effective tax rate on real corporate income because firms deduct nominal interest payments (rather than real interest payments) in calculating taxable profits. Equivalently, corporations are not taxed on the fall in the real value of their debts that results from inflation. Although this argument is valid if one looks only at the taxes paid by the corporation, it is wrong when one considers the taxes paid by creditors and shareholders. As our calculations show, the extra tax paid by the creditors on the inflated interest payments is as large as the tax savings by corporations and their owners. Debt can therefore be ignored in evaluating the net impact of inflation on the total tax burden on corporate capital.

More recently (Feldstein and Poterba 1980), James Poterba and I updated these calculations and extended the analysis to include the taxes paid to state and local governments on the capital used by nonfinancial corporations. We found that the 1979 effective tax rate on the total real capital income[1] of the nonfinancial corporate sector was 69%. Thus taxes now take two-thirds of the total real capital income earned on corporate capital. This represents a return to the tax level of the mid-1950s before accelerated depreciation and the investment tax credit began reducing the total tax burden. Even if attention is limited to federal taxes, our calculation shows that by 1979 the federal government taxes on corporations, their shareholders, and their creditors equaled 65% of the total real capital income of the nonfinancial corporations net of the state and local taxes paid by corporations.

The implication of a 69% total effective tax rate on corporate income is clear. Since the real rate of return on corporate capital before all taxes was 9.0% in 1979 (Feldstein and Poterba 1980), the net rate of return was only about 30% of this, or 2.7%.

## 7.2  Inflation, Tax Rules, and Share Prices

A potentially important way in which inflation can alter the rate of real investment is by changing the cost to the firm of equity capital, i.e. the ratio of share value per dollar of pretax earnings.[2] In a smoothly functioning economy with no distortionary taxes, inflation should have no effect on the cost of equity capital: both the earnings per share and the share price should increase over time at a faster rate because of inflation, but their ratio should be unaffected. In fact, taxes interfere with this neutrality and alter the ratio of the share price to the pretax earnings.

In thinking about the relation between inflation and share prices, it is crucial to distinguish between the effect of a *high* constant rate of inflation and the effect of an *increase* in the rate of inflation expected for the future. When the steady-state rate of inflation is higher, share prices increase at a faster rate. More specifically, when the inflation rate is steady, share prices rise in proportion to the price level to maintain a constant ratio of share prices to real earnings. In contrast, an *increase* in the expected future rate of inflation causes a concurrent fall in the ratio of share prices to current earnings. Although share prices then rise from this lower level at the higher rate of inflation, the ratio of share prices to real earnings is permanently lower. This permanent reduction in the price-earnings ratio occurs because, under prevailing tax rules, inflation raises the effective tax rate on corporate source income.

An important reason for the lower ratio of price to pretax earnings is that an increase in the permanent rate of inflation raises the effective tax rate on equity capital. The magnitude of this increase reflects the role of historic cost depreciation, the use of FIFO inventory accounting, and the extent of corporate debt. A numerical calculation with realistic values will indicate how these separate effects are combined. Consider an economy with no inflation in which each share of stock represents the ownership claim to a single unit of capital (i.e. one dollar's worth of capital valued at its reproduction cost) and to the net earnings that it produces. The marginal product of capital (net of depreciation), $f'$, is subject to a corporate income tax at effective rate $t_1$. In the absence of inflation, this effective rate of tax is less than the statutory rate $(t)$ because of the combined effects of accelerated depreciation and the investment tax credit. The corporation borrows $b$ dollars per unit of capital and pays interest at rate $r$. Since these interest payments are deducted in calculating corporate income that is taxed at the statutory rate $t$, the net cost of these borrowed funds is $(1 - t)br$. The net return to equity investors per unit of capital in the absence of inflation is $(1 - t_1)f' - (1 - t)br$.

What happens to this net return when the inflation rate rises? For simplicity, consider an instantaneous and unanticipated increase to inflation at rate $i$ that is expected to last forever. Under existing United States tax law, inflation raises taxable profits (for any fixed level of real profits) in two ways. First, the value of depreciation allowances is based on the original, or "historic," cost of the asset rather than on its current value. When prices rise, this historic cost method of depreciation causes the real value of depreciation to fall and the real value of taxable profits to rise. Second, the cost of maintaining inventory levels is understated for firms that use the first-in/first-out (FIFO) method of inventory accounting. A linear approximation that each percentage point of inflation increases taxable profits per unit of capital by $x$ implies that the existing treatment of depreciation and inventories reduces net profits by $tx$ per unit of capital.

When there is a positive rate of inflation, the firms' net interest payments $((1 - t)br)$ overstate the true cost to the equity owners of the corporations' debt finance. Against this apparent interest cost it is necessary to offset the reduction in the real value of the corporations' net monetary liabilities. These net monetary liabilities per unit of capital are the difference between the interest-bearing debt $(b)$ and the non-interest-bearing monetary assets $(a)$.

Combining the basic net profits per unit of capital, the extra tax caused by the existing depreciation and inventory rules, and the real gain on net monetary liabilities yields the real net return per unit of capital,

$$(1) \qquad z = (1 - t_1)f' - (1 - t)br - txi + (b - a)i.$$

The effect of inflation on the real net equity earnings per unit of capital $(z)$ depends on the response of the interest rate $(r)$ to the inflation rate $(i)$. In general, the change in equity earnings per unit change in the inflation rate $(dz/di)$ depends on the tax and finance parameters and on the effect of inflation on the interest rate $(dr/di)$ according to

$$(2) \qquad \frac{dz}{di} = - (1 - t)b\frac{dr}{di} - tx + (b - a).$$

Econometric studies indicate that the nominal interest rate has risen approximately point for point with the rate of inflation. Assuming that $dr/di = 1$ implies

(3)
$$\frac{dz}{di} = -(1-t)b - tx + (b-a)$$
$$= t(b-x) - a.$$

Thus equity owners (1) gain $tb$ (per unit of capital) from a rise in inflation because nominal interest expenses are deducted in calculating taxable income; (2) lose $tx$ because of the understatement of cost due to the use of historic cost depreciation and FIFO inventory accounting; and (3) lose $a$ because they hold non-interest-bearing monetary assets.

Recent values of these parameters imply that $dz/di$ is negative and therefore that inflation would reduce the equity earnings per share. In 1977, nonfinancial corporations had a total capital stock of $1,684 billion and owed net interest-bearing liabilities of $509.7 billion,[3] implying that $b = 0.302$. The monetary assets of the NFCs had a value of $54.8 billion, implying that $a = 0.033$. Since the corporate tax rate in 1977 was $t = 0.48$, these figures imply that $dz/di = 0.113 - tx$.

While it is difficult to calculate $x$ as precisely as $t$, $b$, and $z$, it is clear that $tx$ exceeds 0.113 and therefore that $dz/di$ is negative. Recall that $xi$ is the overstatement of taxable profits per dollar of capital caused by inflation at rate $i$. Feldstein and Summers (1979) estimate that in 1977 inflation caused an overstatement of taxable profits of $54.3 billion of which $39.7 billion was due to low depreciation and $14.6 was due to artificial inventory profits. Thus in 1977 $xi = 54.3/1684 = 0.032$. The implied value of $x$ depends on the rate of inflation that was responsible for these additional taxable profits. For the inventory component of the overstated profits, the relevant inflation rate is the one for the concurrent year; for the depreciation component, the relevant inflation rate is a weighted average of the inflation rates since the oldest remaining capital was acquired but with greater weight given to inflation in more recent years. The consumer price index rose 6.8% in 1977, an average of 7.2% in the preceding five years, and 4.5% and 1.9% in the two previous five-year periods.[4] An inflation rate of 7.0% is therefore a reasonable upper bound for the relevant rate and 5.0% is a reasonable lower bound. A value of $i = 0.06$ implies that $x = 0.53$ and therefore that $tx = 0.256$, even at the upper bound of $i = 0.07$, $x = 0.46$, and $tx = 0.22$. Both of these values are clearly above the critical value of 0.113 required for $dz/di$ to be negative.

By itself, the fact that the inflation-tax interaction lowers the net of tax equity earnings tends to depress the price-earnings ratio. This is reinforced by the fact that the nominal increase in the value of the corporation's capital stock induces a capital gains tax liability for shareholders. But the net effect on the share price level depends on the effect of inflation on the investors' opportunity cost of investing in stocks. Because households pay tax on nominal interest income, inflation lowers the real net yield on bonds as an alternative to share ownership. At the same time, the favorable tax rules for investment in land, gold, owner-occupied housing, etc., imply that the real net opportunity cost of shareholding does not fall as much as the real net yield on bonds and may actually rise.[5] In considering these interactions of inflation and tax rules, it is important to distinguish households and nontaxable institutions and to recognize that share prices represent an equilibrium for these two groups.

In Feldstein (1980*c*), I evaluated the effect of inflation on the equilibrium share price, using a very simple model with two classes of investors. That analysis shows that if the opportunity cost that households perceive remains unchanged (at a real net-of-tax 4%), a rise in the inflation rate from 0 to 6% would reduce the share value by 24%.[6] A one-fourth fall in the households' opportunity cost of share ownership (from 0.04 to 0.03) would limit the fall in the equilibrium share value to only 7%.

The real net cost of equity funds rose from about 7% in the mid-1960s to about 10% in the mid-1970s. On balance, I believe that the interaction of inflation and the tax rules is responsible for part, but only part, of this very substantial rise in the real cost of equity capital. Inflation may also depress share prices because of a perceived increase in risk (as Malkiel has stressed) or because investors confuse nominal and real returns (as Modigliani has emphasized). These additional explanations are not incompatible with the tax effect but lie outside the scope of this paper.

### 7.3   Inflation, Tax Rules, and Investment

The rate of fixed business investment in the United States has fallen sharply since the mid-1960s. The share of national income devoted to net fixed nonresidential investment fell by more than one-third between the last half of the 1960s and the decade of the 1970s: the ratio of net fixed nonresidential investment to GNP averaged 0.040 from 1965 through 1969 but only 0.025 from 1970 through 1979. The corresponding rate of growth of nonresidential capital stock declined by an even greater percentage: between 1965 and 1969, the annual rate of growth of the fixed non-residential capital stock averaged 5.5%; in the 1970s, this average dropped to 3.2%.

An important reason for this decline has been the interaction of the high rate of inflation and the existing tax rules. As the discussion in the previous two sections has made clear, the nature of this interaction is complex and operates through several different channels. I have investigated this effect (Feldstein 1980*a*) by estimating three quite different models of investment behavior. The strength of the empirical evidence rests on the fact that all three specifications support the same conclusion.

The simplest and most direct way relates investment to the real net return that the providers of capital can earn on business capital. As I noted in section 7.1, the combined effect of original cost depreciation, the taxation of nominal capital gains, and other tax rules is to raise the effective tax rate paid on the capital income of the corporate sector and thus lower the real net rate of return that the ultimate suppliers of capital can obtain on fixed nonresidential investment. This in turn reduces the incentive to save and distorts the flow of saving away from fixed nonresidential investment. Even when the mechanism by which the financial markets and managerial decisions achieve this reallocation is not specified, the variations in investment during the past decades can be related to changes in the real net rate of return.

The real net rate of return varied around an average of 3.3% in the 1950s, rose by the mid-1960s to 6.5% while averaging 5.0% for the 1960s as a whole, and then dropped in the 1970s to an average of only 2.8%. A simple econometric model (relating net fixed business investment as a fraction of GNP to the real net rate of return and to capacity utilization) indicates that each percentage point rise in the real net return raises the investment–GNP ratio by about one-half a percentage point. This estimated effect is quite robust with respect to changes in the specification, sample period, and method of estimation. It implies that the fall in the real net rate of return between the 1960s and the 1970s was large enough to account for a drop of more than one percentage point in the ratio of investment to GNP, a reduction that corresponds to more than one-third of the net investment ratio in the 1970s.

This general conclusion is supported by two quite different alternative models of investment. The first of these relates investment to the difference between the maximum potential rate of return that the firm can afford to pay on a "standard" project and the actual cost of funds. The second is an extension of the Hall and Jorgenson (1967) investment equation that incorporates all of the effects of inflation and the user cost of capital. Although none of the three models is a "true" picture of reality, the fact that they all point to the same conclusion is reassuring because it indicates that the finding is really "in the data" and is not merely an artifact of the model specification.

### 7.4   The Fiscal Structure and Effects of Monetary Policy

The intellectual tradition in monetary analysis has caused the effects of the economy's fiscal structure to be ignored. Whatever the appropriateness of this division of labor between monetary specialists and tax specialists in earlier decades, it has clearly been inappropriate in more recent years. As I have argued elsewhere (Feldstein 1976, 1980b), the fiscal structure of our economy is a key determinant of the macroeconomic equilibrium and therefore of the effect of monetary policy. The failure to take fiscal effects into account has caused a misinterpretation of the expansionary and distortive character of monetary policy in the 1960s and 1970s.

During the dozen years after the 1951 accord between the Treasury and the Fed, the interest rate on Baa bonds varied only in the narrow range between 3½% and 5%. In contrast, the past fifteen years have seen the Baa rate rise from less than 5% in 1964 to more than 12% at the end of 1979. It is perhaps not surprising therefore that the monetary auhorities, other government officials, and many private economists have worried throughout this period that interest rates might be getting "too high." Critics of what was perceived as "tight money" argued that such high interest rates would reduce investment and therefore depress aggregate demand.

Against all this it could be argued, and was argued, that the *real* interest rate had obviously gone up much less. The correct measure of the real interest rate is of course the difference between the nominal interest rate and the rate of inflation that is *expected* over the life of the bond. A common rule of thumb approximates the expected future inflation as the average inflation rate experienced during the preceding three years. In 1964, when the Baa rate was 4.8%, this three-year rise in the GNP deflator averaged 1.6%; the implied real interest rate was thus 3.2%. By the end of 1979, when the Baa rate was 12.0%, the rise in the GNP deflator for the previous three years had increased to 7.8%, implying a real interest rate of 4.2%. Judged in this way, the cost of credit has also increased significantly over the fifteen-year period.

All of this ignores the role of taxes. Since interest expenses can be deducted by individuals and businesses in calculating taxable income, the net-of-tax interest cost is very much less than the interest rate itself. Indeed, since the *nominal* interest expense can be deducted, the *real net-of-tax* interest cost has actually varied inversely with the *nominal* rate of interest. *What appears to have been a rising interest rate over the past twenty-five years was actually a sharply falling real after-tax cost of funds.* The failure to recognize the role of taxes prevented the monetary authorities from seeing how expansionary monetary policy had become.

The implication of tax deductibility is seen most easily in the case of owner-occupied housing. A married couple with a $30,000 taxable income now has a marginal federal income tax rate of 37%. The 11.4% mortgage rate in effect in the last quarter of 1979 implied a net-of-tax cost of funds of 7.2%. Subtracting a 7.8% estimate of the rate of inflation (based on a three-year average increase in the GNP deflator) leaves a real net-of-tax cost of funds of *minus* 0.6%. By comparison, the 4.8% interest rate for 1964 translates into a 3.0% net-of-tax rate and a 1.4% real net-of-tax cost of funds. Thus, although the nominal interest rate had more than doubled and the real interest rate had also increased substantially, the relevant real net-of-tax cost of funds had actually fallen from 1.4% to a *negative* 0.6%. (See figure 7.1.)

As this example shows, taking the effects of taxation into account is particularly important because the tax rules are so nonneutral when there is inflation. If the tax rules were completely indexed, the effect of the tax system on the conduct of monetary policy would be much less significant. But with existing tax rules, the movements of the real pretax interest rate and of the real after-tax interest rates are completely different. I think that monetary policy in the 1970s was expansionary because the monetary authorities and others believed that the cost of funds was rising or steady when in fact it was falling significantly.

The fall in the real after-tax interest rate has caused a rapid increase in the price of houses relative to the general price level and has sustained a high rate of new residential construction (Poterba 1980). There were, of course, times when the ceilings on the interest rates that financial institu-

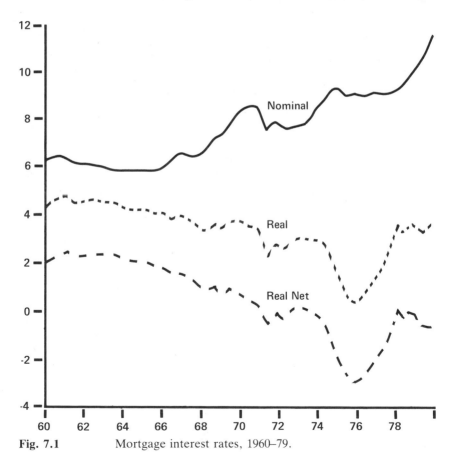

**Fig. 7.1**    Mortgage interest rates, 1960–79.

tions could pay caused disintermediation and limited the funds available for housing. To that extent, the high level of nominal interest rates restricted the supply of funds at the same time that the corresponding low real after-tax interest cost increased the demand for funds. More recently, the raising of certain interest rate ceilings and the development of mortgage-backed bonds that can short-circuit the disintermediation process have made the supply restrictions much less important and have therefore made any interest level more expansionary than it otherwise would have been.

The low real after-tax rate of interest has also encouraged the growth of consumer credit and the purchase of consumer durables. It is not surprising that, with a negative real net rate of interest, house mortgage borrowing has soared to over $90 billion a year, more than double the rate in the early 1970s. More generally, as I noted in section 7.1, even households that do not itemize their tax deductions are affected by the low real after-tax return that is available on savings. Because individuals pay tax on nominal interest income, the real after-tax rate of return on savings has become negative. It seems likely that this substantial fall in the real return on savings has contributed to the fall in the personal saving rate and the rise in consumer demand.

The evidence summarized in the first section shows that the analysis is more complex for corporate borrowers and investors because inflation changes the effective tax rate on investments as well as the real net-of-tax interest rate. More specifically, because historic cost depreciation and inventory accounting rules substantially reduce the real after-tax return on corporate investments, an easy-money policy raises the demand for corporate capital only if the real net cost of funds falls by more than the return that firms can afford to pay. This balance between the lower real net interest cost and the lower real net return on investment depends on the corporation's debt-equity ratio and on the relation between the real yields that must be paid on debt and on equity funds. It is difficult to say just what has happened on balance. In a preliminary study (Feldstein and Summers 1978), Lawrence Summers and I concluded that the rise in the nominal interest rate caused by inflation was probably slightly less than the rise in the maximum nominal interest rate that firms could afford to pay. However, that study made no allowance for the effect of inventory taxation or for the more complex effects of inflation on equity yields that I discussed in section 7.2. My current view, based on the evidence reviewed in section 7.3, is that, on balance, expansionary monetary policy reduced the demand for business investment at the same time that it increased the demand for residential investment and for consumption goods.

It is useful to contrast the conclusion of this section with the conventional Keynesian analysis. According to the traditional view, monetary expansion lowers interest rates, which reduces the cost of funds to investors and therefore encourages the accumulation of plant and equipment. In the context of the United States economy in recent years, this statement is wrong in three ways. First, a sustained monetary expansion raises nominal interest rates. Second, although the interest rate is higher, the real net-of-tax cost of funds is lower. And, third, the lower cost of funds produced in this way encourages investment in housing and consumer durables (as well as greater consumption in general) rather than more investment in plant and equipment. Indeed, because of the interaction of tax rules and inflation, a monetary expansion tends to discourage saving and reduce investment in plant and equipment. The low real net-of-tax rate of interest on mortgages and consumer credit is an indication of this misallocation of capital.

Perhaps the problems of misinterpretation and mismanagement might have been avoided completely if the monetary authorities and others in the financial community, as well as Congress and the economics profession, had ignored interest rates completely and focused their attention on the money supply and the credit aggregates. Presumably, under current Federal Reserve procedures, there will be more of a tendency to do just that. But since the temptation to look at rates as well is very powerful, it is important to interpret the rates correctly. What matters for the household borrower or saver is the real net-of-tax interest rate. A very low or negative real net-of-tax rate is a clear signal of an incentive to overspend on housing and on other forms of consumption. What matters for the business firm is the difference between the real net-of-tax cost of funds (including both debt and equity) and the maximum return that, with existing tax laws, it can afford to pay. The difficulty of measuring this difference should be a warning against relying on any observed rates to judge the ease or tightness of credit for business investment.

## 7.5   The Mix of Monetary and Fiscal Policies

There is widespread agreement on two central goals for macroeconomic policy: (1) achieving a level of aggregate demand that avoids both unemployment and inflation, and (2) increasing the share of national income that is devoted to business investment. Monetary and fiscal policy provide two instruments with which to achieve these two goals. The conventional Keynesian view of the economy has led to the prescription of easy money (to encourage investment) and a tight fiscal policy (to limit demand and prevent inflation). Our low rate of investment and high rate of inflation indicate that this approach has not worked. It is useful to review both the way such a policy is supposed to work and the reason why it fails.

Keynesian analysis, based on a theory developed during and for the Depression, is designed for an economy with substantial slack and essentially fixed prices. This Keynesian perspective implies that real output can be expanded by increasing demand and that the policy mix determines how this increased output is divided between investment, consumption, and government spending. In this context, an increase in the money supply favors investment while a fiscal expansion favors consumption or government spending.

There is a way in which a policy mix of easy money and fiscal tightness could in principle work in a relatively fully employed economy. The key requirement would be a persistent government surplus. Such a surplus would permit the government to reduce the supply of outstanding government debt. This in turn would induce households and institutions to substitute additional private bonds and stocks for the government debt that was removed from their portfolios. The result would be an increased rate of private capital accumulation. Under likely conditions, this substitution of private capital for government debt would require a lower rate of interest and a relative increase in the stock of money.[7]

Unfortunately, the traditional prescription of easy money and a tight fiscal position has failed in practice because of the difficulty of achieving and maintaining a government surplus.[8] As a result, the pursuit of an easy-money policy has produced inflation. Although the inflationary increase in the money supply did reduce the real after-tax cost of funds, this only diverted the flow of capital away from investment in plant and equipment and into owner-occupied housing and consumer durables. By reducing the real net return to savers, the easy-money policy has probably also reduced the total amount of new saving.

The traditional policy mix reflects not only its optimistic view about the feasibility of government surpluses but also its overly narrow conception of the role of fiscal policy. In the current macroeconomic tradition, fiscal policy has been almost synonymous with variations in the net government surplus or deficit and has generally ignored the potentially powerful incentive effects of taxes that influence marginal prices.

An alternative policy mix for achieving the dual goals of balanced demand and increased business investment would combine a tight-money policy and fiscal incentives for investment and saving. A tight-money policy would prevent inflation and raise the real net-of-tax rate of interest. Although the higher real rate of interest would tend to deter all forms of residential and nonresidential investment, specific incentives for investment in plant and equipment could more than offset the higher cost of funds. The combination of the higher real net interest rate and the targeted investment incentives would restrict housing construction and the purchase of consumer durables while increasing the flow of capital into new plant and equipment. Since housing and consumer durables now account for substantially more than half of the private capital stock, such a restructuring of the investment mix could have a substantial favorable effect on the stock of plant and equipment.

A rise in the overall saving rate would permit a greater increase in business investment. The higher real net rate of interest would probably induce such a higher rate of saving. This could be supplemented by explicit fiscal policies that reduced the tax rate on interest income and other income from saving.

In short, restructuring macroeconomic policy to recognize the importance of fiscal incentives and of the current interaction between tax rules and inflation provides a way of both reducing the rate of inflation and increasing the growth of the capital stock.

## Notes

1. This includes both economic profits and the return to creditors.
2. This section is based on Feldstein (1978, 1980c).
3. The capital stock, valued at replacement cost in 1977 dollars, is estimated by the Department of Commerce. The net liabilities are based on information in the Flow of Funds tables. Feldstein and Summers (1979) report the net interest-bearing liabilities of NFCS as $595 billion. For the appropriate debt measure in this work, the value of the net trade credit ($72.7 billion) and government securities ($12.9 billion) must be subtracted from this $595 billion. The subtraction of net trade credit reflects the assumption that the profits of NFCS include an implicit interest return on the trade credit that they extend. The new information is from the *Federal Reserve Balance Sheets of the U. S. Economy.*
4. The index of producer prices for finished goods rose 6.6% in 1977 and an average of 5.9% for the previous decade, essentially the same as the CPI.
5. This point is developed further in Feldstein (1980d, e) and in Hendershott (1979), Hendershott and Hu (1979), and Poterba (1980).
6. This makes no allowance for the effect of the induced reduction of the capital stock on the subsequent pretax return. Summers (1980) shows explicitly how that would reduce the fall in the equilibrium share value.
7. See Feldstein (1980b) for a theoretical analysis in which this possibility is considered.
8. It might be argued that the inflationary erosion of the real government debt means that the government has in fact had real surpluses even though nominal deficits. But such an inflation adjustment also implies an equal reduction in private saving, indicating that private saving has in fact been negative. The conventional government deficit should also be augmented by the off-budget borrowing and the growth of government unfunded obligations in the social security, and civil service and military service pension programs.

## References

Feldstein, M. S. 1976. Inflation, income taxes, and the rate of interest: A theoretical analysis. *American Economic Review.*

————. 1978. Inflation and the stock market. *American Economic Review*, forthcoming. NBER Working Paper no. 276.

————. 1980*a*. Inflation, tax rules, and investment: Some econometric evidence. The Fisher-Schultz lecture of the Econometric Society. *Econometrica*, forthcoming. NBER Working Paper no. 577.

————. 1980*b*. Fiscal policies, inflation, and capital formation. *American Economic Review*.

————. 1980*c*. Inflation, tax rules, and the stock market. *Journal of Monetary Economics*.

————. *1980d*. Inflation, portfolio choice, and the prices of land and corporate stock. *American Journal of Agricultural Economics*, forthcoming. NBER Working Paper no. 526.

————. 1980*e*. The effect of inflation on the prices of land and gold. *Journal of Public Economics*. NBER Working Paper no. 296.

Feldstein, M. S., and Poterba, J. 1980. State and local taxes and the rate of return on non-financial corporate capital. NBER Working Paper no. 508.

Feldstein, M. S., and Slemrod, J. 1978. Inflation and the excess taxation of capital gains on corporate stock. *National Tax Journal*.

Feldstein, M. S., and Summers, L. H. 1978. Inflation, tax rules, and the long term interest rate. *Brookings Papers on Economic Activity*.

————. 1979. Inflation and the taxation of capital income in the corporate sector. *National Tax Journal*.

Hall, R. E., and Jorgenson, D. W. 1967. Tax policy and investment behavior. *American Economic Review*.

Hendershott, P. 1979. The decline in aggregate share values: Inflation and taxation of the returns from equities and owner-occupied housing. NBER Working Paper no. 370.

Hendershott, P., and Hu, S. C. 1979. Inflation and the benefits from owner-occupied housing. NBER Working Paper no. 383.

Poterba, J. 1980. Inflation, income taxes, and owner-occupied housing. NBER Working Paper no. 553.

Summers, L. H. 1980. Inflation, tax rules, and the valuation and accumulation of capital assets. *American Economic Review*, forthcoming.

# 8 Adapting to Inflation in the United States Economy

Stanley Fischer

The costs and effects of inflation depend on the extent to which the institutional structure of the economy has adjusted to its existence. The United States economy has in the seventies made a variety of adjustments that make it easier for individuals to live with inflation, but which also produce complicated side effects.

In this paper I review in detail the major institutional changes in the economy that have made it easier to live with inflation, and briefly describe the most important of the remaining nonadaptations. The economy is now at a stage where most individuals have some protection against inflation, but where inflation still has major economic effects. The economic implications of the increasing indexation of the economy are also analyzed.

Section 8.1 sets the background by examining the historical inflation record, showing that the inflation rate is now high by peacetime historical standards but not especially variable. However, the variability of the inflation rate has been increasing since the early sixties. Variability of inflation matters because uncertainty about the inflation rate creates economic difficulties at least as serious as those caused by high inflation itself. Interest rates have correspondingly been both high and, particularly in the case of long-term rates, variable.

Section 8.2 discusses major innovations in the capital markets in the seventies that have made it easier to live with inflation, while section 8.3

Stanley Fischer is with the Department of Economics, Massachusetts Institute of Technology, and the National Bureau of Economic Research.

The opinions expressed in this paper are those of the author and not the NBER, the National Science Foundation, or MIT. Comments by Robert Hall, Frank Schiff, and Lawrence Summers, and assistance from Jeffrey Miron are acknowledged with thanks. This paper was written at the end of 1980; subsequent institutional adaptation to inflation have not been embodied herein.

169

examines labor market adjustments. The response of government, as well as its failure to adjust the tax laws for inflation, is examined in section 8.4. The effects on the household sector of the innovations described in sections 8.2–8.4 are summarized in section 8.5. Section 8.6 discusses the economic implications of the spreading and uneven indexation of the economy described in sections 8.2–8.4.

## 8.1   The Current Inflation in Historical Perspective

In this section, I set the inflation of the seventies into the historical perspectives of long-term United States price level behavior and that of the post–Korean War period. The annual inflation rate in the United States since 1880 is shown in figure 8.1. It is clear that the current inflation is the most rapid in peacetime during that period; indeed, it is the most rapid peacetime inflation in United States history.

Figure 8.1 also shows a measure of the variability of the inflation rate from year to year.[1] The current inflation is not the most variable peacetime inflation; inflation rates fluctuated more from year to year at the turn of the century and in the Great Depression than they have recently. However, the inflation rate was more variable during the seventies than in the period since the mid-fifties.

From the viewpoint of an individual entering a nominal contract, the payoff of which is specified in dollars, it is the price *level* that determines the real value of the outcome. Uncertainty about the average inflation rate over the period of the contract translates into uncertainty about the price level at the time of payment on the contract. The fact that year to year variability of the inflation rate in figure 8.1 is now relatively low by historical standards suggests that there is more predictability about the behavior of the price level over periods of a year or two than there was in the past. Individuals therefore should not show any greater reluctance to enter contracts of reasonably short duration than they did in earlier periods. However, the increasing variability of the inflation rate in the last decade suggests we should see either shorter contracts or devices to offset price uncertainty—such as indexation—becoming more widespread since the sixties, even for relatively short-term contracts.

There is an important distinction between the predictability of the price level over short and long periods, first emphasized by Benjamin Klein (1975). While there is not now great uncertainty about the price level that will prevail a year from now, uncertainty about the price level in the distant future is probably greater than in the past. Up to World War II it was reasonable to believe that the price level would be more or less stable over very long periods. Rapid inflation was a wartime phenomenon, typically followed by deflation, as at the end of the War of 1812, the Civil War, and World War I. In other words, it used to be reasonable to believe

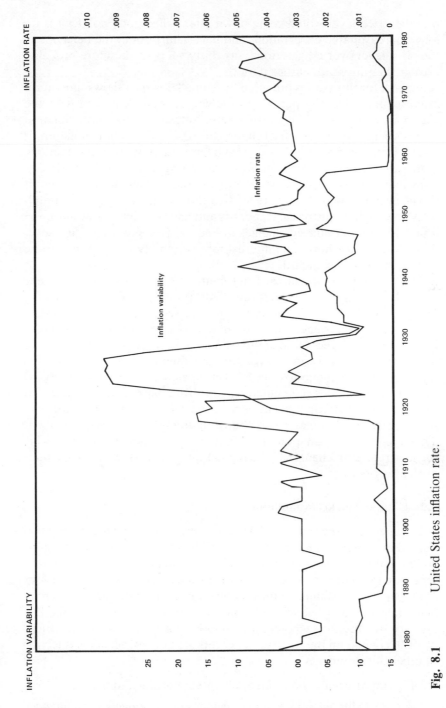

**Fig. 8.1**    United States inflation rate.

that the price level would come down after it had gone up. That is no longer a reasonable expectation, and uncertainty about the behavior of the price level over long periods, say thirty years, is therefore probably greater than it was in earlier periods.

Support for this view is provided by figure 8.2, which shows short-term interest rates over the period since 1880, as well as measures of the variability of short- and long-term interest rates. To a first approximation changes in interest rates reflect changes in expectations about inflation. It is clear from the figure that long-term interest rates are now substantially more variable than in earlier periods, suggesting that changes in expectations about long-term inflation are more frequent than they used to be. It should also be noted from figure 8.2 that short-term interest rate variability is now high by historical standards and has been increasing since the fifties. Recent announced changes in Federal Reserve operating procedure ensure that short-term interest rate variability will continue to be high by historical standards.

The features to emphasize from figure 8.2 are, first, the increasing variability of long-term interest rates, interpreted as reflecting increasing uncertainty about long-term inflation and, second, the rising level of short rates. Greater uncertainty about the price level over long periods is likely to lead to a reduction in the volume of very long-term contracts or to the use of other devices to reduce the vulnerability of participants in long-term arrangements to price level changes. The second feature, rising market interest rates, combined with controls on the rates payable by financial intermediaries, produces financial dislocations, particularly disintermediation, that may be attributed indirectly to increasing inflation. Thus much of the adaptation to inflation discussed in the following sections relates to changes in the regulations under which financial intermediaries operate.

### 8.2   Capital Market Adaptations

The decade of the seventies has seen a series of capital market innovations that either were a response to high inflation and interest rates, and/or make it easier to live with inflation. Taken together, they represent changes in the financial system on a scale comparable to the reforms of the thirties. I examine in turn innovations in the mortgage instrument and other nonbank financial intermediary assets and liabilities, the Depository Institutions Deregulation and Monetary Control Act (DIDMCA) of 1980, changes in the structure of corporate borrowing, and a selection of other developments.

#### 8.2.1   The Mortgage Instrument and Related Innovations

Mortgages, life insurance, and pensions are the longest-term financial arrangements into which most households enter. Changes in the structure

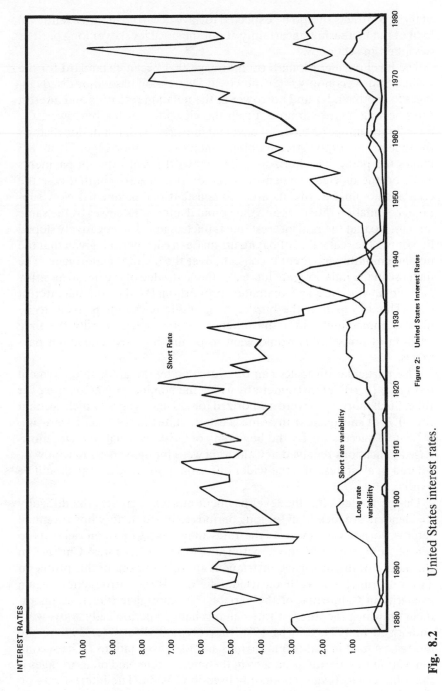

**Fig. 8.2**    United States interest rates.

of these contracts should be expected to have occurred in the seventies in light of the increasing uncertainty about the price level over long periods described in section 8.1.

The level payment long-term mortgage that became standard for the United States economy after the Great Depression has major disadvantages for both lender and borrower as the inflation rate rises and interest rates become more variable. From the viewpoint of the borrower, the main disadvantage of the level payment mortgage is that inflation distorts the time profile of the stream of repayments on the mortgage. Figure 8.3 makes the point. The horizontal line shows the real value of payments made on the mortgage when the inflation rate is zero—in that case the constant nominal payments are also constant real payments. Now suppose the inflation rate rises and the nominal interest rate rises by the same amount, so that the real interest rate is unchanged. The negatively sloped line shows the real value of payments made in each period, given that the nominal monthly payment is constant over the life of the mortgage. The increase in the inflation rate increases the real value of the initial monthly payments, which are approximately proportional to the nominal interest rate. This means that the burden of monthly payments is likely to be highest immediately after the purchase of the house, hardly the time when most households would want to be making their maximum payments.

This particular difficulty can be overcome by the graduated payment mortgage (GPM), an instrument by which the nominal payments rise over time. Such mortgages were authorized for FHA mortgages (which account for 10% of mortgages) in some western states in 1978 and were immediately successful. By the beginning of 1979, over half the FHA mortgage applications received in California were for GPMs. GPMs may now be offered in all states, and the wider diffusion of the instrument should be expected.[2]

On the lender side, the level payment mortgage creates the difficulty that lenders are locked in for long periods to instruments whose nominal returns do not vary even as the rates they have to pay on deposits to remain competitive fluctuate with short-term market rates. Changes in the nature of the mortgage instrument are one way out of this problem. Two experiments have been tried. The first is the introduction, again primarily in California, of the variable rate mortgage (VRM), an instrument on which the interest rate can be changed periodically. VRMs were authorized in 1974, and by 1978 they accounted for over 20% of the mortgages held in California savings and loan associations.[3] The second innovation that permits changes in the interest rate paid on mortgages is the rollover mortgage, commonly used in Canada. The interest rate on this mortgage is renegotiated every five years, with the borrower being guaranteed that refinancing will be available. Both the VRM and rollover

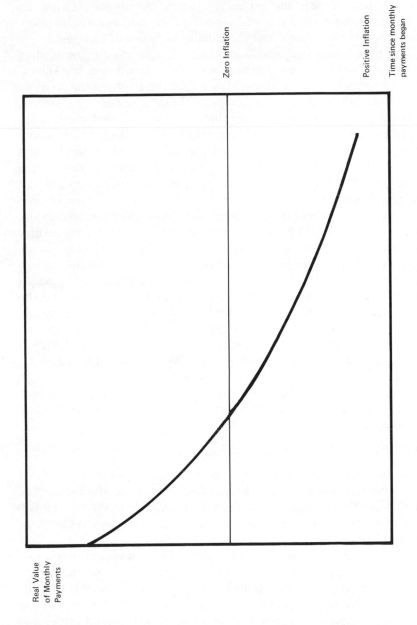

Real Value
of Monthly
Payments

Zero Inflation

Positive Inflation

Time since monthly
payments began

**Fig. 8.3**     Effects of inflation on real value of monthly mortgage payments.

mortgage tend to help the lender (given that borrowers are typically allowed to renegotiate terms when interest rates fall) and are therefore offered at a lower interest rate than the level payment mortgage.

There have been other innovations on both sides of mortgage lending institutions' balance sheets that have made those institutions less vulnerable to interest rate fluctuations. Most important has been the development of secondary markets for mortgages. In the seventies, the financial intermediary system acquired the ability to tap the bond markets for funds, both through the issue of bonds backed by mortgage collateral and through passthrough securities that sell the claims on the income streams financial intermediaries acquire through mortgage lending. The volume of borrowing in these markets now accounts for about a quarter of mortgage lending.[4]

On the liability side of their balance sheets, nonbank financial intermediaries have innovated by issuing new obligations, notably the money market certificate, a six-month instrument with interest rate tied to the Treasury Bill rate, and therefore precisely designed to fight disintermediation. Of course, this innovation required regulatory approval, which was forthcoming in 1978 in time to prevent major disintermediation in the high-interest-rate period at the end of 1979 and in early 1980. By the end of 1979 nearly a quarter of the liabilities of federally insured savings and loan associations were money market certificates.[5] The term and interest rates permissible on other liabilities issued by savings and loan associations have also been rising during the seventies.

In brief, there has been a virtual revolution in the nature of the asset and liability structure of the balance sheets of the major mortgage lending institutions.

### 8.2.2   DIDMCA

The Depositary Institutions Deregulation and Monetary Control Act of 1980 embodies some of the changes discussed in the previous section and makes other changes in the financial intermediary system that will remove most of the Depression-related features of the system except for deposit insurance.

The most significant feature of the act is the removal of interest rate controls, to be phased out over a six-year period. By 1986 the interest rates paid to depositors in financial institutions will be regulated by competition among the institutions. Rates on deposits can be expected to adjust more rapidly and fully to changes in market interest rates—and thus to inflation—than they have in the postwar period. For instance, interest-bearing checking accounts will be permissible nationwide and depositors can then expect to be compensated for rising inflation by receiving interest on their deposits that rises along with the inflation rate. The act also overrides state usury laws.

The act subjects all institutions accepting deposits to the same reserve requirements, dependent only on the types and volume of deposits. The variety of assets that different institutions can hold is being expanded; for instance, savings and loan associations will be able to increase their holdings of consumer installment credit to 20% of their portfolios.[6]

By the mid-eighties, the financial intermediary system will be essentially freed of the regulations that have made it and its depositors vulnerable to changing interest and inflation rates in the postwar period.

## 8.2.3   The Structure of Corporate Debt

The major change in the structure of corporate debt in the post–World War II period has been a move from equity to debt finance.[7] From 1946 to 1960, equity issues accounted for over 4% of total firm financing (including internally generated funds) of nonfinancial corporate business, and credit market debt for about 19%. From 1966 to 1978, equity accounted for about 3% of financing, and debt for about 27.5%.[8]

The above data are potentially misleading in that, as the inflation rate rises, increased debt financing is needed each year merely to maintain constant the real value of outstanding debt. Data on the values of outstanding stocks of debt and equity are thus more relevant to the question of whether there has been a shift to debt finance. Gordon and Malkiel (1980) present data showing that the ratio of the market value of debt to the market value of debt plus equity for a large sample of listed firms rose from an average of 18% for the period 1957–60 to 31% for 1975–78. The ratio reached a peak in their sample period of 1957–78 in 1974, because the market value of equity was then so low. These data confirm the shift to debt finance in the postwar period.

This shift to debt finance is hardly an innovation, but is nonetheless in part a result of increasing inflation. As the nominal interest rate has risen over the postwar period, the value of the tax deductibility of interest payments has risen and made debt finance more attractive.

The second innovation in the structure of corporate finance has been a shift to shorter debt. This shift is a reflection of the increasing uncertainty over long-term inflation that was shown in section 8.1. Long-term debt has fallen from 80% of total credit market debt in 1946–60 to 72.5% in 1979, with short-term debt rising correspondingly.[9] These data treat bank borrowing as partly short- and partly long-term debt. However, since bank borrowing is increasingly on a floating rate basis, part of debt that is counted as long-term bank borrowing has interest rates that are adjusted weekly.[10] This is yet another response to the increasing volatility of interest rates.

Along similar lines, there has been a shortening of the maturity of outstanding debt within the structure of long-term corporate debt. This shortening for the period through 1972 is documented by Klein (1975), who shows a small effect of increasing inflation uncertainty on the maturity of debt issues. Since 1972, when Klein calculated the average maturity of outstanding corporate debt at 19.1 years, the average maturity has fallen by about another 1.5 years.[11] Thus there has been a continuing decline in the maturity of outstanding corporate bonds, which complements the shift from long-term to short-term debt described in the preceding paragraph.

Finally, it should be emphasized that the effective maturity of a coupon bond changes when the inflation rate rises. For the reasons described in discussing the level payment mortgage, the real value of coupon payments on a standard bond falls over time if the inflation rate is positive. Thus, even if the real interest rate on a bond stays unchanged, the time shape of the stream of payments the corporation promises shifts toward the present as the inflation rate rises. Effectively, the maturity of the bond becomes shorter.

The conclusion is that the shortening of the structure of outstanding corporate debt in response to high and uncertain inflation is more pronounced than the above listed data on the division between long and short debt and the stated maturity of the debt appear to indicate. The introduction of the floating rate bank loan, as well as floating rate borrowing by some corporations, represents another response in corporate finance to uncertain inflation.

### 8.2.4   Other Changes

Other changes in the capital markets will affect the ability of the economy to deal with inflation. First, there have been changes in regulations which now require listed corporations to publish inflation-adjusted accounts alongside their regular accounts. As is well known, profits calculated under the two accounting schemes may differ widely. Inflation adjustments to 1979 profits for three large corporations are shown in table 8.1. The column Profits₁ shows profits as adjusted for the effects of inflation on the costs of goods sold and for depreciation. In each case

| Table 8.1 | | Effect of Inflation on Corporate Profits, 1979 | | |
|---|---|---|---|---|
| Company | Reported Profits | (1) Profits$_1$ (adjusted for general inflation) | (2) Capital Gain on Outstanding Debt | Profits$_2$ (sum of (1) + (2)) |
| AT&T | 5,674 | 1,837 | 6,841 | 8,678 |
| Exxon | 4,295 | 3,052 | 998 | 4,050 |
| General Motors | 2,893 | 1,776 | 182 | 1,958 |

Source: Company annual reports. Data are in millions of dollars.

profits are reduced, for the three companies together by 48%. $Profits_2$ adds to $Profits_1$ the capital gains the company obtains because the real value of its outstanding nominal obligations falls with inflation. $Profits_2$ is a measure of the income accruing to the equity holders of the firms; the inflation adjustment in this case raises total revenue by 14%. The change is obviously greatest for utility companies which use debt extensively. $Profits_2$ remains lower than reported profits, calculated using historical cost data, for Exxon and GM. The publication of the new accounts should give the investing public a firmer basis for portfolio decisions.

Second, I turn to the other major long-term contracts which households typically enter: life insurance and pensions. In both cases there have been inflation-related changes, but no major innovations. Life and other insurance policies now frequently contain cost-of-living adjustment clauses that permit automatic changes in the nominal amount of coverage (along with changes in premiums) without any need to enter a new contract. In the case of long-term term life insurance, this simple innovation does remove a major inflation distortion. For whole life policies, however, there remains a distortion resulting from the fact that the annuities payable do not adjust with inflation once payouts begin.[12]

Turning to private pensions, there is effectively indexation that will correct against any major changes in the price level to the extent that the pension benefit is based on wages at the time of retirement; if the benefits of existing beneficiaries are linked to those of new beneficiaries, the indexation extends also to those currently receiving benefits. But it is not known how many individuals fall into the categories that are effectively indexed. Recently some private pension plans have made voluntary adjustments to individual pensions in response to changes in the price level (e.g. Dupont). But there has been no systematic move to indexation of private pensions, and it is indeed difficult to see how such a change could be made in the absence of an indexed asset for pension funds to hold as a means of guaranteeing their ability to meet indexed liabilities.[13]

Indexation of social security and governmental and railroad pension benefits will be discussed in section 8.4 below.

## 8.3 Factor Markets

Formal indexation arrangements in the form of COLA (cost-of-living adjustment) clauses are prominent in the labor market. The extent of the inclusion of indexation clauses in formal labor contracts has mirrored the behavior of the Consumer Price Index in the postwar period, as can be seen in figure 8.4. The basic pattern is that indexation was predominant in the late fifties, that COLA clauses began to disappear in the early part of the sixties as the inflation rate stabilized at a low level and then tended to reappear as the inflation rate rose in the late sixties and early seventies.

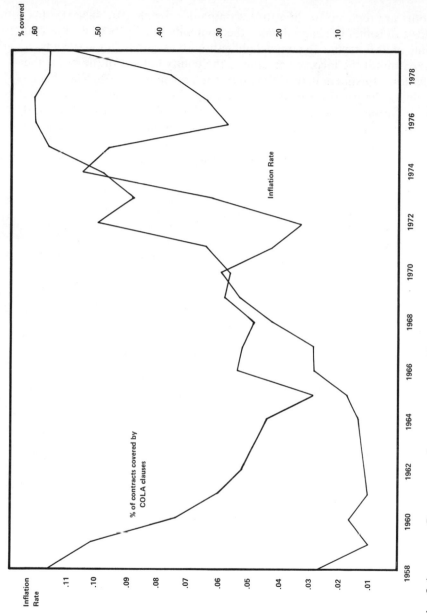

**Fig. 8.4**  Percentage of contracts covered by COLA clauses.

Since 1975, the proportion of workers in major union contracts (covering 5,000 or more employees) who have been protected by a cost-of-living clause has been stable at around 60%. However, there should be no illusion that the mass of the working force is formally covered by COLA clauses. First, only about 10% of the labor force is covered by collective bargaining agreements involving more than 5,000 employees, so that the 60% shown for 1979 in figure 8.3 in fact refers to a group of workers amounting to only 6% of the total labor force.

Second, existing COLA clauses do not provide 100% compensation against inflation. A typical indexed labor contract will include some nominal increase in wages that is independent of the inflation rate and then provides partial coverage against price increases. For example, wages might be scheduled to rise by 5% plus 0.5% for every 1% increase in the price level. In this way the firm and the workers share the risks of unanticipated inflation.

Third, existing COLA clauses do not provide full protection against inflation because there are inevitably lags in the application of the adjustments. Most COLA adjustments take place every three months, but in some contracts the adjustment is only annual.

The questions that naturally arise after discussion of union contracts are: first, whether the formal indexation that exists for 60% of the workers covered by major contracts is special, applying to 6% of the labor force; and second, whether the increasing indexation of labor contracts in the past decade has had important effects on the behavior of the economy. The answer to the first question is that indexation of labor contracts is not widespread. Federal government employees are not formally covered by COLA clauses, but about 25% of state and local employees are (or were in a 1978 survey). There is little need for employees on contracts of a year or shorter to be covered by indexation clauses since price level behavior is reasonably predictable in the short run. And most contracts, whether formal or informal, last for a year or less. Given the conclusion that indexation clauses are not yet widespread in labor contracts, their existence cannot have had important effects on the overall behavior of the economy. But it should be stressed that the nature of the current inflation—in which short-term price developments can be forecast quite well—does not suggest a great demand for indexation in short-term labor contracts.

There is little documentation of the extent of indexation in long-term contracts other than those for labor, though there is much informal evidence of considerable use of indexation. It is common in long-term industrial contracts for prices to be escalated by an index that relates to the cost of production or the market price of the commodity being exchanged. Similarly, long-term rent contracts that include revenue participation implicitly involve a form of indexing.

## 8.4   Government

The indexation of social security benefits was introduced in 1972. Estimates of the value of the existing obligations incurred by the social security system are currently in the range of $3 trillion ($3 $\times$ $10^{12}$), far in excess of the marketable national debt. Given the indexation of benefits, it thus appears that most workers own a substantial indexed retirement benefit.

However, social security cannot be directly compared to an indexed obligation of the government. The indexation of social security benefits can always be overridden by Congress, and applies only for those years in which Congress does not make any explicit adjustments to the benefits. But the establishment of formal indexation reduces the likelihood that Congress will permit the value of real benefits to existing beneficiaries to fall, and thus increases the inflation protection afforded by social security. It is in this sense that most individuals are protected from the worst effects of inflation.

Aside from the question of whether there is any legal obligation to maintain the real value of social security benefits, there is an economic question of how individuals value their social security assets. Since the system is on a pay-as-you-go basis, the benefits receivable in the future by existing workers will be paid for by future workers, who are the children of the beneficiaries. To the extent that recipients of the benefits are concerned about the welfare of their children, any increase in benefits carries with it an implied offset in the form of the reduction of the welfare of the then contributors to the system. Of course, precisely the same issue exists with regard to the question of whether the national debt should be regarded as a debt or an asset or, on balance, neither, by current economic agents. This is still a matter of controversy.

Federal government pension benefits, including those of the military, are formally indexed to the Consumer Price Index. Federal, including military, employees make up about 5% of the labor force. About a third of state and local government employees are covered by indexed pensions, adding another 4% of the labor force that has such benefits. But the indexation for state and local government employees is typically only partial as compared to the full federal indexing. The pensions of railroad employees are also price-indexed.

Some estimates indicate that over 50% of federal expenditures are indexed.[14] However, given Congress's ability to override indexation, as it sometimes does, any such number should be regarded as suggestive rather than definitive. For instance, the 50% estimate above includes federal wages for civilian and military employees, which in 1979 were increased less than the inflation rate.

There is no formal indexation of taxes. Purely proportional taxes would in effect be indexed, but the tax system is far from neutral to inflation. The best-know failure of the tax system to index relates to "bracket-creep," whereby rising prices without adjustment of tax brackets increase real taxes even if real income does not rise. But the most serious failure to index the tax system lies in the treatment of returns to capital.[15]

## 8.5   The Household Balance Sheet and Income Statement

Sections 8.2–8.4 have described a variety of innovations and adaptations that influence the way in which inflation affects the economy. But do these changes add up to a major shift, or do they rather represent piecemeal adjustments to the new era of high and uncertain inflation and fluctuating interest rates? To set the changes in perspective, we present in this section the household sector's balance sheet at the end of 1979 and its income statement, to show which household sector transactions have been affected by the innovations and where the remaining nonadaptations to inflation are to be found.

Table 8.2 shows the household sector balance sheet for the end of 1979. The housing stock is the main tangible asset of the household sector. Correspondingly, the major financial liability is mortgages. As noted above, there have been innovations in the form of the mortgage instrument. But it should be noted that these innovations have occurred mainly

**Table 8.2**     **Balance Sheet of the Household Sector, 1979**

|  |  | $ trillion |
|---|---|---|
| Tangible assets |  |  |
| Residential structures |  | 2.76 |
| Consumer durables |  | .89 |
| Financial assets |  | 3.83 |
| Deposits* | 1.45 |  |
| Credit market instruments | 0.55 |  |
| Equities | 0.91 |  |
| Life insurance reserves | 0.21 |  |
| Pension fund reserves | 0.62 |  |
| Other | 0.08 |  |
| Financial liabilities |  | 1.33 |
| Mortgages* | 0.88 |  |
| Consumer installment credit | 0.31 |  |
| Other | 0.14 |  |
| Memo: Personal disposable income, 1979 |  | 1.62 |

Source: Financial assets and liabilities, Federal Reserve Board, *Flow of Funds Accounts*, Assets and Liabilities Outstanding, 1969–79, February 1980. Household sector is "Households, Personal Trusts, and Nonprofit Organizations." Tangible assets: Federal Reserve System, *Balance Sheets for U.S. Economy*, June 1980.
*Affected by institutional changes in the last decade.

in California and a few other western states, and that most home financing is still done through the level payment mortgage. The advantages of home ownership are of course heavily affected by taxation, but there have been no major changes in the tax rules relating to home ownership in the postwar period, despite the potent effects of inflation in reducing the after-tax real cost of home purchases. Consumer durables represent the second major household asset category. There have been few innovations in the financing of consumer durable purchases, but since these are financed through relatively short-term consumer installment credit, the need for change is less. The tax benefit of borrowing rises with the nominal interest rate (assuming the pretax real rate is unchanged), but there have been no tax changes here either.

The major financial assets are deposits. The changes that have occurred here will substantially reduce the effect of inflation on the costs of holding funds in the traditional financial institutions. Innovations covering the remaining 62% of financial assets have been minimal—though in the case of equities little innovation should be expected.

Table 8.3 shows that the major source of personal income is wages and salaries. The effects of inflation on this source of income have been

**Table 8.3**      **Sources and Disposition of Personal Income, 1979**

| Personal Income | $ billion 1923 | % of Personal Income 100 |
|---|---|---|
| Sources | | |
| Wages and salaries* | | 63.8 |
| Other labor income (largely fringe benefits) | | 6.4 |
| Proprietors' income | | 6.8 |
| Rental income of persons | | 1.4 |
| Personal interest income* | | 10.0 |
| Dividends | | 2.7 |
| Transfer payments* of which (as % of transfer payments) | | 13.1 |
| OASDI and health insurance benefits | 52.5 | |
| Govt. employee retirement benefits | 14.8 | |
| Veteran benefits | 5.7 | |
| Other | 27.0 | |
| Less: Personal contributions for social insurance | | 4.2 |
| Disposition | | |
| Personal tax and nontax payments | | 15.6 |
| Personal consumption expenditures | | 78.5 |
| Interest paid to business | | 2.1 |
| Personal saving | | 3.8 |

Source: *Economic Report of the President, 1980*, tables B-20 and B-21.
*Affected by recent innovations.

changed to a small extent by the increasing indexation of labor contracts. The innovations discussed earlier also change the relation between inflation and personal interest income, and of course between inflation and transfer payments. Thus the innovations have strongly affected the relation between inflation and at least 25% of personal income, and also have had some impact on the relation between inflation and wage and salary income.

Little innovation should have been expected on the disposition side of the income statement, except in the case of taxes. As previously noted, such innovation has not been forthcoming, and its absence is likely to have significant effects on the economy's rates of capital accumulation and growth.[16]

The data presented in this section confirm the impression that the most important of the innovations discussed in sections 8.2–8.4 are those relating to the structure of the financial intermediary system. The other changes described are distinctly sporadic and incomplete.

## 8.6   Economic Implications

Despite their unevenness, the changes that have taken place in the institutional structure of the economy in the last decade can be described as having reduced the use of long-term nominal contracts in the economy and as having increased the extent of indexation. Formal indexation has increased chiefly in labor contracts, though even here it will be recalled that the indexation is less than 100%.

What are the consequences of increasing indexation? It is easiest to start by comparing an economy that is fully indexed with one that is not indexed. Suppose that in the fully indexed economy all contracts involving future payment tie the nominal payments to be made to an index such as the Consumer Price Index. Such an economy is well suited to handle the effects of an inflation that results purely from an increase in the quantity of money. In this case, the real economic situation can be restored by an equiproportionate rise in all prices, which is the type of price change that indexation will produce. An increase in the quantity of money should be expected, in a fully indexed economy, to lead to a rapid rise in all prices with minimal real effects on other variables.

A change in the quantity of money would have different effects in an economy in which prices were not indexed, however. In this case prices would probably take time to adjust, would adjust at different times and to different extents, and therefore would have effects on real economic activity.

A fully indexed economy affected by a shock requiring changes in relative prices as well as the aggregate price level—such as the oil price shock—might have considerable difficulty in adjusting. This would be the case if contracts essentially attempted to fix real magnitudes, such as the real wage, over lengthy periods. A nonindexed economy could do a better job of adjusting to a change in its real circumstances.

It is in this latter sense that indexation is sometimes argued to be inflationary. The notion is that any increase in a price—such as that of oil—that is required to restore the economy to equilibrium is likely under indexation to produce automatic increases in wages and therefore in other prices. Such changes would be less likely to occur in a nonindexed economy. It is not, however, generally recognized that it should be easier to reduce the inflation rate through monetary policy in an indexed econcally.

While indexation is theoretically attractive in isolating an economy from real effects caused by a "pure" money-supply-caused inflation, such inflations are unlikely to occur. There is no record of a pure inflation in which the money supply started growing essentially at the whim of the monetary authority. There is usually a real economic reason the government has turned to inflationary policy. In these circumstances, contracts indexed to the Consumer Price Index are likely to hamper adjustment rather than help. Further, no indexation scheme is free of lags and so perfect indexation is in any event unattainable.

So far we have been comparing a fully indexed economy with one that is not indexed. But the worst of all worlds is likely to be one in which the economy has made some adjustments to inflation by increasing indexation, but has not adjusted in other areas. Then inflation is likely to worsen the distortions of relative prices that occur in the absence of indexation. Some sectors would be sheltered from the inflation while others would have to bear the adjustments that the economy as a whole had to make.

To take an important example of the possible distortions from uneven adjustments to inflation, consider housing. As noted above, there have been extensive changes in the methods of financing home purchase, which are beginning to remove the difficulties caused by the interaction of the level payment mortgage with inflation. But under inflationary conditions, the tax laws strongly favor home ownership (assuming interest rates rise about one for one with inflation, as they have). With the financing distortion removed, the effects of inflation on the demand for housing will now be more distortionary than they were before.

Because the tax laws in the United States have made little accommodation to inflation, inflation has serious distorting effects on investment and financing decisions. If the tax system is not adjusted as continued inflation brings further private sector institutional adaptation to inflation, the costs of inflation may well increase rather than decrease, despite institutional changes induced by the inflation.

# Notes

1. The measure of inflation variability for each year is the standard deviation of the inflation rate over the past decade.
2. See McFarlin and Vitek (1980).
3. See Thompson (1978) and Melton and Heidt (1979).
4. See Sivesind (1979) and Jaffee and Rosen (1980) for further details. GPMs have not been as well received in the secondary markets as by borrowers, and their spread may therefore be slowed, at least until further experience allows for improved evaluation of default risk.
5. Zabrenski (1980).
6. The contents of the act are summarized in the *Federal Reserve Bulletin*, June 1980, pp. 444–53.
7. Trends in corporate financing in the post–World War II period are comprehensively surveyed by Friedman (1980).
8. The data, based on Flow of Funds statistics, are taken from Friedman (1980, table 5).
9. Data for 1946–60 from Friedman (1980), for 1979 from *Flow of Funds Accounts* of the Federal Reserve System. Long-term debt is defined as bonds, mortgages, and 40% of bank loans. Short-term debt is remaining credit market borrowing.
10. Since the Federal Reserve's survey of terms of bank lending was first made in 1977 (see *Federal Reserve Bulletin*, May 1977), there has been an increase in the proportion of loans in all categories that carry floating rates. The increase was greatest for long-term commercial and industrial loans, 66% of which had a floating rate in February 1980, as opposed to 51% in 1977. However, the increase has been smallest for the largest category of loans, short-term commercial and industrial, which rose from 45% to 51% with floating rates.
11. Calculation based on data on outstanding securities contained in Salomon Brothers Memorandum, "The Anatomy of the Secondary Market in Corporate Bonds: Year-End, 1979 Update," 2 April 1980.
12. There is a general question of why graduated payment (as opposed to indexed) annuities are not available.
13. Equity participation mortgages may be an important real asset for funds to hold in this regard, though real estate is a far riskier real asset than government indexed bonds would be. The recent proposal to allow thrifts to issue equity participation mortgages could put them in the position of having real assets in their portfolios. But the tax aspects of such mortgages—which reduce tax deductible interest payments at the expense of reduced capital gains for the homeowner—make it unlikely that they will achieve much market penetration.
14. See the 1979 report by the Comptroller General to the Congress, "An Analysis of the Effects of Indexing for Inflation on Federal Expenditures."
15. See Fischer and Modigliani (1978) for a description of some of the effects of inflation on taxes on capital, and also Boskin and Shoven (1980). Feldstein's chapter in the present volume (chapter 7) provides a discussion of the interactions of taxes and inflation.
16. See, again, Feldstein's chapter in this book.

# References

Boskin, M. J., and Shoven, J. B. 1980. Issues in the taxation of capital income in the United States. *American Economic Review Papers and Proceedings* 70:164–70.

Fischer, S., and Modigliani, F. 1978. Towards an understanding of the real effects and costs of inflation. *Weltwirtschaftliches Archiv*, band 114, heft 4; also available as NBER Reprint no. 47.

Friedman, B. M. 1980. Post-war changes in the American financial markets. In M. S. Feldstein, ed., *The American economy in transition*. Chicago: University of Chicago Press.

Gordon, R. H., and Malkiel, B. G. 1980. Taxation and corporation finance. Unpublished manuscript, Princeton University.

Jaffee, D. M., and Rosen, K. T. 1980. The use of mortgage passthrough securities. In *New sources of capital for the savings and loan industry*. San Francisco: Federal Home Loan Bank Board.

Klein, B. 1975. The impact of inflation on the term structure of corporate financial instruments: 1900–1972. In W. L. Silber, ed., *Financial innovation*. Lexington, Massachusetts: Lexington Books.

McFarlin, E., and Vitek, T. 1980. The graduated payment mortgage. *Federal Home Loan Bank Board Journal*, January, pp. 14–17.

Melton, W. C., and Heidt, D. L. 1979. Variable rate mortgages. *Federal Reserve Bank of New York Quarterly Review*, Summer, pp. 23–31.

Sivesind, C. M. 1979. Mortgage-backed securities: The revolution in real estate finance. *Federal Reserve Bank of New York Quarterly Review*, Autumn, pp. 1–10.

Thompson, L. J. 1978. All quiet on the western VRM front. *Federal Home Loan Bank Board Journal*, October, pp. 10–13.

Zabrenski, S. T. 1980. Changes in S & L account structure. *Federal Home Loan Bank Board Journal*, January, pp. 22–29.

# 9 United States Inflation and the Dollar

Jacob A. Frenkel

## 9.1 Introduction

Following the move to generalized floating in 1973, United States inflation accelerated, interest rates rose, the value of the dollar in the market for foreign exchange fluctuated and the volatility of exchange rates between the United States dollar and major foreign currencies reached new heights. These developments pose several questions which are dealt with in this paper.[1] Among these questions are (i) What are the causes for the large fluctuations in exchange rates? (ii) What are the causes for the large divergences between the external and internal values of the dollar? (iii) Have exchange rates fluctuated excessively? (iv) Did the move to a flexible exchange rate regime contribute to the deterioration of the dollar? (v) What would be the implications of restoring fixed parities for the dollar? (vi) What would be the implications of adopting an intervention rule in the foreign exchange market? (vii) What role could the external value of the dollar play in determining the course of the Federal Reserve's policy? and (viii) How could macroeconomic policy contribute to stabilizing the internal and the external values of the dollar?

## 9.2 The Record

To set the stage for the analysis it is useful to start with a brief review of the empirical record. This review concentrates on the evolution and the interrelation of exchange rates, prices, and interest rates during the

Jacob A. Frenkel is with the Department of Economics, University of Chicago, and the National Bureau of Economic Research.

The opinions expressed in this paper are those of the author and not the University of Chicago, the NBER, or the National Science Foundation.

1970s. Subsequent sections contain the interpretation of these facts as well as the policy implications.

The first set of relevant facts concerns the turbulence of the foreign exchange market. A simple measure of such turbulence is the average absolute monthly percentage changes in the various exchange rates over some interval of time. Table 9.1 reports such measures for three major exchange rates: the dollar/pound, the dollar/French franc and the dollar/ DM for the period June 1973–July 1979. In all cases the average absolute change exceeded 2% per month. In comparison the average absolute monthly percentage changes of wholesale and consumer price indices and of the ratios of national price levels were only about half that of the exchange rate.

The second set of facts concerns the predictability of these changes in exchange rates. If the forward premium on foreign exchange is regarded as a measure of the market's prediction of the future change in the exchange rate, then a comparison between actual changes and the forward premium may reveal the extent to which the market was successful in predicting these changes. Figures 9.1–9.3 present plots of predicted and realized monthly percentage changes of exchange rates for the three pairs of currencies where the predicted change is measured by the lagged forward premium. The key fact emerging from these figures is that predicted changes in exchange rates account for a very small fraction of actual changes. This phenomenon is also reflected in the comparison between the variances of actual and predicted changes: in all cases the variances of the monthly percentage changes in exchange rates exceeded the variances of the monthly forward premiums by a factor larger than 20.

If exchange rates moved in accord with relative national price levels as suggested by a simple version of the purchasing power parity theory, the

**Table 9.1**    **Mean Absolute Percentage Changes in Prices and Exchange Rates, Monthly Data for June 1973 to July 1979**

| Country | WPI | COL | Stock Market | Exchange Rates against the Dollar Spot | Exchange Rates against the Dollar Forward | COL/COL$_{US}$ |
|---|---|---|---|---|---|---|
| United States | .009 | .007 | .037 | — | — | — |
| United Kingdom | .014 | .012 | .066 | .021 | .021 | .007 |
| France | .011 | .009 | .054 | .020 | .021 | .003 |
| Germany | .004 | .004 | .030 | .024 | .024 | .004 |

Note: All variables represent the absolute values of monthly percentage changes in the data. WPI denotes the wholesale price index, and COL denotes the cost-of-living index. Data on prices and exchange rates are from the IMF tape (May 1979 version). The stock market indices are from *Capital International Perspective*, monthly issues.

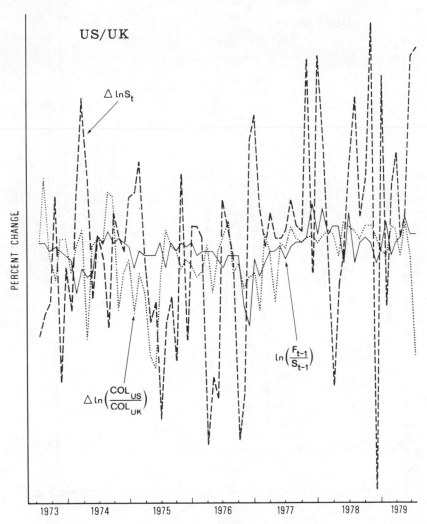

**Fig. 9.1**     Monthly percentage changes of the US/UK consumer price indices [Δ ln (COL$_{US}$/COL$_{UK}$)] and of the dollar/pound exchange rate (Δ ln $S_t$), and the monthly forward premium [ln ($F_{t-1}$/ $S_{t-1}$)], July 1973–July 1979.

volatility of exchange rates would be regarded as a manifestation of the forces underlying the volatility of national inflation rates and the turbulence of exchange rates would probably not be regarded as an additional source of social cost. The third set of facts relevant for this issue concerns the relation between exchange rates and prices. As illustrated in figures 9.1–9.3, short-run changes in exchange rates have not been closely linked to short-run differentials in the corresponding national inflation rates.

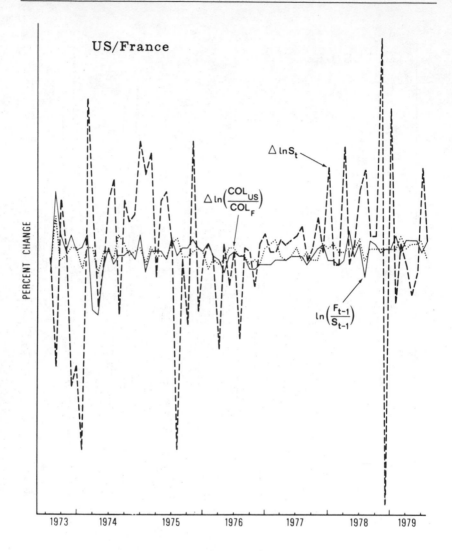

**Fig. 9.2**    Monthly percentage changes of the US/France consumer price indices [Δ ln (COL$_{US}$/COL$_F$)] and of the dollar/French franc exchange rate (Δ ln $S_t$), and the monthly forward premium [ln ($F_{t-1}/S_{t-1}$)], July 1973–July 1979.

Furthermore, this loose link seems to be cumulative. As illustrated in figures 9.4–9.6, divergences from purchasing power parities, measured in terms of the relation between exchange rates and the ratio of consumer price indices, seem to persist.

The fourth and final set of facts concerns the relation between the value of the dollar and the rate of interest. The record of the 1970s (at least up to mid-1979) shows that a rise in the rate of interest in the United States

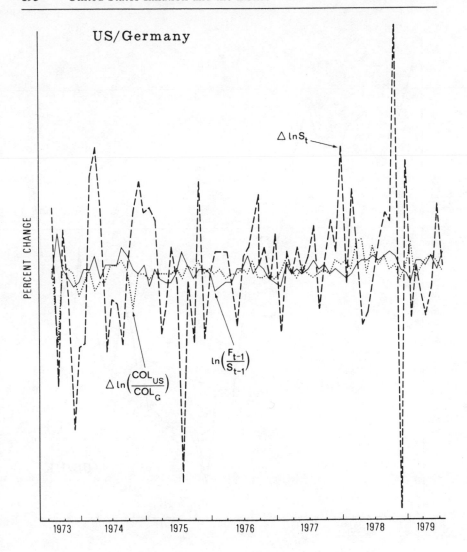

**Fig. 9.3**     Monthly percentage changes of the US/German consumer
price indices [$\Delta \ln (\mathrm{COL_{US}}/\mathrm{COL_G})$] and of the dollar/DM exchange rate ($\Delta \ln S_t$), and the monthly forward premium
[$\ln (F_{t-1}/S_{t-1})$], July 1973–July 1979.

(relative to the foreign rate of interest) has been associated with a
depreciation of the dollar. This fact, which is in contrast to the view that a
high interest rate yields a strong dollar, is illustated in figure 9.7.[2] Since
mid-1979 the rise in the United States relative rate of interest has been
associated with an appreciation of the dollar.

In summary, the record of the 1970s shows that (i) the foreign exchange
value of the dollar was highly volatile, (ii) by and large changes in

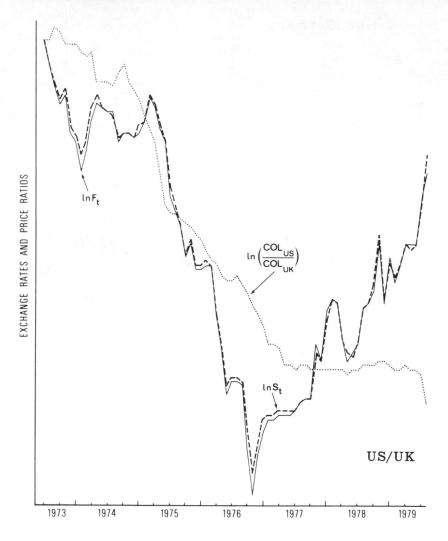

**Fig. 9.4**    Monthly observations of the dollar/pound spot (ln $S_t$) and forward (ln $F_t$) exchange rates and the ratio of the US/UK cost-of-living indices [ln (COL$_{US}$/COL$_{UK}$)(scaled to equal the spot exchange rate at the initial month)], June 1973–July 1979.

exchange rates were unpredictable, (iii) the fluctuations in exchange rates did not conform closely to movements in national price levels, and (iv) for most of the 1970s the rise in the United States (relative) rate of interest was associated with a decline in the foreign exchange value of the dollar, while beginning in mid-1979 this relationship reversed itself.

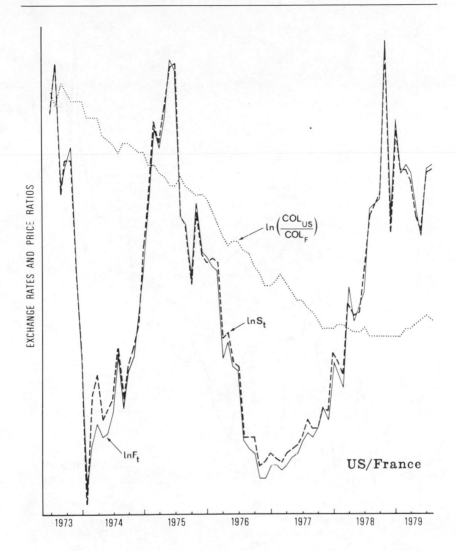

EXCHANGE RATES AND PRICE RATIOS

$\ln\left(\dfrac{COL_{US}}{COL_F}\right)$

$\ln S_t$

$\ln F_t$

US/France

1973     1974     1975     1976     1977     1978     1979

**Fig. 9.5**          Monthly observations of the dollar/French franc spot ($\ln S_t$) and forward ($\ln F_t$) exchange rates and the ratio of the US/French cost-of-living indices [$\ln (COL_{US}/COL_F)$(scaled to equal the spot exchange rate at the initial month], June 1973–July 1979.

## 9.3   An Interpretation of the Record

In this section I interpret the record of the United States dollar in terms of the modern "asset market theory" of exchange rate determination.

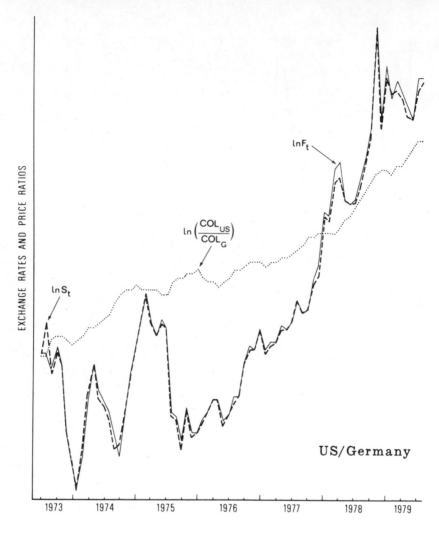

**Fig. 9.6**         Monthly observations of the dollar/DM spot (ln $S_t$) and forward
(ln $F_t$) exchange rates and the ratio of the US/German cost-of-
living indices [ln (COL$_{US}$/COL$_G$)(scaled to equal the spot exchange rate at the initial month], June 1973–July 1979.

### 9.3.1   Why Was the Foreign Exchange Value of the
Dollar Volatile and Unpredictable?

The central insight of the modern approach to the analysis of exchange
rates is the notion that the exchange rate, being the relative price of two
durable assets (monies), can be best analyzed within a framework that is
appropriate for the analysis of asset prices. The volatility and the unpre-

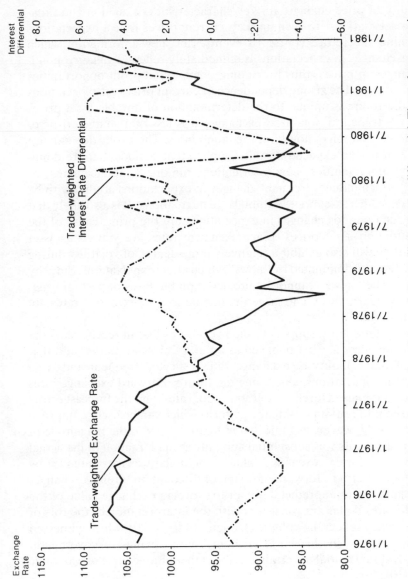

**Fig. 9.7**  Foreign exchange value of the US dollar and interest rate differential. The exchange rate is a trade-weighted average of the foreign currency value of the dollar; the interest differential is the US three-month commercial paper rate minus a trade-weighted foreign rate. The weights are from the *Federal Reserve Bulletin*, August 1978, p. 700.

dictability of price changes are key characteristics of auction and organized asset markets. In such markets current prices reflect expectations concerning the future course of events, and new information which induces changes in expectations is immediately reflected in corresponding changes in prices, thus precluding unexploited profit opportunities from arbitrage. The strong dependence of current prices on expectations about the future is unique to the determination of durable asset prices which are traded in organized exchange; it is less of a characteristic of price determination of nondurable commodities. The strong dependence of asset prices on expectations also implies that periods that are dominated by uncertainties, new information, rumors, announcements, or "news" which induces frequent changes in expectations are likely to be periods in which asset prices exhibit large fluctuations. It is also likely that during such periods changes in expectations are the prime cause of the fluctuations in asset prices. Since exchange rates are viewed as asset prices, they will also exhibit a relatively large degree of volatility during periods that are dominated by "news" which alters expectations. Since by definition the "news" cannot be predicted on the basis of past information, it is clear that by and large the fluctuations in exchange rates are unpredictable.

The evidence lends support to the hypotheses that in recent years the foreign exchange market behaved as an efficient asset market and that much of the volatility of exchange rates reflected frequent and large changes in expectations concerning the future. Forward exchange rates seem to be unbiased forecasts of future spot rates, and the forecast errors do not seem to contain systematic patterns which can be used to improve predictions. However, as indicated in figures 9.1–9.3, the magnitude of the forecast errors was substantial and only a small fraction of the actual change in the foreign exchange value of the dollar was accounted for by the previous period's forward premium or discount on foreign exchange. The volatility and unpredictability of the foreign exchange value of the United States dollar are consistent with the interpretation of the role of "news." They reflect the volatile character of the 1970s, which witnessed great turbulence in the world economy, large swings in government policy, and substantial uncertainties about the future course of economic and political events.

### 9.3.2    Why Did the Foreign Exchange Value of the Dollar Deviate from Purchasing Power Parities?

One of the striking facts concerning the relation between the price level and the foreign exchange value of the dollar during the 1970s (as exhibited in figures 9.1–9.6) has been the poor performance of the predictions of the simple versions of the purchasing power parity doctrine. As is known, when applied to aggregate national price levels, purchasing power parities can be expected to hold in the long run only if most of the shocks to the system are of a monetary origin and do not require changes in relative prices. To the extent that most of the shocks reflect "real" changes (like differential growth rates among sectors), the required changes in sectoral relative prices may result in a relatively loose connection between exchange rates and aggregate price levels. The 1970s was a decade in which real shocks were not in shortage. In the context of the United States dollar, the experience during the 1970s illustrates clearly the extent to which "real" shocks (the oil embargo, supply shocks, commodity booms and shortages, shifts in the demand for money, differential productivity growth) result in systematic deviations from purchasing power parities. These "real" shocks necessitated changes in real exchange rates and resulted in the persisting deviations from purchasing power parities which were illustrated in figures 9.4–9.6.

It is pertinent to note, however, that in addition to these factors there is a presumption that, at least in the short run, as illustrated by the evidence in figures 9.1–9.3, exchange rate fluctuations would not be matched by corresponding fluctuations in aggregate price levels. The arguments in section 9.3.1 emphasized that in periods which are dominated by "news" which alters expectations, exchange rates are likely to be highly volatile. Aggregate price indices on the other hand are not expected to reveal such a degree of volatility since they reflect the prices of goods and services which exhibit some "stickiness" and which are less durable and therefore less sensitive to the "news." It follows therefore that in periods during which there is ample "news" which induces large fluctuations in exchange rates, there will also be large deviations from purchasing power parities. There is thus an intrinsic difference between exchange rates and national price indices. Exchange rates reflect not only current circumstances but also expectations concerning the *future*. In contrast, the prices of national outputs reflect to a large extent *present* and *past* circumstances as they are embedded in existing contracts. Consequently, when there are large and frequent changes in expectations, it is likely that the future will be expected to differ greatly from the present and the past. Under such circumstances one may find large and frequent deviations from purchasing power parities when the latter are computed using current prices.

### 9.3.3   Why Did the High Interest Rate Fail to Strengthen the Dollar?

Prior to accounting for the empirical facts outlined in section 9.2 it is useful to recall the arguments of the typical analysis which predicts that high rates of interest are likely to be associated with currencies that are strong in international money markets. According to the typical explanations a higher rate of interest attracts foreign capital, which induces a surplus in the capital account of the balance of payments and thereby induces an appreciation of the domestic currency. Another variant of this approach states that the higher rate of interest lowers spending and thus induces a surplus in the current account of the balance of payments which results in an appreciation of the currency. A third variant claims that the higher rate of interest implies (via the interest parity theory) a higher forward premium on foreign exchange and that, to the extent that at a given point in time the forward exchange rate is predetermined by past history (an assumption that is clearly rejected by the evidence on the co-movements of spot and forward rates, as illustrated in figures 9.4–9.6), the required rise in the forward premium will be brought about by an appreciation of the domestic currency. Whatever the route, this approach predicts a positive relation between the rate of interest and the foreign exchange value of the domestic currency.

While such a prediction might be appropriate for noninflationary environments, it is entirely inappropriate for inflationary environments like the one prevailing in the United States in recent years. Indeed, as indicated by figure 9.7, this prediction is inconsistent with the record. During the 1970s (up to mid-1979) the secular rise in the rate of interest in the United States (relative to the foreign rate of interest) has been associated with a secular depreciation of the dollar. The same broad facts emerge from an examination of the circumstances prevailing in a cross section of countries. Generally, countries with relatively low rates of interest (Germany, Switzerland) have relatively strong currencies while countries with relatively high rates of interest (Canada, Italy) have relatively weak currencies.

The explanation is straightforward. In an inflationary environment the primary cause for variations in rates of interest is variations in inflationary expectations. In such an environment a relatively rapid rise in prices is associated with high *nominal* rates of interest as well as with a *depreciation* of the currency in terms of foreign exchange. In an inflationary environment a rise in the nominal rate of interest may just compensate for the erosion of purchasing power without providing for a higher *real* return. Under these circumstances, a rise in the United States rate of interest may not attract foreign capital. Capital markets are much more sophisticated than what is presumed by some of the simplistic theories. The evidence indicates that higher nominal rates of interest are associated with a forward discount on the currency in foreign exchange markets without necessarily raising *real* yields and without necessarily attracting foreign capital (except, possibly, for the very short run). The reversal of the relation between interest rates and the external value of the dollar which has taken place in the United States since mid-1979 indicates that from mid-1979 to the present (mid-1981), the prime cause for the fluctuations in United States interest rates has not been variations in inflationary expectations but rather variations in the *real* rate of interest.

## 9.4 Policy Implications

The high and variable world and United States inflation resulted in high and variable rates of interest and in a depreciated dollar. The induced turbulence of the foreign exchange value of the United States dollar as indicated by the large and unpredictable fluctuations, which did not conform closely to movements in relative national price levels, is costly. It generates capital gains and losses for holders of assets denominated in different national monies; it induces asset holders to alter behavior and expend resources in an attempt to reduce risk; it interferes with the efficiency of the price system in guiding resource allocation; and it may result in economically inappropriate patterns of production, consumption, and trade. A relevant question therefore is how can government policy be managed to stabilize the dollar and reduce its costly and undesirable volatility? This section analyzes the implications of alternative policies.

### 9.4.1 Implications of Fixed Parities

Very few economists recommend fighting inflation by pegging the price level through direct intervention in commodity markets. Similar (though not identical) arguments could be made against fighting the external depreciation of the dollar by pegging the exchange rate. Both dimensions of the deteriorating dollar are reflections of macroeconomic policies, and both can be handled with the aid of macroeconomic policies. Prices and exchange rates are the manifestation of policies rather than tools that should be manipulated as instruments of policy.

It is clear that as a *technical* matter policy can reduce the fluctuations of the dollar even to the extent of a complete pegging of the rate. If the source of evil was the variability of exchange rates, then pegging the rate would have been the simple and feasible solution. The experience with the Bretton Woods system indicates that this is not the case. It must not be assumed that policies which are successful in pegging the exchange rate for a period of time are also successful in eliminating the ultimate cause that underlies the fluctuations. Such policies may only transfer the effects of disturbances from the foreign exchange market to somewhere else in the economic system. For example, it is clear that a commitment to peg the rate of exchange implies a reduced control over the course of monetary policy, which would have to be adjusted so as to ensure the fixity of the rate. In that case the attempt to reduce variability of exchange rates would result in an increased variability of the money supply. It follows that the relevant choice is not between costly turbulence and free tranquility but rather between alternative outlets to the underlying turbulence. This is one of the important constraints that the openness of the economy to international trade in goods and capital imposes on the effectiveness of monetary policy. One could argue, however, that the obligation to peg the rate would alter the conduct of policy fundamentally by introducing discipline. Experience seems to suggest, however, that national governments are unlikely to adjust the conduct of domestic policies so as to be disciplined by the exchange rate regime. Rather, it is more reasonable to assume that the exchange rate regime is more likely to adjust to whatever discipline national governments choose to introduce.

Could one make a case for transferring the effects of disturbances from the foreign exchange market? Here it is important to emphasize that there is no presumption that transferring disturbances will reduce their overall impact and lower their social cost. On the contrary, since the foreign exchange market is a market in which risk can easily be bought and sold, it may be sensible to concentrate disturbances in this market rather than transfer them to other markets, such as labor markets, where they cannot be dealt with in as efficient a manner.

### 9.4.2    The Implications of a
Purchasing Power Parity Rule

As was indicated in section 9.2, the foreign exchange value of the United States dollar has been far more volatile than the various aggregate price indices. This different degree of volatility resulted in large deviations from purchasing power parities, and by these standards it seems that exchange rate variations were excessive. In view of the large divergences from purchasing power parities, various proposals were made concerning rules for intervention in the foreign exchange market. Some of these proposals are variants of a purchasing power parity rule according to which the authorities are expected to intervene in the market for foreign exchange so as to ensure that the path of exchange rates conforms with the path of the general price level.

There are fundamental difficulties with a purchasing power parity rule. First, as indicated in section 9.3.2, there are intrinsic differences between the characteristics of exchange rates and the price of national outputs. These differences, which result from the much stronger dependence of exchange rates (and other asset prices) on expectations, suggest that in assessing whether exchange rate volatility was excessive, a relevant yardstick should be variations in other asset prices like those of securities rather than variations in price levels. As shown in table 9.1, the variability of exchange rates was about half that of the various stock market indices. This of course does not imply that exchange rates as well as stock market indices have not been too volatile; rather, it indicates that in determining whether volatility was excessive it is not enough to point to the fact that exchange rates have moved more than the price level.

Second, since in the short run the prices of national outputs do not adjust fully in response to shocks, intervention in the foreign exchange market which ensures conformity with purchasing power parities would be a mistaken course of policy. When commodity prices are slow to adjust to current and expected economic conditions, it may be desirable to allow for "excessive" adjustment in some other prices.

Third, it is important to note that changes in real economic conditions requiring adjustment in the equilibrium relative prices of different national outputs occur continuously. Under these circumstances what may seem to be divergences from purchasing power parities may just reflect equilibrating changes. Further, if there is short-run stickiness of prices of domestic goods in terms of national monies, then rapid exchange rate adjustments are capable of changing the relative prices of different national outputs and are a desirable response to the changing real economic conditions. An intervention rule which links changes in exchange rates rigidly to changes in domestic and foreign prices in accord with purchasing power parity ignores the occasional need for equilibrating changes in relative prices.

### 9.4.3    The Rate of Interest Is a Poor Monetary Indicator

The interpretation of the relation between the rate of interest and the foreign exchange value of the dollar during the 1970s rested on the distinction between nominal and real rates of interest—a distinction that is critical during inflationary periods. That discussion also provides an illustration of the potential danger in using the wrong monetary indicator. Traditionally, the criterion for assessing whether monetary policy was easy or tight has been the height of the rate of interest: a high interest rate was interpreted as indicating a tight monetary policy while a low interest rate was interpreted as indicating an easy monetary policy. By now it is recognized that during an inflationary period it is vital to draw a distinction between nominal and real rates of interest and, as a result, during inflationary periods the rate of interest may provide a very misleading interpretation of the stance of monetary policy. The same logic also applies with respect to the analysis of the relation between exchange rates and interest rates. A rise in the interest rate will strengthen the currency if it is due to a rise in the real rate, and it will weaken the currency if it is due to a rise in inflationary expectations. In this context inflationary expectations play a central role. As a result, policies which attempt to induce an appreciation of the dollar could be successful only if they reduced inflationary expectations. The reduction in inflationary expectations would halt the depreciation of the currency in terms of goods and in terms of foreign exchange, and would result in lower nominal rates of interest while maintaining (or even raising) real rates of interest.

### 9.4.4 Policies Which Reduce Inflation Will Strengthen the Dollar

The recognition of the link between inflation, the nominal rate of interest, and the depreciation of the dollar is fundamental for the analysis of policy. An excessive growth of the supply of dollars relative to the demand for dollars (for given behavior of foreign monetary aggregates) reduces the value of the dollar in terms of domestic goods and services (as reflected by the domestic inflation rate) as well as in terms of foreign exchange (as reflected by the decline in the external value of the currency). Since the higher inflation rate and the higher rate of depreciation of the dollar are both symptoms of the same fundamental cause, there should be no conflict whatsoever between policies that are aimed at lowering domestic inflation and policies that are aimed at halting the external depreciation of the dollar.

Emphasis on the fact that the external and the internal values of the dollar are both endogenous variables is important in view of the recent allegation that the move to a regime of flexible exchange rates has been inflationary. Both the external and the internal values of the dollar respond to the same set of shocks, and both can be influenced by a similar set of policies. The finding that typically a depreciation of the external value of the dollar precedes and exceeds the depreciation of its internal value does not imply that as an economic matter the chain of causality runs from exchange rates to prices. Rather, it may just reflect the intrinsic difference between exchange rates and prices: exchange rates adjust faster and to a larger extent to shocks than national price levels. It seems therefore that the attribution of the rise in United States inflation to the move to a flexible exchange rate regime may reflect to some extent the fallacy of a belief in post hoc, ergo propter hoc.

The perspective that policies which strengthen the domestic value of the dollar are consistent with policies which strengthen its external value implies that the qualitative differences between policies that are introduced through the domestic desk and the external desk at the Fed are not as large as might have been thought. Domestic monetary policies like open market operations involve sales (or purchases) of dollars against securities. External intervention policies like nonsterilized interventions in foreign exchange markets ultimately involve sales (or purchases) of dollars against foreign exchange. Both policies result in changes in the relative supplies of United States dollars, and both therefore are expected to alter the domestic as well as the external value of the dollar. Under these circumstances the degree of coordination between the domestic and the external desks becomes an important issue. It is relevant to note that the degree of coordination between the various activities of the Fed is also important when the official intervention in foreign exchange markets alters only the supplies of nonmonetary assets available to the public. Such policies may influence exchange rates through portfolio effects and possibly more importantly through signaling to the public the intentions of the government concerning future policies. If the policies of the domestic and the external desks are coordinated, then such signals of the external desk of the Fed should be consistent with the signals provided through the policies of the domestic desk.

The foregoing arguments discussed the role of monetary policy and the conduct of the Fed. It is important to note that this emphasis does not reflect the belief that the source of the depreciation of the dollar was exclusively of a monetary origin. On the contrary, it is clear that "real" shocks were responsible for a significant share of the economic difficulties of the 1970s. It is believed, however, that macroeconomic policy can do little to offset changes in equilibrium levels of real income resulting from changes in relative prices of internationally traded goods (and the recent rise in the relative price of oil is a case in point). Further, while the depreciation might have been caused to some extent by "real" shocks, there is little doubt that the conduct of monetary policy is critical in influencing the internal and the external values of the dollar.

### 9.4.5   The Role of the Dollar in the Design of Monetary Policy

As was already indicated, exchange rates are influenced by the whole array of (actual and expected) government policies, especially policies which affect the demand and supply of different national monies. Exchange rates, however, are not instruments of policy that may be manipulated independently of other policy tools.

The close association between policies aimed at lowering inflation and those aimed at strengthening the dollar in foreign exchange markets raises the question of the role of the dollar in the design of monetary policy. It seems that the simultaneous achievement of domestic price stability and a stable value of the dollar in terms of foreign currencies need not imply that the external value of the dollar must play an important role in guiding the course of monetary policy.

While this implication may seem to be a revival of the "benign neglect" attitude which became popular during the fixed exchange rate era, the opposite is the case. One of the major arguments for the "benign neglect" attitude was that the United States economy was relatively closed and the foreign trade sector was relatively unimportant. The typical statistic which was used to justify this position was the low share of imports in GNP. This argument was inappropriate in the past and is even less appropriate under present circumstances. The United States has always been an open economy. The relevant measure of openness to international trade in goods and services is not the share of actual trade in GNP but rather the share of tradable commodities in GNP (i.e. of potential trade), which is by far larger than that of actual trade. Furthermore, one of the main linkages of the United States to the world economy is operating through world capital markets with which the United States is clearly well integrated.

This implication is based on the notion that the United States *is* an open economy, that the external value of the dollar *is* important, and that the restoration of price stability will automatically strengthen the external value of the dollar. Policy which views the exchange rate as an independent target or, even worse, as an independent instrument is likely to result in unstable prices. Furthermore, if monetary policy succeeds in achieving price stability, it might be useful to allow for fluctuations in the exchange rate which provide for a partial insulation from misguided foreign monetary policies.

It is of interest to note that this view that policy which ensures domestic price stability also creates an environment that is conducive for a stable dollar was also advocated by Henry Simons over thirty years ago:

> The major need for international monetary stabilization will be simply the internal stabilization of the dollar itself. This is the central prescription from which hopeful planning should proceed . . . If the dollar again is violently unstable in purchasing power or commodity value, and especially if it is again debased irresponsibly by tragically inopportune tariff increases or devaluations, world economic order, large international trade, and decent national behavior in commercial policies or practices will be unattainable. If we can securely and closely stabilize our own price level and prevent recurrent aberrations of inflation and deflation, we can thereby eliminate the major obstacle to reasonable stability of foreign-exchange rates. Here is perhaps the best single contribution we can make to resumption of orderly international trade—to the ending of arbitrary exchange controls (rationing of foreign exchange), bilateralism, discrimination, and direct national control of governmental monopolizing of foreign trade . . . serving well our national interest in this matter, we may also serve well the cause of world order and reconstruction, and conversely. [Simons 1948, p. 262.]

Even when monetary policy is not guided by exchange rate targets, it might attempt to offset disturbances arising from shifts in the demand for money. Such shifts in demand may be especially pronounced under a regime of flexible exchange rates. A policy which accommodates such demand shifts by offsetting supply shifts would reduce the need for costly adjustments of exchange rates and national price levels. The difficulty with implementing this policy is in identifying when a shift in money demand has occurred. Here the exchange rate may be useful as an indicator for monetary policy, especially when frequent changes in inflationary expectations make nominal interest rates an unreliable indicator of fluctuations in money demand. Accordingly, a combination of rising nominal interest rates and an appreciation of the dollar may indicate a rise in the demand for dollars that should be accommodated by an increase in supply, whereas the combination of rising nominal interest rates and a depreciation of the dollar may indicate a rise in inflationary expectations that should obviously not be fueled by an accommodative change in supply.

### 9.4.6   Low and Stable Rates of Monetary Expansion Would Contribute to Economic Stability

An important way in which government policy can make a positive contribution to restoring price stability and reducing costly and unnecessary turbulence in foreign exchange rates is by reducing high and variable rates of monetary expansion which, for example, result from misguided attempts to stabilize nominal interest rates. This is especially important because exchange rates are affected not only by current policy actions but also by current expectations of future policy. If expectations of future policy are highly sensitive to current policy, then instability of policy can have a magnified effect on exchange rates and on the relative prices of different national outputs, thereby generating significant social costs. If, as I believe, the instability and unpredictability of policy, particularly monetary policy, has contributed significantly to the turbulence of exchange rates since 1973, then the turbulence and its associated cost can be reduced. In order to restore order and effectiveness to economic policies it is important that such policies be perceived as being consistent and permanent. A track record of erratic policies that are based on attempts to fine-tune the economy will not promote such a perception.

An open economy under fixed exchange rates cannot have a monetary rule which ensures a stable growth of nominal balances. In such an economy the autonomy of the monetary authorities is lost to the commitment to peg the rate of exchange. This autonomy is regained under a flexible exchange rate regime, but, as was noted above, shifts in the demand for money are likely to occur. Since it might be desirable to accommodate such demand shifts, the monetary rule should be formulated with some flexibility so as to allow for occasional accommodations.

During a stabilization program it is likely that some sectors will be harmed more than others. The principles of the division of responsibilities between monetary and fiscal policies suggest that since monetary policy is an aggregate policy, it need not be guided by intersectoral considerations. These intersectoral considerations are, however, extremely important. The proper instrument for dealing with sectoral difficulties is fiscal rather than monetary policy.

Recognition of these principles is critical since very frequently the period of time that the economic system needs for adjustment is likely to be longer than the period of time the political system is willing to provide.

In the past this conflict resulted in stop-and-go policies with subsequent acceleration of the rate of inflation. These costs can be avoided if the Fed maintains its independence from political pressures.

Once the Fed adopts a stable course of policy, it will minimize the costly side effects. Put differently, money is felt when it is out of order; when it is in order, it only serves as a veil over the real equilibrium of the economy. This unique property of money was best summarized by John Stuart Mill:

> There cannot, in short, be intrinsically a more insignificant thing, in the economy of society, than money; except in that the character of a contrivance for sparing time and labour. It is a machine for doing quickly and commodiously, what would be done, though less quickly and commodiously, without it: and like many other kinds of machinery, it only exerts a distinct and independent influence of its own when it gets out of order [Mill 1862, book 3, chapter 7, sec. 3.]

Following a predictable stable course of policy will ensure that money is in order. Adopting such a course will not eliminate variations of exchange rates nor will it ensure that exchange rates conform with the predictions of the purchasing power parity theory. It will, however, reduce some of the unnecessary and costly fluctuations which are induced by unstable and erratic policies.

## Notes

1. Some of the arguments in this paper draw on Frenkel (1981a, b) and on Frenkel and Mussa (1980, 1981).
2. I am indebted to Dallas S. Batten for preparing this figure.

## References

Frenkel, J. A. 1981a. Flexible exchange rates, prices, and the role of "news": Lessons from the 1970s. *Journal of Political Economy* 89, no. 4 (August): 665–705.

———. 1981b. The collapse of purchasing power parities during the 1970s. *European Economic Review* 16, no. 1 (May): 145–65.

Frenkel, J. A., and Mussa, M. L. 1980. The efficiency of foreign exchange markets and measures of turbulence. *American Economic Review* 70, no. 2 (May): 374–81.

———. 1981. Monetary and fiscal policies in an open economy. *American Economic Review* 71, no. 2 (May): 253–58.

Mill, J. S. 1862. *Principles of political economy*. 5th ed. London: Parker & Co.

Simons, H. C. 1948. *Economic policy for a free society*. Chicago: University of Chicago Press.

# 10 Public Concern about Inflation and Unemployment in the United States: Trends, Correlates, and Political Implications

Douglas A. Hibbs, Jr.

> I think Dick's going to be elected President but I think he's going to be a one-term President. I think he's really going to fight inflation, and that will kill him politically.
>
> Dwight D. Eisenhower, 1968.

## 10.1 The Economy as a Public Issue

Although former President Eisenhower's forecast turned out to be wrong, numerous empirical studies show that macroeconomic performance has an important impact on mass political support for elected officials.[1] Moreover, during recent years economic issues (principally inflation, the energy crisis, and unemployment) have overshadowed other problem areas as sources of public concern. Indeed, not since the Great Depression of the 1930s and the immediate post–World War II reconversion scare has the state of the economy occupied such a salient place on the public agenda. As the Gallup Poll time-series data in figure 10.1 show, in every year since completion of the American withdrawal from Vietnam more than 70% of the public identified an economic issue as "the most important problem facing the country today."

In view of macroeconomic developments during the 1970s this comes as no surprise. The tight labor markets accompanying the Vietnam War boom and the Johnson administration's attempt to obscure the war's true cost through a policy of hidden deficit finance (abandoned too late with

Douglas A. Hibbs, Jr., is professor of government, Harvard University.

The research described in this paper was supported by National Science Foundation Grants soc77-20693 and soc78-27022. Nicholas Vasilatos and Jonathan Nagler provided valuable assistance, and Jerry Hall and Elizabeth Welch typed the manuscript. Edward Tufte kindly supplied data from the *New York Times*/CBS News Polls.

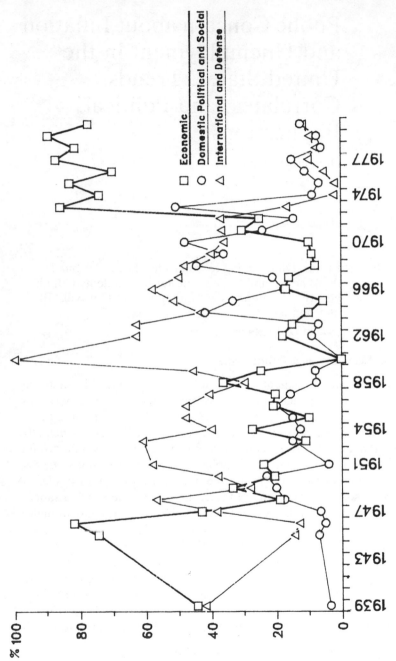

**Fig. 10.1**  Aggregate responses to the question, "What is the most important problem facing the United States today," (approximate wording)? Source: George Gallup, *The Gallup Poll, Public Opinion: 1935–71*, vols. 1–3 (New York: Random House, 1972), and American Institute for Public Opinion, *The Gallup Opinion Index*, various issues.

the 1968 tax surcharge) left the incoming Nixon administration facing accelerating prices. The new Republican administration pursued a deflationary macroeconomic policy to check the inflation. The high-employment budget surplus grew by about 20 billion (constant 1972) dollars in 1969 and showed an average constant dollar level of more than 5 billion for 1969–70.[2] Dr. Arthur Burns, Nixon's appointee as chairman of the Federal Reserve, accommodated the administration's fiscal policy; the nominal M2 money supply decelerated in 1969 and 1970, and the real money supply (deflated M2) increased by only 0.76% in 1969 and decreased by nearly 2% in 1970.[3] The policy worked, helping produce the 1970–71 recession and reducing the consumer price inflation rate by more than 1.5 percentage points between early 1970 and mid-1971.

By late 1971 wage and price controls were imposed and the policy of fiscal and monetary restraint was jettisoned in a successful attempt to stimulate an election-year boom.[4] In 1972 the real high-employment deficit was increased by more than 8 billion dollars, nominal M2 was expanded by nearly 12%, and real M2 grew by 8.5%. However, new crises soon rocked the economy. This time the shocks were exogenous: dramatic increases in the world prices of food and raw materials in 1972–73 and the OPEC–induced quadrupling of the price of petroleum in late 1973 contributed to unprecedented double-digit rates of inflation throughout 1974. The Ford administration responded by launching the "Whip Inflation Now" media campaign and, more tangibly, by cutting back sharply the high-employment budget deficit, which in 1974 was reduced by about 9 billion 1972 dollars from the average of the preceding two years. Dr. Burns again accommodated the fiscal authority's policy of restraint, proclaiming that the shortage was "of oil not money"; nominal M2 decelerated substantially, and real M2 declined by a crushing 4.5% during 1974.

The consequence was at the time the most severe recession in postwar United States history. Unemployment stood at nearly 9% by the middle of 1975. Consumer price inflation declined from the double-digit rates of 1974 to the 5 to 6% per annum range in 1976.

The severity of the recession prompted the Ford administration to pursue expansionary policies in late 1975 and 1976, but the President apparently remained committed to his earlier priorities, declaring to a cheering Wall Street audience during the campaign that "after all, unemployment affects only 8% of the people while inflation affects 100%."

These priorities were reversed during the first years of the Carter administration, which emphasized the traditional liberal Democratic goal of moving the economy toward full employment. Over 1976–77 nominal M2 growth proceeded at a rate in excess of 12%, real M2 increased at a brisk 5.9% rate during 1977, and the high-employment budget deficit continued to rise, peaking at 29 billion 1972 dollars in 1977:4 after

Congress in May 1977 passed the tax cuts proposed by the administration to stimulate the economy. Fueled by these policy actions and no doubt also by the economy's endogenous recuperative capability, the rate of unemployment declined continuously, falling by about two percentage points between the end of 1976 and the beginning of 1979.

However, the cost was a steady acceleration of prices. The annualized rate of change of consumer prices increased from less than 5% in 1976:4 to more than 8.5% in 1978:4. Following the second great OPEC shock of 1979, which more than doubled the price of petroleum, consumer prices continued to accelerate sharply and inflation was running at more than 13% per year during the first two quarters of 1980.

The escalation of inflation to politically (and economically?) hazardous rates produced a dramatic policy reversal in late 1978 that continued through 1979 and into the election year. The administration implicitly acknowledged that the voluntary wage-price guidelines plan announced on 24 October 1978 was unlikely by itself to decelerate prices significantly, and the earlier commitment to achieving a sustained low rate of unemployment was for practical purposes abandoned. The high-employment budget deficit was reduced by 9 billion (1972) dollars in 1978 and by more than 11 billion (1972) dollars in 1979 and averaged a comparatively modest 4–5 billion during late 1979 and early 1980—the smallest high-employment deficits since 1974. On two occasions, 1 November 1978 and 6 October 1979, the discount rate was increased by a full percentage point and, perhaps more important, with the encouragement of the administration the monetary authorities refused to accommodate the inflationary pressures. Consequently, the nominal M2 growth rate was flat and real M2 declined in every quarter after 1978:3. The 1979/78 year on year decline in real M2 was over 2%, and the 1980/79 annual decline was a bruising 4%.

The macroeconomic history of the Carter administration looks like a "political business cycle" run backward: rising inflation, falling unemployment, and a favorable real income growth rate during the first twenty-four to thirty-six months of the administration were followed by negative growth rates, sharply increased unemployment, and, during the last two quarters, as the election approached, slightly decelerating consumer prices. Although the OPEC shock of 1979 was obviously beyond the administration's control, this is nonetheless somewhat ironic because William Nordhaus, an economist who wrote a seminal paper on electorally motivated macroeconomic policy cycles (1975), served on the President's Council of Economic Advisers during 1977–78. In any case recent events suggest that the assumption of stylized political business cycle theories that an expansionary policy is the politically optimal election-year strategy may be erroneous during periods of high and rising inflation. I return to this point below.

## 10.2   Public Concern about Inflation and Unemployment

The Gallup data in figure 10.1 were organized in a way that shows the "economy" has become the dominant public issue in recent years, but inflation, unemployment, and to a lesser degree the energy crisis (except in 1974 and possibly 1979)[5] are the variables preoccupying both policy-makers and the mass public. Unfortunately, the Gallup data chronically confuse the "high cost of living" with "rising prices," that is, the price level and standards of living with the inflation rate, and therefore the Gallup series cannot be used to assess unambiguously public concern about unemployment and inflation.[6]

However, at intermittent periods between 1971:3 and 1974:4 and once every quarter thereafter surveys undertaken by the Survey Research Center at the University of Michigan have asked national samples of American households "which of the two problems—inflation or unemployment—do you think will cause the more serious economic hardship for people [may have the more serious consequences for the country] during the next year or so?"[7] These questions encourage people to acknowledge (implicitly) the difficult choice that has been at the heart of recent macroeconomic policy debates and provide the best available time-series evidence on the public's relative concern about inflation and unemployment during the critical 1971–80 period.

Figure 10.2 shows (a) the aggregate responses to the Michigan inflation/unemployment question along with (b) the actual rates of inflation, unemployment, and growth of per capita real personal disposable income in the macroeconomy. Nothing in neoclassical economic theory adequately explains the high levels of public concern about inflation revealed by the data in figure 2a. The principal economic costs of anticipated inflation are the resources devoted to economizing cash balances and fixed-interest rate assets. However, this is likely to be a trivial matter when viewed in relation to the costs of unemployment (but see Feldstein 1979).

The menu of costs associated with unanticipated inflation is longer and more interesting, but in my view it does not provide a convincing explanation of the public's aversion to rising prices. The existing empirical evidence suggests that the aggregate wage and salary income share is not eroded by inflation (Bach and Stephenson 1974) and that rising prices have no dramatic effects on the size distribution of income (Blinder and Esaki 1978). Unanticipated price increases do of course arbitrarily redistribute wealth from nominal creditors to nominal debtors, and the aggregate amounts involved are probably large. But at the microlevel a great deal of "canceling" must also take place. People lose on some accounts (fixed price assets) and gain on others (fixed price liabilities). Empirical work suggests that the rich (and perhaps the very poor) are net losers

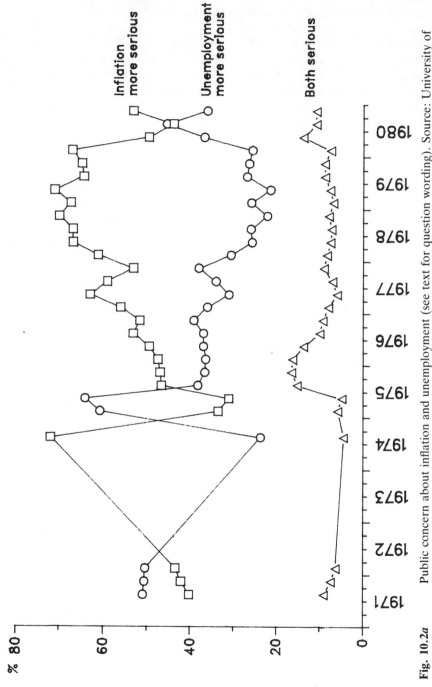

**Fig. 10.2a** Public concern about inflation and unemployment (see text for question wording). Source: University of Michigan, Survey of Consumer Sentiment.

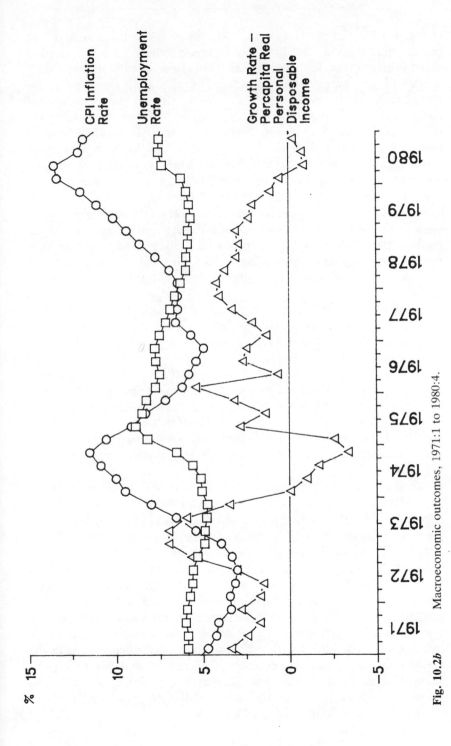

**Fig. 10.2b**   Macroeconomic outcomes, 1971:1 to 1980:4.

(Minarik 1979; Palmer and Barth 1978), which is consistent with public opinion data showing that high-income households are more concerned about inflation than low- and middle-income households (Hibbs 1975).

One of the major inflation-induced wealth redistributions is intergenerational: from the old and retired, who are likely to be net creditors, to the young and economically active, who are likely to be net debtors (Bach and Stephenson 1974; Palmer and Barth 1978). Surprisingly, however, microanalysis of the Michigan public opinion data shows that retirees were less concerned about inflation (more concerned about unemployment) than the young (Hibbs 1979). Perhaps this is true because retirees in surveys taken in the 1970s were old enough to have experienced the Great Depression and the event was traumatic enough to counteract their current economic self-interest. In theory, the aged poor—retirees whose welfare depends on social security—are perhaps the most exposed to inflation. Since 1974, however, social security has been indexed to inflation, thus limiting the adverse effects of rising prices on the aged poor.

To the extent that state revenue is raised by direct taxation based on progressive nominal schedules, inflation increases the effective rate of income taxation (inflationary fiscal drag) unless the authorities take compensatory action. Although discretionary tax cuts have neutralized much of the potential gross transfer to the state,[8] it probably is true that inflation has made possible a growth of government revenue higher than politicians could have achieved by making explicit real claims on the electorate. The (unobserved) difference between the historical time path of effective tax rates and what would have occurred in a world of stable prices (or indexed taxes) may explain some of the public's concern about inflation.

However, neither the income, wealth, nor tax effects of inflation appear large enough to explain widespread public aversion to rising prices, and therefore less tangible and partly psychological factors are probably more important than easily identified objective costs. As Okun has argued, sustained high rates of inflation may undermine "the foundations of habit and custom," forcing people "to compile more inflation and to try to predict the future—costly and risky activities that they are poorly qualified to execute and bound to view with anxiety" (Okun 1975, p. 383). Empirical evidence does indicate that high rates of inflation are associated with high variability of the inflation rate, and that these quantities are correlated with variations in relative prices and with the variance of inflationary expectations (Cukierman and Wachtel 1979; Klein 1976; Parks 1978; Vining and Elwertowski 1976). Presumably this heightens uncertainty about the future stream of prices and leads to greater incidence of unanticipated inflation.

It is also possible that people fail to credit inflation-induced windfall gains, for example, on fixed-interest liabilities such as home mortgages, against the losses incurred on such money-valued assets as pension and life insurance reserves. Perhaps more important, the connection between rising wages and rising prices may not be well understood by the mass public. Although there is no solid empirical evidence supporting this conjecture, it is possible that inflation tends to be viewed as an arbitrary tax that chips away the purchasing power of nominal income increases which people believe they deserve to enjoy fully. For example, between 1975:4 and 1976:4 nominal personal disposable income per person rose by about 7.5%, but prices increased by about 4.9%, leaving a more modest 2.6% real gain. Perhaps some people entertained the mistaken idea that their standard of living could have risen by 7.5%, or nearly so, if it were not for the "evil" of inflation.

Since 1973 one important factor contributing to popular concern about inflation has probably been the decline in real income experienced by the consumers of food, raw materials, and especially petroleum as a result of the shift in the terms of trade in favor of the producers of these commodities. It is likely that many people blamed rising prices for the shrinkage of their real income, even though the immediate post–OPEC inflationary burst was to a large extent merely the mechanism of a change in relative prices. In the third quarter of 1974, for example, per capita real personal disposable income declined by almost 2%, inflation was running at double-digit levels, and more than 70% of the public considered inflation a more serious problem than unemployment. Inflation, however, was hardly the root cause of the erosion of real income. Had the real loss absorbed by the oil-consuming nations taken place about a stable price level, the pain would not have been any less unpleasant, but inflation could not have been held responsible. However, if people were confused, it is understandable: as James Tobin (1976) has pointed out, neither President Ford, nor his economic advisers, nor the Federal Reserve Authorities, and very few outside economists told the public that anti-inflationary policies could not restore the former terms of trade or the real income loss.

It is no mystery why people are concerned about high and rising unemployment rates—after all, unemployment is a real quantity representing lost real output and underutilized human resources. Remember too that the measured unemployment rate is just that—a rate—and a far larger fraction of the labor force experiences bouts of actual unemployment during any given time interval than the average percentage numbers might suggest. In a twelve-month period the fraction is likely to be about three times the average "official" rate. Moreover, in addition to households touched directly by some form of unemployment or underemployment, an even larger number will be aware of unemployment among relatives, friends, neighbors, and, of course, workmates.

When inflation is viewed in this light, it is perhaps puzzling that the public is so concerned about it. Indeed, in the Michigan data people who were actually unemployed at the time of the interviews often expressed *less* concern about unemployment than did some (employed) blue-collar groups (see Hibbs 1979). This implies that for many individuals fear of future unemployment, the memory of past unemployment, or the aggregate social costs of unemployment are more powerful influences than the pain of contemporaneous personal experience. One of the reasons must be that unemployment no longer poses an economic disaster for many of those affected directly.[9] In the 1930s the unemployed often went hungry. Today public transfers to the unemployed provide a significant cushion against the economic pain and most suffer only temporary reductions in income.[10] In other words, as Feldstein (1978) has emphasized, the private costs of unemployment are much lower now than in the past.

Turning again to the aggregate survey and economic data in figures 2*a* and 2*b*, it is obvious that the public's relative concern about inflation responds to the prevailing macroeconomic situation. In late 1971 and early 1972 as the recession was coming to an end, the conjunction of comparatively low and falling inflation rates and modest real income growth rates produced popular majorities more concerned about unemployment than inflation. However, by the summer of 1974 inflation was raging at more than 10% per annum, real income per capita was falling by nearly 2% on an annual basis, and almost three-quarters of the public viewed inflation as the more serious economic problem.

The situation was reversed six months later. The inflation rate was falling sharply, unemployment increased to its highest level since the Great Depression, and only one person out of every three expressed greater concern about inflation than unemployment. As the economy moved from severe recession into "stagflation" for the eighteen months encompassing late 1975 and 1976, popular concern about inflation increased sharply and hovered about the 50% mark.

During the first year of the Carter administration, unemployment fell dramatically, the annualized inflation rate increased to about 6.5%, and public concern about inflation drifted upward averaging 58% for the year. Over the next eight quarters unemployment stabilized at just under 6%, and beginning in 1978:1 consumer prices *accelerated* in *every* subsequent quarter until the third quarter of 1980. Predictably, the public's relative concern about inflation shot upward. During 1978 and 1979 only about one person in four was more concerned about unemployment than inflation, and two-thirds or more of the public typically identified inflation as the more serious economic problem. The situation changed with the onset of the recession that began in 1980. The unemployment rate rose sharply between 1980:1 and 1980:2, and during the third quarter the inflation rate declined from its mid-year peak. Consequently, by 1980:3 the fractions of the electorate viewing unemployment and inflation as the more serious problem were approximately the same—about 45%. By the election quarter unemployment had stabilized, however, and 53% of the public saw inflation as the more serious problem.

Regressing the percentages of the public more concerned about inflation than unemployment on the actual rates of inflation, unemployment, and per capita real personal disposable income growth yields more systematic information about the response of public opinion to macroeconomic developments. Such statistical analyses support the following conclusions.[11]

1. Relative concern about the problem of inflation is quite insensitive to the prevailing *level* of the unemployment rate. Indeed, if real income per capita is growing at the usual rate (2.3% per year, the 1970–80 average), then at any *stable* unemployment rate within the range experienced during the last decade a solid majority of the public is likely to be more concerned about inflation than unemployment *if* the rate of inflation runs higher than 5.0–6.0% per annum.

2. However, changes in the unemployment rate are associated with sizable movements in the opinion distribution. Each percentage point increase in the rate of unemployment produces a decline of about twelve percentage points in public concern about inflation. Great fluctuations in the public's view of inflation and unemployment are therefore associated with movements of the economy into and out of recessions.

3. As indicated in (1) above, public opinion does appear to be sensitive to the inflation rate level. Each percentage point of inflation adds about 1.4 points to the percentage of the public believing inflation to be a more serious problem than unemployment. Since this effect was estimated in the presence of the per capita real disposable income growth rate (see below), it implies that people find rising prices distasteful even when money income adjusts fully to cost-of-living increases.

Public sensitivity to the inflation rate is even greater when rising prices are accompanied by declining per capita real disposable personal income. In these circumstances (prices rising, real income falling) each percentage point of inflation adds about 1.4 plus 0.7 times the rate at which real income is decreasing to the percentage of the public more concerned about inflation than unemployment.[12]

4. Changes in the inflation rate (accelerations and decelerations of prices) have quite dramatic effects on public opinion. A 1% increase of the inflation rate typically yields a transitory upward movement of about eleven percentage points to public concern about inflation. Since the best autoregressive predictors of this quarter's inflation rate are the inflation rates one and two quarters ago, this result may partly reflect the public's aversion to *unanticipated* movements in prices.[13]

5. Aside from the consequences of the (unusual) conjunction of high

inflation and falling real income, the growth rate of real income alone typically has a positive association with popular concern about inflation. When real income is rising, each percentage point of the growth rate adds approximately two points to the percentage of the public more concerned about inflation than unemployment. When real income is declining, the public's relative concern about inflation changes on the margin by 2.0 times the marginal income change minus 0.7 times the inflation rate.

These results suggest that recession rather than inflation typically is viewed as the more important threat to living standards and that, therefore, when real income is increasing at a brisk pace, the public's attention turns away from the unemployment issue toward the problem of inflation. Conversely, declining real income generally increases public concern about the unemployment issue.

## 10.3    Political Implications

If one believes, as I do, that economic policy is responsive to and constrained by public views of economic developments, then the public opinion data discussed earlier help illuminate the political environment facing macroeconomic policy officials. More direct evidence on the political implications of macroeconomic outcomes, however, is available from econometric models of how economic conditions affect mass political support for the President.

Figure 10.3 shows the elasticities of political support with respect to real and nominal macroeconomic performance for every President since Kennedy.[14] (The political support index is the percentage of the public responding "approve" to the well-known Gallup Poll question "Do you approve or disapprove of the way [the incumbent] is handling his job as President?") The elasticities give the long-run proportional changes in political support expected from unit proportional changes in the economic performance variables that are sustained indefinitely. (Practically speaking, given the dynamic structure of the model from which the elasticities were computed, "indefinitely" means five to six years.)

The elasticities implicitly reveal the public's long-run, proportional aversion to various economic outcomes. So that persistent developments are not obscured by short-run realizations of the variables, the time plots show four-quarter moving averages of the long-run elasticities implied at each period. For convenience figure 10.3 displays absolute values of the moving averages, though of course the underlying unemployment and inflation parameters are negative and the real income growth rate parameter is positive. Notice also that the "real" elasticities are the sum of the absolute values of the unemployment real income growth rate elasticities.

Several patterns are apparent from the data in figure 10.3. First, the

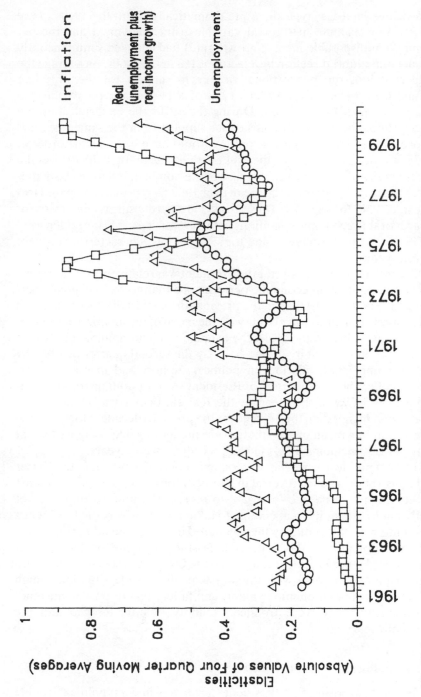

**Fig. 10.3**  Implied long-run elasticities of political support with respect to nominal and real macroeconomic outcomes.

elasticities increase, typically quite dramatically, from the 1960s to the 1970s. For example, if the real variables (unemployment and the per capita real disposable income growth rate) had changed simultaneously in an unfavorable direction by a factor of 1% in the 1960s, on average the expected long-run proportional decline in support for the President would have been on the order of 0.3 of a percentage point (the real elasticity mean for 1960–69). During the 1970s the expected long-run proportional decline in the President's support from the same sustained movement in the real macroeconomy would have been on the order of 0.55 of a percentage point (the real elasticity mean for 1970-79). As the figure indicates, the upward increase of the nominal, inflation elasticities over time is even greater: the mean over 1960-69 is 0.14 as compared to a mean of 0.46 for 1970-79. These results are hardly surprising in view of the favorable economic conditions in the 1960s—virtually a "golden age" of economic performance—and the "stagflation" characteristic of more recent years.

Second, popular support for the President was relatively more sensitive to nominal, inflation economic performance than to real economic performance in the 1970s than in the previous decade. In the 1960s the mean of the real elasticities was about twice the mean of the inflation elasticities (0.3 versus 0.14); in the 1970s the average real and nominal elasticities were both in the vicinity of one-half. By the second quarter of 1980 the relative impact of inflation on political support had increased enormously. For the four quarters of President Carter's administration spanning 1979:3–1980:2 the mean of the real elasticities was about 0.66— somewhat higher than the average for the previous decade. However, the corresponding mean of the inflation elasticities was 0.88—higher than at any period (including 1974) in the preceding twenty years.[15]

From a political as well as an economic point of view, then, the Carter administration's policy reversal in late 1978 comes as no surprise. But the policy change came late—too late to reverse the upward trajectory of inflation by a margin great enough to influence decisively the President's standing with the public by the election. However, the administration's anti-inflation policies did manage successfully to create an election-year recession. Hence President Carter and the Democratic party went before the electorate in 1980 with the worst of all possible situations—high inflation, increased unemployment, and falling real disposable income. As a result, they were trounced soundly by Mr. Reagan and the Republicans.[16]

## 10.4   Politically Feasible Policies

It is not surprising that President Carter was in deep political trouble because of high and rising inflation rates. Since the late 1960s solid pluralities (more recently majorities) of the public have identified "Government" as opposed to "Business" or "Labor" as the institution most responsible for inflation (see figure 10.4), and great majorities regularly agree that the federal government "spending more money than it takes in" and "printing money with nothing to back it up" are "extremely important" particular causes of inflation. (For example, the percentages of the public agreeing that government spending and money creation are extremely important causes were 79 and 74 respectively in the April 1980 *New York Times*/CBS News Poll.) On this score the public is in general agreement with the economics profession's diagnosis of the proximate sources of inflation. Today few economists dissent from Milton Friedman's assertion that the *proximate* cause of inflation "is always and everywhere a monetary phenomenon resulting from and accompanied by a rise in the quantity of money relative to output" (Friedman 1966). As the public opinion data seem implicitly to acknowledge, the most important indicator of fiscal pressure on the money supply and therefore on the inflation rate is the size of the budget deficit.

The anti-inflation policy favored by the majority of economists is straightforward: contract the supply of money and credit thereby raising interest rates and unemployment and reducing the rate of growth; that is, induce a recession to depress inflationary expectations and, ultimately,

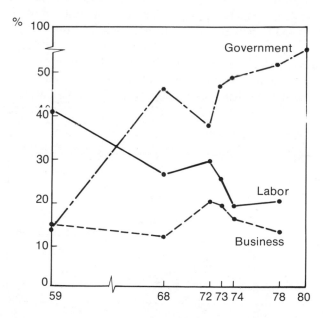

**Fig. 10.4**     Responses to the question, "Which is the most responsible for inflation—government, business, or labor?" Source: Gallup Polls and 1980 *New York Times*/CBS Poll.

actually reverse price acceleration. Here the public and the economics profession part company. Sizable majorities in the opinion surveys repeatedly oppose letting interest rates and unemployment rise to fight inflation,[17] preferring instead, as the data in figure 10.5 suggest, a policy of wage and price controls. Indeed, there is solid popular support for controls even if the policy means a reduction in real wages. Fifty-one percent of the respondents in the April 1980 *New York Times*/CBS News Poll were willing to accept government limitations on their wage increases "to a rate considerably lower than the present rate of inflation" (39% were "not willing"), and the July 1978 Harris/ABC News Poll found 68% of the respondents willing to accept a pay raise "less than the cost of living" if there were "some assurance" that it would contribute to bringing inflation under control.

With the exception of unorthodox thinkers such as Galbraith, Lekachman, and Heilbroner, and a few of the more conventional economists such as Bator and Tobin, the American economics profession has generally opposed incomes policies on the grounds that they introduce distortions and inefficiencies in labor and product markets and confer no long-run benefits in the form of reduced inflation. (See the econometric evidence on the 1971–73 experience in, for example, Gordon 1975, 1977.) Yet the pain associated with the economists' policy of deflation via recession will be enormous. By Hall's (1979) reading of the econometric evidence, the year on year underlying (wage) inflation rate falls one-half a percentage point for every percentage point that the actual unemployment rate stands above the "natural" rate. Hall judges the "natural" rate to be a staggering 6.8%, which, given an underlying inflation rate in the vicinity of 10% per annum, implies that it might take as long as ten years of 8.8% unemployment to restore price stability. By Okun's law this would mean a real GNP loss (gap) of about 5% in *each* year.[18] Of course

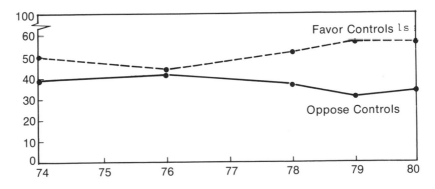

**Fig. 10.5**    Responses to the question, "Would you favor or oppose having the government bring back wage and price controls?" Source: Gallup Poll.

inflation might well respond more quickly to economic slack than such simple calculations imply, but there is little doubt that the employment and real output costs of significant disinflation will be high. (See chapter 1, Robert J. Gordon's contribution to this volume.)

The public would not endure the costs and therefore elected, politically accountable officials are unlikely to pursue the necessary draconian policies for any sustained period of time. Instead, unless inflation miraculously abates without policy intervention in the near future, it is quite possible that President Reagan, notwithstanding his ideological inclinations, will yield to political pressures and introduce statutory wage and price controls, or some form of a tax-based incomes policy. Perhaps the preferences of the people (and the possible actions of the politicians) are on sounder ground than the views of most economists. The costs of orthodox disinflationary policies described above justify quite a lot of incomes policy–induced distortion and inefficiency in the marketplace. Moreover, we have no solid empirical evidence that wage-price controls (or tax-based incomes policies) are ineffective *when* accompanied by monetary and fiscal policies consistent with the lower rates of wage and price change encouraged or imposed on the economy by tax incentives or statutory controls.[19] It is at least arguable that the combination of an incomes policy and fiscal and monetary restraint would produce more disinflation per unit of foregone real output and employment than orthodox alternative policies. In other words the politically feasible policy may also be the economically efficient one.

# Notes

1. This section updates the introductory part of Hibbs (1979).

2. The budget figures are based on the Federal Reserve Bank of St. Louis high-employment surplus/deficit series. The real series are nominal data divided by the GNP deflator with a 1972 base year.

3. "New" M2 deflated by the CPI.

4. For a detailed empirical analysis of the "electoral business cycle" in general and the 1972 experience in particular, see Tufte (1978).

5. See *Public Opinion*, December/January 1980, p. 40.

6. When responding to open-ended survey questions, many people apparently do not differentiate between high and rising prices and use the terms interchangeably (see Kiewiet 1980). The Michigan survey questions described ahead refer explicitly to inflation and therefore are less likely to confuse respondents.

7. The alternative wording in brackets was used in the 1971:3, 1971:4, and 1972:1 surveys.

Notice that the question refers to "people" generally (or to the "country") and not to the respondent *personally*. Questions pertaining to *personal* economic concerns invariably yield more mentions of inflation and fewer mentions of unemployment than questions pertaining to respondents' assessment of *national* economic problems.

For example, in February 1980 the Harris survey asked a national cross section: "If you had to choose, which do you think is a more serious problem

(1) for you and your family today—
(2) for the country today—

rising prices or high unemployment?"

|  | Rising Prices | High Unemployment | Both |
|---|---|---|---|
| (1) Problem for you and your family | 82% | 10% | 7% |
| (2) Problem for the country | 46% | 44% | 17% |

*Harris Survey*, 20 March 1978.

Research shows that *national* economic concerns have far greater influence on political behavior than *personal* economic concerns (see, for example, Kiewiet 1980 and Kinder and Kiewiet 1979, 1981), and therefore the former are more useful for my purposes.

8. See Sunley and Peckman (1976) on the stability of effective federal tax rates.

9. For a broader view of the strain and personal dissatisfaction produced by unemployment experience, see Schlozman and Verba (1979).

10. Gramlich (1974) provides estimates of unemployment-induced earnings loses of various demographic groups.

11. The conclusions are based on the following regression results from available data over the period 1971:3–1980:4:

$$Y_t = 38.5 - 12.3(U_t - U_{t-1}) + 1.38P_t$$
$$\quad (3.9) \quad (3.1) \qquad\qquad (0.37)$$
$$\quad + 11.1(P_t - P_{t-1}) + 2.01R_t - 0.72(P_tR_t^*),$$
$$\quad\quad (1.2) \qquad\qquad (0.75) \quad (0.24)$$
$$R^2 = 0.89 \quad \text{DW}(2) = 1.61, \quad \text{SER} = 4.27,$$

where $Y$ = percentage of the public more concerned about inflation than unemployment (graphed in figure 10.2a); $P$ = rate of inflation of consumer prices; $U$ = rate of unemployment; $R$ = growth rate of per capita real personal disposable income (nominal income deflated by the personal consumption deflator); $R^* = R$ if $R < 0$ and $R^* = 0$ otherwise; standard errors are in parentheses; and all rates of change are formed $\ln(X_t/X_{t-4}) \cdot 100$.

The level of the unemployment rate has a small, statistically insignificant effect on public opinion as the following regression results indicate:

$$Y_t = 40.2 - 0.25U_t - 12.3(U_t - U_{t-1}) + 1.39P_t$$
$$\quad (9.9) \quad (1.3) \qquad (3.2) \qquad\qquad (0.38)$$
$$\quad + 10.8(P_t - P_{t-1}) + 1.99R_t - 0.71(P_tR_t^*),$$
$$\quad\quad (1.8) \qquad\qquad (0.78) \quad (0.25)$$
$$R^2 - 0.89, \quad \text{DW}(2) = 1.57, \quad \text{SER} = 4.37.$$

The aggregate results above and the discussion in the text are broadly consistent with the nonlinear, disaggregated analyses reported in Hibbs (1979).

12. This estimate is based on limited experience and therefore should be interpreted cautiously.

Surprisingly, in all statistical analyses the consumer prices inflation rate performed better than the inflation rate of the personal consumption deflator, even though the latter probably has measured the actual inflation experience of consumers more accurately in recent periods. This implies either that people use a "fixed basket/fixed weight" standard in developing opinions about the relative importance of the inflation issue or, more likely, that opinions are to some extent affected by the media, since media coverage focuses heavily on movements of the Consumer Price Index.

13. Cf. the earlier discussion. Over the period 1971:1–1980:4 the best autoregressive equation for the CPI inflation rate is

$$P_t = 0.52 + 1.69 P_{t-1} - 0.76 P_{t-2},$$
$$(0.23)\ (0.11)\qquad (0.12)$$
$$R^2 = 0.97,\quad \text{DW} = 1.97,\quad \text{SER} = 0.57,$$

where $P_t = \ln(\text{CPI}_t / \text{CPI}_{t-4}) \cdot 100$.

14. The results in figures 10.3 and 10.4 are based on Hibbs (1982).

15. Since the elasticities are a nonlinear function of all variables driving political support (see the model in Hibbs 1982), they do not necessarily track closely their associated economic variables. As it turns out, the inflation and real income growth rate elasticities have high shared variation with the rate of inflation and real income growth respectively (the $r^2$ through 1980:1 are 0.91 and 0.86), whereas the shared variation between the unemployment elasticity and the unemployment rate is a more modest $r^2 = 0.41$.

16. For evidence showing that the 1980 election outcome represented a repudiation of the Carter administration's macroeconomic performance rather than a fundamental "shift to the right" of the electorate's preferences on domestic social issues, see Hibbs 1982a.

17. For example, in an April 1980 *New York Times*/CBS News Poll 69% of the public opposed "letting unemployment rise to try to fight inflation" (34% were in favor) and in the January 1980 poll 56% opposed "letting interest rates go up."

18. Here I have accepted Hall's very high estimate of the "natural" unemployment rate, and I have assumed that $(Y^* - Y)/Y = 2.5(U - U^*)$, where $U$ and $U^*$ are the actual and "natural" rates of unemployment, and $Y$ and $Y^*$ are actual and "natural" levels of real output, respectively. For recent estimates of Okun's law coefficient, see Perry (1977) and the comments and discussion of that paper.

19. Virtually all the evidence relevant to a peacetime United States economy is from 1971 to 1973 when fiscal and monetary policy was excessively expansionary. Consequently, the inflation rate increased sharply when the Nixon controls were lifted.

# References

Bach, G. L., and Stephenson, J. B. 1974. Inflation and the redistribution of wealth. *Review of Economics and Statistics* 61, no. 1: 1–13.

Blinder, A. S., and Esaki, H. Y. 1978. Macroeconomic activity and income distribution in the postwar United States. *Review of Economics and Statistics* 60: 604–9.

Cukierman, A. and Wachtel, P. 1979. Differential inflationary expectations and the variability of the rate of inflation. *American Economic Review* 69, no. 4: 595–609.

Feldstein, M. 1978. The private and social costs of unemployment. *American Economic Review* 68, no. 2: 155–58.

———. 1979. The welfare cost of permanent inflation and optimal short-run economic policy. *Journal of Political Economy* 87, no. 4: 749–68.

Friedman, M. 1966. What price guideposts? In G. P. Schultz and R. Z. Aliber, eds., *Guidelines, informal controls, and the market place.* Chicago: University of Chicago Press.

Gordon, R. J. 1975. Can the inflation of the 1970s be explained? *Brookings Papers on Economic Activity* 3:613–62.

————. 1977. The impact of aggregate demand on prices. *Brookings Papers on Economic Activity* 1: 253–76.

Gramlich, E. M. 1974. The distributional effects of higher unemployment. *Brookings papers on Economic Activity* 2: 293–336.

Hall, R. 1979. Labor market in recession and recovery. In NBER 1979 Research Conference: A summary. Cambridge: NBER.

Hibbs, D. A., Jr. 1975. *Economic interest and the politics of macroeconomic policy.* Cambridge: MIT, Center for International Studies.

————. 1979. The mass public and macroeconomic performance: The dynamics of public opinion toward unemployment and inflation. *American Journal of Political Science* 23, no. 4: 705–31.

————. 1982. On the demand for economic outcomes: Macroeconomic performance and mass political support in the United States, Great Britain, and Germany. *Journal of Politics* (May).

————. 1982a. President Reagan's mandate from the 1980 elections: A shift to the right? *American Politics Quarterly* (October).

Kiewiet, D. R. 1980. *The electoral effects of economic issues*, Ph.D. dissertation, Yale University.

Kinder, D. R., and Kiewiet, R. 1979. Economic discontent and political behavior: The role of personal grievances and collective economic judgements in congressional voting. *American Journal of Political Science* 23, no. 3: 495–527.

————. 1981. Sociotropic politics: The American case. *British Journal of Political Science* 11, no. 2: 129–62.

Klein, B. 1976. The social costs of the recent inflation: The mirage of steady 'anticipated' inflation. *Journal of Monetary Economics,* suppl. series, 3: 185–212.

Minarik, J. J. 1979. Who wins, who loses from inflation? *Challenge,* January–February, pp. 26–31.

Nordhaus, W. 1975. The political business cycle. *Review of Economic Studies* 42, no. 2: 169–89.

Okun, A. M. 1975. Inflation: Its mechanics and welfare costs. *Brookings Papers on Economic Activity* 2: 351–401.

Palmer, J. L., and Barth, M. C. 1978. Distributional effects of inflation and higher unemployment. In M. Moon and E. Smolensky, eds., *Improving measures of economic well-being,* pp. 201–39. New York: Academic Press.

Parks, R. W. 1978. Inflation and relative price variability. *Journal of Political Economy* 86: 79–96.

Perry, G. 1977. Potential output and productivity. *Brookings Papers on Economic Activity* 1: 11–47, 48–60.

Schlozman, K. L., and Verba, S. 1979. *Injury to insult: Unemployment, class, and political response.* Cambridge: Harvard University Press.

Sunley, E. M., Jr., and Peckman, J. A. 1976. Inflation adjustment for the individual income tax. In H. J. Aaron, ed., *Inflation and the income tax*. Washington: Brookings.

Tobin, J. 1976. Inflation control as social priority. Paper delivered to the Conference on the Political Economy of Inflation and Unemployment in Open Economies, Athens, Greece.

Tufte, E. 1978. *Political control of the economy*. Princeton: Princeton University Press.

Vining, D. R., and Elwertowski, T. C. 1976. The relationship between relative prices and the general price level. *American Economic Review* 66, no. 4: 699–708.

# 11     Inflation, Corporate Profits, and the Rate of Return to Capital

Jeremy I. Bulow and John B. Shoven

## 11.1   Introduction

In the 1960s and 1970s the United States experienced a substantial increase in both the rate of inflation and the variance of this rate. This fact has made conventional nominal financial accounts difficult to interpret, and it has made accounting for inflation and changing prices an important subject for both economists and accountants. Assertions have been made that distorted inventory profits and the failure to index depreciation allowances for inflation have caused reported corporate profit figures to be exaggerated and have increased the tax rate on real corporate earnings. The results of this paper show that this view was predicated on incomplete adjustments for inflation, and our real profit measures contradict the commonly held conclusion that profits have been overstated. If one wants to calculate complete and consistent inflation-adjusted accounts, the liabilities of the firm must be included in the process in addition to the tangible assets which receive the most attention.

In this paper we briefly discuss the value of adjusting profit figures for inflation and describe two alternative approaches (one based on balance sheets and the other on income statements). We discuss the individual factors involved and describe the supplementary inflation accounting information now being required by the Financial Accounting Standards Board (FASB) and the Securities and Exchange Commission (SEC). These reporting requirements will soon vastly increase the amount known about how inflation has affected large American corporations since 1975. The

Jeremy I. Bulow is with the Graduate School of Business, Stanford University, and the National Bureau of Economic Research. John B. Shoven is with the Department of Economics, Stanford University, and the National Bureau of Economic Research.

The authors thank Larry Summers for helpful advice and Margo Nelson and Laura Childs for research assistance.

full impact of the requirements is effective with the 1980 annual reports, which must include a summary of five years' worth of inflation adjustments. Given that the "micro" information is in a state of flux and rapidly improving, we concentrate in this paper on presenting a macro–time series of the aggregate importance of these adjustments for nonfinancial corporations. In doing so, we utilize the as yet unpublished aggregate balance sheets recently compiled by the Flow of Funds division of the Board of Governors, Federal Reserve System.[1] A time series of balance sheets is available from 1946 to 1979 for the household sector, the financial sector, and the nonfinancial corporate sector. We compute several alternative measures of nonfinancial corporate profits, present estimates of the return to corporations, tabulate the effective average corporate tax rate, and derive a new series for $q$, the ratio of the market value to replacement cost of capital. We conclude with a summary of our findings.

## 11.2    Why Adjust Corporate Accounts?

Adjusting corporate profits for inflation is important for at least three reasons. First, inflation accounting may entail supplemental disclosures on the part of the firm. Such disclosures may provide valuable new information about the status of corporate operations. This may be useful as a guide to investment allocation, in assessing management performance, and, in aggregate, in determining the state of the economy and the distribution of income. Second, adjustments to already available data may make such information more usable and understandable. This assemblage of already available data serves the same purpose as presenting historical accounting data in balance sheet, income statement, and sources and uses of funds formats, rather than serving just as a collection of raw data. Providing data in a usable and standardized form is essential for analyzing firms. Third, in addition to helping gauge the financial status of the corporate sector, inflation accounting can be quite useful in developing policy guidelines, most obviously in the area of corporate tax policy. To date, all the required inflation accounting adjustments are purely supplementary information for book purposes. The tax base is still conventional nominal corporate net income.[2]

Inflation distorts not only the reported income flows of corporations but also their balance sheet entries, including the bottom line net worth figure. Revising the balance sheet statistics to reflect current prices is useful in assessing the distribution of wealth in the country. Further, the current value figures are necessary to implement most fundamental investment analysis techniques and theories of investment based on asset market equilibrium such as Brainard and Tobin's "$q$" theory. Their variable $q$ is the ratio of the market value of a firm's assets (the total of the bond and stock market value) to the replacement cost of those assets (hence, the need for inflation-adjusted figures). They logically assert that as long as this ratio exceeds unity, acquiring physical assets and selling paper claims is a profitable real investment activity which will be engaged in. On the other hand, if $q$ is less than one, real investment is unprofitable. We compute a new series for the average $q$ of the nonfinancial corporate sector.

## 11.3 Balance Sheet and Income Statement Approaches

In analyzing inflation adjustments, one can take either of two approaches. One method, the traditional one, is to emphasize the income statement, with the balance sheet serving a secondary role. With such a method, each income statement item is adjusted to calculate a total effect on profits. Some income statement procedures designed to correct for inflation (such as LIFO inventory accounting) actually make the balance sheet less reflective of current values at the same time that they improve the income figure. In the next section we review the major adjustments which are needed to comprehensively follow the income statement approach. An alternative method is to adjust the balance sheet, with the income statement being a residual. Such a method is consistent with the Haig-Simons definition of income as the change in real net worth plus net disbursements. If income statement items are each adjusted in such a way as to reflect the change in the firm's net worth, the two methods will be identical. However, we find it simpler to begin with the balance sheet method. Also, we feel that the balance sheet method makes it easier to be sure of adjusting all items in a consistent manner. None of the new inflation accounting supplemental reporting requirements of the FASB and SEC, which basically follow the income statement approach, are fully comprehensive. The SEC requirements in particular deal only with the asset side of the balance sheet. We will discuss the balance sheet approach in some detail later, treating the nonfinancial corporate sector as essentially one firm. The real income of that sector is calculated there using the balance sheet residual approach.

## 11.4 Major Income Statement Adjustments

Because it is the way in which most of the literature approaches the subject, we will begin by discussing the major income statement adjustments. These issues were more fully detailed in our previous two articles on this subject (Shoven and Bulow 1975, 1976).

The adjustment which receives the most attention is the depreciation deduction, which reflects the effects of wear, tear, and obsolescence on the value of the firm's physical assets. Conventional accounts base depreciation deductions on the historical acquisition cost of the asset. The original cost of the asset is really an irrelevant number as a balance sheet entry or as the basis of an income statement adjustment. This cost is sunk and in a world of rapid inflation and relative price moves may bear little resemblance to current value or economic wealth.

Corporations deduct the historical acquisition cost over time according to the several alternative schedules which are permitted. Over the past thirty years the IRS has generally shortened the lifetime assumptions it will permit and also has accelerated the permissible schedules. Many of these changes may have been made to reflect inflationary expectations (as argued by Beaver 1979), although they offset inflation correctly only for certain firms and for a particular rate of inflation. The recent push for extreme lifetime shortening and simplification (ten-year lives for plant, five for equipment, and three for motor vehicles) certainly was fueled by the perception that inflation was eroding the value of existing original cost depreciation allowances. One feature of depreciation accounting, never fully justified, is that a firm need not use the same technique for book (i.e. annual report, SEC 10-K) and tax-reporting purposes. The usual practice is to use straight-line depreciation for book purposes and accelerated depreciation techniques for tax accounts. The difference can result in firms reporting far lower profit figures to the Treasury than to their shareholders.

Higher rates of inflation reduce the real value of depreciation deductions based on historical cost and therefore increase reported profits and taxes. In our earlier papers we showed that the magnitude of this effect was greater for firms with longer-lived assets. We also showed that if true economic depreciation followed a straight line pattern, then the accelerated original cost methods permitted could be as generous as the straight-line replacement cost for growing firms with modest rates of inflation. In general, however, the empirical analysis of that earlier work showed that inflation had reduced even tax depreciation figures below what would result from using a straight-line current cost basis.

At least three forms of inflation-adjusting depreciation allowances have been suggested. They would all be identical if relative prices remained stable and there was no technical change. The first form is termed a "general value," "constant dollar," or "general purchasing power" adjustment. With it, the original cost basis is increased according to the increase in a general measure of inflation between the present and the acquisition date. The second form of adjustment is usually termed "current cost," although terminology is not as precise in the field as would be desirable. The current cost basis of an asset is the cost of an identical asset today. To implement a current cost depreciation plan, one would use a specific price index for each type of capital asset. The final scheme is termed "replacement cost." The replacement cost of an asset is the lowest cost of obtaining a new asset of equivalent operating capacity or productive capability. Unlike current cost, replacement cost takes technical change into account, and hence, in general, replacement cost figures will be the same as or lower than current cost figures.

In adjusting the basis from original cost to one of these figures which more closely approximate present values, one would almost certainly want to unwind the acceleration which has been permitted on tax accounts. Of course, as we already stated, to date none of the adjustments have been utilized by the tax authorities. Further, if one were trying to measure the accrual or Haig-Simons income of corporations, the proper depreciation figure would be the change in the real value of the asset. If the relative price of an asset had increased (decreased), you not only would want to raise (lower) the depreciation basis of that item, but also would record the holding gain (loss). This point will be made clearer when we discuss the balance sheet approach.

The second income statement adjustment, that involving inventory evaluation, also receives a great deal of attention. With first-in, first-out (FIFO) inventory accounting and other essentially equivalent methods, the nominal appreciation of inventoried stock is treated as part of corporate income. This is because with these techniques the cost of goods sold or utilized is taken as the cost of the oldest of the inventoried items. No account is made of the fact that the acquisition cost was in older dollars of more purchasing power. Firms are offered an alternative inventory accounting technique, last-in, first-out (LIFO), which does not record inventory appreciation as a profit. With this method the cost of goods sold or utilized is taken as the cost of the newest inventoried items (which approximates replacement cost). One drawback of LIFO is that it results in inappropriate balance sheet valuations for inventories, as items may be carried at extremely old prices. Further, if the inventory of a company appreciates in real terms (e.g. oil or gold in recent years), a reasonable argument can be made that real profits should be recorded. The LIFO system will fail to do so, while the FIFO method will report the full nominal appreciation rather than the lower real increase in value.

One of the puzzles of corporate behavior is why corporations continue to use FIFO as widely as they do. The national income and products accounts (NIPA) report the impact that universal adoption of LIFO would have on nonfinancial corporate profits in their inventory valuation adjustment (IVA) figures, and the estimate for 1979 was that reported profits would have been $41.9 billion lower. From the Federal Reserve's current cost balance sheet we have determined the total inventory appreciation or holding gains. Table 11.1 shows that less than half of aggregate inventory appreciation is sheltered through the adoption of LIFO and that there has been no strong trend in that direction. Significantly, the IRS and SEC require consistency of inventory accounting techniques between the

Table 11.1    Distribution of Inventory Holding Gains
between LIFO and FIFO Method Firms

|  | Revaluation of Inventories | Inventory Valuation Adjustment | LIFO Sheltered Inventory Profits |
|---|---|---|---|
| 1967 | 4.0 | 1.2 | 2.7 |
| 1968 | 4.9 | 3.4 | 1.5 |
| 1969 | 9.0 | 5.5 | 3.5 |
| 1970 | 5.7 | 5.1 | 0.6 |
| 1971 | 6.8 | 5.0 | 1.8 |
| 1972 | 9.1 | 6.6 | 2.5 |
| 1973 | 29.5 | 18.6 | 10.9 |
| 1974 | 59.2 | 40.4 | 18.8 |
| 1975 | 12.5 | 12.4 | 0.1 |
| 1976 | 24.8 | 14.6 | 8.2 |
| 1977 | 23.6 | 15.2 | 8.4 |
| 1978 | 42.1 | 25.2 | 16.8 |
| 1979 | 76.0 | 41.9 | 34.0 |

annual report books and the tax accounts, so this means that, in aggregate, corporations could have lowered their 1979 tax base by $41.9 billion and their tax bill by $19.2 billion by adopting LIFO, assuming the marginal rate as the statutory 46%. It should be emphasized here that the choice is only a matter of what numbers to write down on these accounts; no real behavior need be altered. The bill of almost $20 billion for the right to use FIFO seems a little steep for the explanations we offer.

Nonetheless, some attempts at explaining the preference for FIFO can be made. First, the adoption of LIFO lowers reported earnings and in the long run will make the firm's ratio of assets to liabilities appear worse (because of the lower value placed on the inventoried stock). Managers may not believe in the efficiency of financial markets in "seeing through" this. Further, a firm commonly faces constraints in its dividend and borrowing policies by the terms of its existing bonds and bank credits. These constraints may become binding sooner or with higher probability with LIFO accounting figures. Also, the management's profit sharing or bonus arrangement may well depend on reported earnings. Changing these plans to offset a new system of accounts may be institutionally difficult. Finally, it is asserted, although not documented, that LIFO is computationally more expensive than FIFO or equivalent techniques. We leave it to the reader to assess whether these factors add up to $20 billion.

Many discussions of inflation accounting stop right here. The major categories of tangible assets have been covered (except those which do not depreciate such as land). However, the treatment of financial assets and liabilities is of equal importance.

Financial assets and liabilities (nonfinancial corporations are net debt-ors) undergo a change in real value under inflation via two quite different mechanisms. First, debt with the same nominal market value at the end of the year as at the beginning is less of a real liability if the general price level is higher. Another way of looking at the same thing is to recognize that the inflation premium component of the interest payments repre-sents real debt repayment. It should be emphasized that this adjustment of adding the real depreciation of nominal liabilities to profit figures is appropriate independent of inflationary expectations. The second mechanism results from changes in nominal interest rates which may or may not be due to changes in inflationary expectations. Generally, one does expect interest rates to rise with inflationary expectations, and on average that has certainly occurred since about 1950. Changes in interest rates affect the value of long-term bonds and therefore the value of a firm's financial assets and liabilities. Because (1) most innovations in inflationary (and interest rate) expectations have been positive since about 1950 and (2) in periods when interest rates have unexpectedly fallen, bond price increases have been limited by call provisions, the market value of publicly held debt has consistently been below par value for that period. It is difficult to evaluate complex private debt agreements (e.g. some capitalized lease contracts), but qualitatively the effect has doubtless been the same.

With a Haig-Simons accrual definition of real income these changes in market value should be considered a part of income in the year they occur. Currently, they are taken into income over the life of the debt. For example, assume that debt with a par value of $50 million falls in market value from $50 to $40 million over the course of a year. The reason for the fall would be that the present value of the interest payments to be made on this debt would be $10 million less than on debt with an equal par value issued at the end of the year. The company has made a $10 million gain at the expense of its bondholders in the sense that it can buy up its obligation (or similar obligations of other companies) for $40 million.

Two aspects of this proposal should be clarified. First, it may seem paradoxical for the case of a fall in bond values due to a perceived deepening of default risk. Such a change may correspond to a decrease in value of the assets of the firm that clearly makes the equity holders worse off and which, under the purchasing-power-accrual concept of income, would be reported as a loss. However, to the extent that the greater risk of bankruptcy depreciates the value of the bond liabilities, some of this loss is transferred from the equity holders to the bondholders. As a result, stockholders realize a partially offsetting gain, which would be recorded as accrual income with the procedures described in this section.

Second, as with depreciation and inventory accounting, market value reporting of financial liabilities involves the timing of income (and presumably tax payments). If the bond is not repurchased prematurely, its price will return to 100 (percent of issue price).[3] The net change in value will be zero, and the tax payments over the life of the bond will be the same with or without market value reporting. Firms offer many bond issues, some with rather long maturities, and the empirical data presented in our earlier papers show that the long run is long enough that the adoption of market value statements would have a sizable effect on earnings.

As has already been stated, firms do not now revise the value of their outstanding liabilities to the market level. In terms of present value, this omission is compensated for by the deduction of interest expense according to the historical coupon rate and not the market rate, but the timing of reported income diverges from that of the actual accrual of economic power. To clarify this phenomenon, consider a firm that issues a ten-year, $10,000 bond at 4% interest. If interest rates jump to 10% immediately after the bond is issued, its market value falls to $6,313. If the company does not repurchase this obligation, current accounting practice would have it report $400 annual interest expense on a $10,000 loan, $600 less interest than what would be required at the market rate. With a 10% discount rate, the present value of this $600 annual "saving" for the next ten years is $3,687, exactly the amount of the drop in market value. Thus the gain is spread over the life of the obligation. With market value accounting, a $3,687 profit would be recorded when the spurt in the interest rate occurred. If the 10% rate persists, the value of the bond would be $6,544 after one year and $6,798 after two. Following the extraordinary (one-shot) gain of $3,687, the firm would report $400 in interest and a $231 rise in obligations the first year (for a total of $631, or 10% of $6,313), and $400 plus a $254 increase in obligations during the second year. The total debt cost would always be consistent with the market interest rate and the market value of the debt, and the profits or losses due to interest rate changes would be reported when they were experienced. Proponents of accrual accounting would argue that these calculations more accurately reflect the income flows and economic position of the business enterprise.

This second adjustment "marks to market" the nominal value of bonds and simply records a loss in value as a profit if the bond is a liability and as a loss should it be an asset. In fact, nonfinancial corporations hold few long-term financial assets, so that most of these adjustments come from financial liabilities. Also, the second type of adjustment depends on *changes* in interest rates which may occur because of *changes* in the rate of inflationary expectations and not the level of inflation, so that even the sign of the adjustment varies over time. The first adjustment to financial assets and liabilities simply converts changes in nominal values to changes in real values. Both of these adjustments are numerically significant as will be seen in the aggregate figures we display later.[4]

While this completes the major income statement inflation adjustments, there are a couple of special items worthy of mention. These are the accounting treatment for pension liabilities and for foreign assets and liabilities. All accrued pension liabilities of a firm are nominal. Such liabilities are calculated with only the knowledge of the worker's past history with the firm and the knowledge of the term structure of nominal interest rates. Even if workers have their pensions tied to their final salary, the firm's pension obligation is still nominal—unless there is an implicit contract between the worker and the firm that provides the worker a given real *salary* (not a given level of real total compensation) in future years. For more details concerning why these liabilities are nominal, see chapter 5 of this volume, by Jeremy Bulow.

Pension fund liabilities, as very long-term corporate debts, change dramatically in value when interest rates change. As pointed out by Bulow in chapter 5, defined benefit pension plans currently hold surpluses in the tens of billions of dollars, principally because of increases in nominal interest rates.

The treatment of foreign assets and liabilities is complex and will not be dealt with here in any detail. Generally, the accrual definition of corporate income would require that foreign assets and liabilities first be stated at current value in whatever currency they are denominated, and then converted to dollars at the present exchange rate. There are a number of FASB proposals to calculate the holding gains on foreign assets, but none precisely implements this concept.

## 11.5   The FASB and SEC Reporting Requirements

Three types of inflation accounting data are now required of certain large firms.[5] Two of these requirements are due to the FASB, with the final being SEC Accounting Series Release (ASR) 190. Beginning with fiscal years ending after 25 December 1979, FASB Statement No. 33 required firms to provide certain general price level financial information. For years after 25 December 1980 data must also be disclosed on a current cost basis. The SEC requires statements of costs of goods sold, depreciation, inventory, and property, plant, and equipment on the basis of replacement cost. The FASB does include the first of the two adjustments to financial assets and liabilities mentioned earlier (that is, it does reflect the fact that a liability with a fixed nominal value through time has a decreasing real value with inflation), but does not mark financial items to current market value. The SEC requirements do not apply to financial items.

The FASB general price level computation procedures are meant to adjust the value of assets and liabilities for general inflation, but not to allow for differential price movements. The Consumer Price Index for all urban consumers (CPI-U) is prescribed to measure changes in general purchasing power. This choice of index is probably unfortunate as the CPI's shortcomings have become more apparent in recent years. The general restatement rule is (constant dollar amount) = (historical cost amount) × [(average for the year CPI-U)/(date of purchase CPI-U)]. Constant dollar amounts of inventory and property, plant, and equipment must be reduced to the recoverable amount[6] if there has been a material and permanent reduction in the value of the asset to the enterprise. (This is also true for the current cost method.)

Some reasonable approximations are allowed in performing these computations. For example, in dealing with property, plant, and equipment it is permissible to assume that any asset acquired before 1945 was acquired at that time, because such a cutoff does not introduce material distortions into companies' data.

The FASB also requires that entries in historical cost financial statements expressed in a foreign currency first be translated into historical cost financial statements expressed in United States dollars in accordance with FASB Statement No. 8. The resulting amounts are then restated to constant dollar amounts using the CPI-U.

Unlike the general price level–adjusted statements, the current cost method is meant to take into account relative as well as general price movements. The current cost of assets may be obtained either through direct pricing—using (1) current invoice price, (2) vendors' firm price lists or other quotations or estimates, or (3) standard manufacturing costs that approximate current costs—or through indexing—using either externally or internally generated indices of the cost changes for the class of assets being considered.

The FIFO value of inventories may be used as a reasonable measure of current cost, except for slow inventory turnover items such as tobacco and wine. Property, plant, and equipment will often be adjusted by the use of specific price indices rather than the general CPI-U used for the general price level statements. Foreign assets are handled by first estimating current cost in the foreign market and then translating that cost into United States dollars at the current rate of exchange.

The SEC replacement cost disclosure requirements are similar in spirit to the FASB current cost requirements, but they differ in several respects. The most important difference is that replacement cost is based on the cost of acquiring a new asset with equivalent productive capability whereas current cost is based on the cost of producing an *identical* asset currently.

Also, ASR 190 may or may not require a replacement cost measure of assets related to a contract or project, depending primarily on whether the contract or project is of a recurring nature. The FASB requires current cost estimates for all such assets, as of the date of use on or commitment to the contract.

The SEC requires firms to use straight-line depreciation when assets are being depreciated on any time-expired basis (as opposed to use basis) for historical cost purposes. FASB 33 requires the use of the same depreciation methods for current cost purposes as are used for historical purposes, unless accelerated methods were chosen for historical purposes to offset in part the effect of inflation on depreciation deductions.

Detailed information about the various requirements can be found in FASB (1979) and Deloitte, Haskins, and Sells (1979).

### 11.6    Aggregate Profits of the Nonfinancial Corporate Sector: A Balance Sheet Approach

The balance sheet is meant to present the value of a firm's assets and liabilities with net worth representing the residual of assets less liabilities. A very condensed balance sheet is shown below:

BALANCE SHEET

| Tangible Assets | | 70 | Total Liabilities | | 55 |
|---|---|---|---|---|---|
| Plant and Equipment | 40 | | Long-term Debt | 40 | |
| Inventories | 20 | | Short-term Debt | 15 | |
| Land | 10 | | Net Worth | | 45 |
| Financial Assets | | 30 | | | |
| Total Assets | | 100 | = Liabilities + Net Worth | | 100 |

The change in net worth between the end of the current year and the end of the year before represents the increase in the value of the equity holders' claim. The profit of equity holders equals the increase in the value of their claim plus the net disbursements made by the firm to equity holders. Thus

$$\text{profit} = \Delta\text{net worth} + \text{dividends} - \text{new issues},$$

where new issues would be the net of share repurchases by the corporation.

The problem in implementing this profit formula is determining the appropriate definition for net worth and hence the change in net worth. We begin by assembling two sets of balance sheets for the nonfinancial corporate sector using the new data set compiled by the Federal Reserve

System. The first set bases the valuation of all assets and liabilities on historical cost. The second set of balance sheets values all assets and liabilities at current cost. In table 11.2 we present a time series of these two balance sheets and compute nine different definitions of corporate income. Several of these income measures differ in which of the balance sheet items are adjusted to current value figures in the determination of net worth and the change in net worth. Two of the income measures are based on the performance of equity markets.

Historical profits are determined from the net worth figures of traditional historical cost balance sheets. Capital maintenance income has been defined as that amount of money (or purchasing power) over and above what is necessary to keep capital intact. This definition has been propounded by Pigou and Marshall and would exclude real holding gains on tangible and financial assets. It is not consistent with the balance sheet determination of income. For example, the capital maintenance concept calls for the use of LIFO inventory accounting. For depreciable assets it uses a replacement cost basis, but does not recognize changes in the asset value for balance sheet reporting. Financial items are not "marked to market," but the correction for the change in general purchasing power is made.

Our "SEC" profits attempt to capture the impact of ASR 190–type adjustments. Tangible assets are stated at current value[7] while financial items are unadjusted. The FASB figures in table 11.2 are derived from balance sheets in which tangible assets are carried at current cost and a general value adjustment is made to financial items.

National Income Account profit figures are presented in table 11.2 for comparison with our constructed series. The real current cost income figures are derived from balance sheets with both the asset and liability sides adjusted to current values, and both beginning and end-of-year balance sheets are stated in end-of-year dollars. The resulting change in net worth represents the real increase in the current value of the net asset position of equity holders. This figure is the most consistent with the Haig-Simons definition of accrual income. The seventh income definition, nominal current cost, calculates the change in the *nominal* net worth in the equity holders position, not adjusting the beginning balance sheet to end-of-year dollars. Finally, the nominal and real stockholder gain adds the change in firm stock market values and net disbursements to shareholders.

In examining the alternative profit figures of table 11.2, one is first struck by the stability of historical and National Income Account (NIA) profits relative to the other measures. It comes as no surprise, of course, that the measures based on the stock market are highly volatile. The "SEC" measure is frequently low, indicating the inappropriateness of partial adjustments. If only such adjustments were made for tax purposes, this would, obviously, be highly advantageous for owners of corporate equities. The most noteworthy feature of table 11.2 is the volatility of the sixth series, real Haig-Simons income or real current cost profits. In 1971, this definition of profits yields a loss of $0.6 billion for the nonfinancial corporate sector (while the NIA figure is a $33.4 billion profit). In 1974, the relative positions are reversed, with the accrual figure being $169.3 billion profit versus the NIA figure of $60.2 billion. It is no surprise that recording holding gains as profits adds volatility, but the extent of the addition is very large.

Comparison of the NIA and real current cost profits yields one particularly striking result. In the years from 1949 through 1972 National Income Accounts profits were consistently a little higher than real current cost, by a total of roughly $60 billion. However, since 1973 aggregate NIA profits have understated our real current cost income figures by a total of about $160 billion. Thus official profits were overstated relative to real accrual profits in the relatively low-inflation early part of the sample and are actually being understated in the current high-inflation period.

Table 11.3 presents average tax rates and corporate rates of return for our alternative profit figures. In general, real accounting rates of return, while volatile, have not declined. Stockholder returns have, of course, fallen sharply over the period. The result is summarized in the Brainard-Tobin "$q$" measure, which is also shown in table 11.3.

The first $q$ series measure is simply the ratio of the market value of equity and net financial liabilities to the current cost value of tangible assets. The remaining three measures simply take inventories out of the numerator and denominator, the first at full value, the second at 90 cents per dollar, and the last at 75 cents per dollar. Several of the $q$ series figures were constructed from a relatively small sample of firms, so that an advantage of this set is that it is for the entire nonfinancial corporate sector.

The $q$ series data yield several interesting results. First, $q$ is low at the beginning of our sample with a 0.48 value in 1949. If inventories are removed at full current value, then the remaining tangible assets are valued in financial markets at only 33 cents per dollar. The $q$ ratio rises fairly steadily through the 1950s and ranges slightly above unity during the 1960s. This is a substantially lower value for $q$ for these peak years than other investigators have derived. The fall in $q$ after 1972 is extremely sharp, its value more than halving in just two years. The 1979 figures range from 0.435 to 0.573 depending on the inclusion of inventories. One possible reason for the low 1979 values of $q$ is that the significant relative price changes of the 1970s reduced the value of much equipment in place, even if the cost of replacing such equipment had risen. Such adjustments

**Table 11.2  Aggregate Balance Sheets and Profits for Nonfinancial Corporations, 1949–79**

*a)* 1949–55

| | 1949 | 1950 | 1951 | 1952 | 1953 | 1954 | 1955 |
|---|---|---|---|---|---|---|---|
| | Historical Balance Sheet for Nonfinancial Corporations | | | | | | |
| (1) Tangible assets | 147.0 | 166.2 | 187.8 | 199.5 | 213.8 | 222.8 | 241.9 |
| (2) residential structures | 2.5 | 2.7 | 2.8 | 2.9 | 3.0 | 3.2 | 3.3 |
| (3) property, plant, equipment | 90.2 | 99.1 | 110.5 | 121.1 | 133.0 | 143.0 | 154.7 |
| (4) inventories | 45.3 | 55.1 | 64.9 | 66.1 | 67.9 | 66.3 | 73.0 |
| (5) land | 9.0 | 9.3 | 9.6 | 9.4 | 9.9 | 10.3 | 10.9 |
| (6) Financial assets | 85.6 | 102.4 | 110.5 | 116.0 | 119.1 | 124.6 | 142.1 |
| (7) Long-term debt | 48.1 | 50.9 | 55.1 | 60.8 | 65.1 | 70.2 | 74.9 |
| (8) Short-term debt | 53.7 | 73.9 | 83.9 | 84.1 | 84.6 | 83.8 | 100.7 |
| (9) Net worth | 130.8 | 143.8 | 159.3 | 170.6 | 183.2 | 193.4 | 208.4 |
| (10) change in net worth | 9.7 | 13.0 | 15.5 | 11.3 | 12.6 | 10.2 | 15.0 |
| (11) + dividends | 6.4 | 7.9 | 7.7 | 7.8 | 8.0 | 8.2 | 9.4 |
| (12) − new issues | 1.2 | 1.3 | 2.1 | 2.3 | 1.8 | 1.6 | 1.7 |
| (13) = profits | 14.9 | 19.6 | 21.1 | 16.8 | 18.8 | 16.8 | 22.7 |

## Current Cost Balance Sheet for Nonfinancial Corporations

|  |  |  |  |  |  |  |  |
|---|---|---|---|---|---|---|---|
| (1) Tangible assets | 222.3 | 249.0 | 277.5 | 291.6 | 304.6 | 314.1 | 342.5 |
| (2) residential structures | 5.2 | 5.5 | 5.7 | 5.8 | 5.8 | 5.9 | 6.1 |
| (3) property, plant, equipment | 127.6 | 141.3 | 156.8 | 166.7 | 176.4 | 184.7 | 202.0 |
| (4) inventories | 50.2 | 61.0 | 71.1 | 72.1 | 73.9 | 72.2 | 79.3 |
| (5) land | 39.3 | 41.2 | 43.9 | 47.0 | 48.5 | 51.3 | 55.1 |
| (6) Financial assets | 85.6 | 102.4 | 110.5 | 116.0 | 119.1 | 124.6 | 142.1 |
| (7) Long-term debt | 46.7 | 50.6 | 51.3 | 58.5 | 62.0 | 69.8 | 68.7 |
| (8) Short-term debt | 53.7 | 73.9 | 83.9 | 84.1 | 84.6 | 83.8 | 100.7 |
| (9) Net worth | 207.5 | 226.9 | 252.8 | 265.0 | 277.1 | 285.1 | 315.2 |
| (10) change in net worth | 7.4 | 19.4 | 25.9 | 12.2 | 12.1 | 7.9 | 30.1 |
| (11) + dividends | 6.4 | 7.9 | 7.7 | 7.8 | 8.0 | 8.2 | 9.4 |
| (12) − new issues | 1.2 | 1.3 | 2.1 | 2.3 | 1.8 | 1.6 | 1.7 |
| (13) = profits | 12.6 | 26.0 | 31.5 | 17.7 | 18.3 | 14.5 | 37.8 |

## Alternative Definitions of Income for Nonfinancial Corporations

|  |  |  |  |  |  |  |  |
|---|---|---|---|---|---|---|---|
| (1) Historical | 14.9 | 19.6 | 21.1 | 16.8 | 18.8 | 16.8 | 22.7 |
| (2) Capital maintenance | 12.9 | 11.1 | 17.3 | 13.7 | 14.3 | 13.8 | 19.6 |
| (3) "SEC" | 16.2 | 22.9 | 11.3 | 15.9 | 12.8 | 13.0 | 25.1 |
| (4) "FASB" | 16.0 | 23.3 | 13.2 | 16.2 | 13.3 | 13.4 | 25.8 |
| (5) National Income Accounts | 15.5 | 21.5 | 17.8 | 15.9 | 16.4 | 16.4 | 21.8 |
| (6) Real current cost | 14.4 | 22.0 | 16.3 | 14.7 | 14.1 | 10.7 | 31.5 |
| (7) Nominal current cost | 12.6 | 26.0 | 31.5 | 17.7 | 18.3 | 14.5 | 37.8 |
| (8) Nominal stockholder | 13.5 | 31.0 | 27.3 | 17.1 | 1.1 | 77.8 | 60.9 |
| (9) Real stockholder | 14.3 | 29.2 | 19.5 | 15.4 | −1.3 | 75.8 | 56.1 |

*(Table continues on the following pages)*

**Table 11.2** (continued)

b) 1956-63

|  | 1956 | 1957 | 1958 | 1959 | 1960 | 1961 | 1962 | 1963 |
|---|---|---|---|---|---|---|---|---|
| Historical Balance Sheet for Nonfinancial Corporations | | | | | | | | |
| (1) Tangible assets | 266.0 | 285.2 | 294.5 | 313.8 | 331.3 | 347.3 | 368.2 | 389.3 |
| (2) residential structures | 3.6 | 3.9 | 4.3 | 4.9 | 5.6 | 6.6 | 7.9 | 9.4 |
| (3) property, plant, equipment | 169.8 | 185.8 | 195.5 | 206.4 | 218.5 | 228.7 | 241.1 | 252.9 |
| (4) inventories | 80.5 | 82.6 | 80.3 | 86.5 | 89.7 | 92.4 | 97.8 | 103.7 |
| (5) land | 12.1 | 12.9 | 14.4 | 16.0 | 17.5 | 19.6 | 21.4 | 23.3 |
| (6) Financial assets | 147.2 | 151.9 | 163.5 | 178.7 | 181.7 | 194.6 | 206.6 | 222.2 |
| (7) Long-term debt | 80.1 | 88.1 | 96.6 | 102.6 | 108.7 | 117.4 | 126.4 | 135.1 |
| (8) Short-term debt | 108.8 | 110.3 | 111.8 | 124.2 | 129.9 | 137.1 | 145.0 | 158.5 |
| (9) Net worth | 224.3 | 238.7 | 249.6 | 265.7 | 274.4 | 287.4 | 303.4 | 317.9 |
| (10) change in net worth | 15.9 | 14.4 | 10.9 | 16.1 | 8.7 | 13.0 | 16.0 | 14.5 |
| (11) + dividends | 10.1 | 10.4 | 10.2 | 10.8 | 11.5 | 11.7 | 12.7 | 14.0 |
| (12) − new issues | 2.3 | 2.4 | 2.0 | 2.1 | 1.4 | 2.1 | 0.4 | −0.3 |
| (13) = profits | 23.7 | 22.4 | 19.1 | 24.8 | 18.8 | 22.6 | 28.3 | 28.8 |

Current Cost Balance Sheet for Nonfinancial Corporations

| | | | | | | | | |
|---|---|---|---|---|---|---|---|---|
| (1) Tangible assets | 380.9 | 405.2 | 415.2 | 434.4 | 448.6 | 462.5 | 482.5 | 499.0 |
| (2) residential structures | 6.3 | 6.6 | 7.2 | 7.8 | 8.5 | 9.5 | 10.7 | 12.2 |
| (3) property, plant, equipment | 225.3 | 242.8 | 250.1 | 257.6 | 264.6 | 269.8 | 278.2 | 287.4 |
| (4) inventories | 87.5 | 89.3 | 87.0 | 92.0 | 94.8 | 97.8 | 102.7 | 109.3 |
| (5) land | 61.8 | 66.5 | 70.9 | 77.0 | 80.7 | 85.4 | 90.9 | 90.1 |
| (6) Financial assets | 147.2 | 151.9 | 163.5 | 178.7 | 181.7 | 194.6 | 206.6 | 222.2 |
| (7) Long-term debt | 70.0 | 77.6 | 86.0 | 85.9 | 93.9 | 103.5 | 114.0 | 122.2 |
| (8) Short-term debt | 108.8 | 110.3 | 111.8 | 124.2 | 129.9 | 137.1 | 145.0 | 158.5 |
| (9) Net worth | 349.3 | 369.2 | 380.9 | 403.0 | 406.5 | 416.5 | 430.1 | 440.5 |
| (10) change in net worth | 34.1 | 19.9 | 11.7 | 22.1 | 3.5 | 10.1 | 13.5 | 10.4 |
| (11) + dividends | 10.1 | 10.4 | 10.2 | 10.8 | 11.5 | 11.7 | 12.7 | 14.0 |
| (12) − new issues | 2.3 | 2.4 | 2.0 | 2.1 | 1.4 | 2.1 | 0.4 | −0.3 |
| (13) = profits | 41.9 | 27.9 | 19.9 | 30.8 | 13.6 | 19.7 | 25.8 | 24.7 |

Alternative Definitions of Income for Nonfinancial Corporations

| | | | | | | | | |
|---|---|---|---|---|---|---|---|---|
| (1) Historical | 23.7 | 22.4 | 19.1 | 24.8 | 18.8 | 22.6 | 28.3 | 28.8 |
| (2) Capital maintenance | 19.3 | 19.2 | 16.1 | 22.5 | 17.7 | 21.4 | 30.7 | 31.6 |
| (3) "SEC" | 27.4 | 14.2 | 13.7 | 15.2 | 8.5 | 16.5 | 18.6 | 16.5 |
| (4) "FASB" | 28.7 | 15.8 | 14.4 | 16.3 | 9.5 | 17.0 | 19.8 | 17.6 |
| (5) National Income Accounts | 21.8 | 20.7 | 17.5 | 22.3 | 20.2 | 19.7 | 23.0 | 25.5 |
| (6) Real current cost | 32.2 | 15.7 | 14.3 | 22.0 | 7.2 | 16.0 | 17.9 | 17.9 |
| (7) Nominal current cost | 41.9 | 27.9 | 19.9 | 30.8 | 13.6 | 19.7 | 25.8 | 24.7 |
| (8) Nominal stockholder | 27.8 | −38.7 | 107.8 | 27.9 | 2.9 | 83.8 | −26.8 | 81.2 |
| (9) Real stockholder | 19.5 | −48.8 | 104.2 | 20.0 | −2.9 | 80.6 | −34.9 | 75.0 |

(Table continues on the following pages)

**Table 11.2** (continued)

*c*) 1964–71

|  | 1964 | 1965 | 1966 | 1967 | 1968 | 1969 | 1970 | 1971 |
|---|---|---|---|---|---|---|---|---|
|  | Historical Balance Sheet for Nonfinancial Corporations | | | | | | | |
| (1) Tangible assets | 414.9 | 450.5 | 497.1 | 536.7 | 578.9 | 630.7 | 670.9 | 712.2 |
| (2) residential structures | 10.9 | 12.4 | 13.7 | 14.8 | 16.4 | 18.4 | 20.2 | 22.3 |
| (3) property, plant, equipment | 268.0 | 289.9 | 316.8 | 341.7 | 368.6 | 399.5 | 427.5 | 456.0 |
| (4) inventories | 110.7 | 120.3 | 136.4 | 147.8 | 159.2 | 173.9 | 182.6 | 191.4 |
| (5) land | 25.3 | 27.9 | 30.2 | 32.4 | 34.7 | 38.9 | 40.6 | 42.5 |
| (6) Financial assets | 237.1 | 258.8 | 272.3 | 288.6 | 319.2 | 351.1 | 369.6 | 406.0 |
| (7) Long-term debt | 142.8 | 152.1 | 166.7 | 185.8 | 204.9 | 222.1 | 248.5 | 278.2 |
| (8) Short-term debt | 172.3 | 198.5 | 219.1 | 230.9 | 264.0 | 300.6 | 314.4 | 332.5 |
| (9) Net worth | 336.9 | 358.7 | 383.6 | 408.6 | 429.2 | 459.1 | 477.6 | 507.5 |
| (10) change in net worth | 19.0 | 21.8 | 24.9 | 25.0 | 20.6 | 29.9 | 18.5 | 29.9 |
| (11) + dividends | 15.3 | 17.1 | 18.1 | 18.8 | 20.7 | 20.6 | 19.8 | 20.0 |
| (12) − new issues | 1.1 | 0.0 | 1.3 | 2.4 | −0.2 | 3.4 | 5.7 | 11.4 |
| (13) = profits | 33.2 | 38.9 | 41.7 | 41.4 | 41.5 | 47.1 | 32.6 | 38.5 |

## Current Cost Balance Sheet for Nonfinancial Corporations

|  |  |  |  |  |  |  |  |  |
|---|---|---|---|---|---|---|---|---|
| (1) Tangible assets | 524.8 | 566.6 | 622.5 | 675.8 | 731.3 | 807.5 | 871.5 | 925.7 |
| (2) residential structures | 13.8 | 15.3 | 16.6 | 18.6 | 22.0 | 25.4 | 27.7 | 30.2 |
| (3) property, plant, equipment | 302.0 | 326.9 | 360.9 | 394.6 | 435.3 | 486.1 | 534.0 | 576.4 |
| (4) inventories | 116.5 | 126.7 | 143.1 | 155.9 | 167.7 | 185.0 | 194.1 | 204.5 |
| (5) land | 92.5 | 97.7 | 101.9 | 106.7 | 106.3 | 111.0 | 115.7 | 114.6 |
| (6) Financial assets | 237.1 | 258.8 | 272.3 | 288.6 | 319.2 | 351.1 | 369.6 | 406.0 |
| (7) Long-term debt | 131.8 | 138.9 | 140.7 | 152.5 | 168.5 | 160.2 | 200.7 | 250.2 |
| (8) Short-term debt | 172.3 | 198.5 | 219.1 | 230.9 | 264.0 | 300.6 | 314.4 | 332.5 |
| (9) Net worth | 457.8 | 488.0 | 535.0 | 581.0 | 618.0 | 697.8 | 726.0 | 749.0 |
| (10) change in net worth | 17.3 | 30.2 | 47.0 | 46.0 | 37.0 | 79.9 | 28.1 | 23.1 |
| (11) + dividends | 15.3 | 17.1 | 18.1 | 18.8 | 20.7 | 20.6 | 19.8 | 20.0 |
| (12) − new issues | 1.1 | 0.0 | 1.3 | 2.4 | −0.2 | 3.4 | 5.7 | 11.4 |
| (13) = profits | 31.5 | 47.3 | 63.8 | 62.4 | 57.9 | 97.1 | 42.2 | 31.7 |

## Alternative Definitions of Income for Nonfinancial Corporations

|  |  |  |  |  |  |  |  |  |
|---|---|---|---|---|---|---|---|---|
| (1) Historical | 33.2 | 38.9 | 41.7 | 41.4 | 41.5 | 47.1 | 32.6 | 38.5 |
| (2) Capital maintenance | 36.5 | 42.6 | 47.3 | 47.0 | 48.7 | 53.9 | 39.3 | 44.2 |
| (3) "SEC" | 25.9 | 33.6 | 31.7 | 37.0 | 23.7 | 34.2 | 13.6 | 7.8 |
| (4) "FASB" | 27.1 | 35.6 | 35.6 | 40.8 | 30.6 | 43.0 | 23.8 | 18.1 |
| (5) National Income Accounts | 30.7 | 37.1 | 39.9 | 37.5 | 38.2 | 35.1 | 27.9 | 33.4 |
| (6) Real current cost | 24.9 | 37.2 | 47.2 | 46.9 | 31.1 | 65.5 | 5.3 | −4.6 |
| (7) Nominal current cost | 31.5 | 47.3 | 63.8 | 62.4 | 57.9 | 97.1 | 42.2 | 31.7 |
| (8) Nominal stockholder | 67.6 | 61.3 | −32.7 | 164.0 | 106.1 | −72.9 | 16.6 | 119.7 |
| (9) Real stockholder | 60.8 | 50.1 | −51.5 | 149.4 | 76.1 | −110.5 | −17.7 | 87.2 |

(Table continues on the following pages)

**Table 11.2** (continued)

*d*) 1972–79

Historical Balance Sheet for Nonfinancial Corporations

|  | 1972 | 1973 | 1974 | 1975 | 1976 | 1977 | 1978 | 1979 |
|---|---|---|---|---|---|---|---|---|
| (1) Tangible assets | 765.6 | 850.0 | 965.7 | 1015.9 | 1102.0 | 1212.2 | 1347.7 | 1513.1 |
| (2)  residential structures | 25.1 | 28.5 | 30.5 | 31.0 | 31.4 | 32.1 | 33.3 | 35.3 |
| (3)  property, plant, equipment | 489.2 | 532.7 | 582.0 | 627.7 | 680.1 | 748.8 | 830.3 | 926.9 |
| (4)  inventories | 205.9 | 238.9 | 299.4 | 302.2 | 331.9 | 368.4 | 416.1 | 477.0 |
| (5)  land | 45.4 | 49.9 | 53.8 | 55.0 | 58.6 | 62.9 | 68.0 | 73.9 |
| (6) Financial assets | 455.5 | 526.0 | 516.7 | 557.6 | 610.4 | 664.8 | 756.7 | 869.9 |
| (7) Long-term debt | 307.9 | 337.0 | 371.9 | 413.0 | 451.7 | 495.3 | 541.4 | 590.1 |
| (8) Short-term debt | 373.1 | 456.1 | 443.9 | 438.9 | 473.8 | 531.7 | 631.5 | 765.7 |
| (9) Net worth | 540.1 | 582.9 | 666.6 | 721.6 | 786.9 | 850.0 | 931.5 | 1027.2 |
| (10) change in net worth | 32.6 | 42.8 | 83.7 | 55.0 | 65.3 | 63.1 | 81.5 | 95.7 |
| (11) + dividends | 21.6 | 23.8 | 25.9 | 28.3 | 32.9 | 37.0 | 41.6 | 46.8 |
| (12) − new issues | 10.9 | 7.9 | 4.1 | 9.9 | 10.5 | 2.7 | 2.6 | 3.5 |
| (13) = profits | 43.3 | 58.7 | 105.5 | 73.4 | 87.7 | 97.4 | 120.5 | 139.0 |

Current Cost Balance Sheet for Nonfinancial Corporations

| | | | | | | | | |
|---|---|---|---|---|---|---|---|---|
| (1) Tangible assets | 1008.9 | 1166.1 | 1393.9 | 1512.7 | 1649.7 | 1815.3 | 2045.7 | 2344.2 |
| (2) residential structures | 34.7 | 41.3 | 46.7 | 50.3 | 54.7 | 61.5 | 69.3 | 78.4 |
| (3) property, plant, equipment | 625.5 | 717.3 | 847.6 | 947.5 | 1026.7 | 1124.3 | 1256.8 | 1422.1 |
| (4) inventories | 221.2 | 264.0 | 336.1 | 338.2 | 373.9 | 416.7 | 478.5 | 571.5 |
| (5) land | 127.5 | 143.5 | 163.5 | 176.7 | 194.4 | 212.8 | 241.1 | 272.2 |
| (6) Financial assets | 455.5 | 526.0 | 516.7 | 557.6 | 610.4 | 664.8 | 756.7 | 869.9 |
| (7) Long-term debt | 281.7 | 288.8 | 283.9 | 347.5 | 438.3 | 461.3 | 467.9 | 470.7 |
| (8) Short-term debt | 373.1 | 456.1 | 443.9 | 438.9 | 473.8 | 531.7 | 631.5 | 765.7 |
| (9) Net worth | 809.6 | 947.2 | 1182.8 | 1283.9 | 1348.0 | 1487.1 | 1703.0 | 1977.7 |
| (10) change in net worth | 60.6 | 137.5 | 235.6 | 101.2 | 64.1 | 139.1 | 215.8 | 274.8 |
| (11) + dividends | 21.6 | 23.8 | 25.9 | 28.3 | 32.9 | 37.0 | 41.6 | 46.8 |
| (12) − new issues | 10.9 | 7.9 | 4.1 | 9.9 | 10.5 | 2.7 | 2.6 | 3.5 |
| (13) = profits | 71.3 | 153.4 | 257.4 | 119.6 | 86.5 | 173.4 | 254.8 | 318.1 |

Alternative Definitions of Income for Nonfinancial Corporations

| | | | | | | | | |
|---|---|---|---|---|---|---|---|---|
| (1) Historical | 43.3 | 58.7 | 105.5 | 73.4 | 87.7 | 97.4 | 120.5 | 139.0 |
| (2) Capital maintenance | 48.9 | 57.4 | 89.9 | 77.8 | 75.3 | 91.9 | 114.1 | 124.0 |
| (3) "SEC" | 34.2 | 73.0 | 109.2 | 6.8 | 61.5 | 57.1 | 81.1 | 96.2 |
| (4) "FASB" | 43.7 | 88.5 | 137.0 | 35.3 | 77.5 | 78.1 | 111.9 | 138.0 |
| (5) National Income Accounts | 42.2 | 52.6 | 60.2 | 60.4 | 77.2 | 83.9 | 97.3 | 115.2 |
| (6) Real current cost | 39.9 | 106.5 | 169.3 | 4.9 | 21.0 | 95.2 | 144.8 | 171.6 |
| (7) Nominal current cost | 71.3 | 153.4 | 257.4 | 119.6 | 86.5 | 173.4 | 254.8 | 318.1 |
| (8) Nominal stockholder | 108.5 | −161.4 | −157.9 | 207.3 | 184.2 | −20.2 | 99.4 | 162.9 |
| (9) Real stockholder | 76.6 | −211.2 | −221.2 | 158.7 | 149.0 | −69.6 | 40.4 | 89.1 |

**Table 11.3**    Average Tax Rates, Alternative Rates of Return, and Tobin's $q$ for Nonfinancial Corporations, 1949–79

a) 1949–55

| | 1949 | 1950 | 1951 | 1952 | 1953 | 1954 | 1955 |
|---|---|---|---|---|---|---|---|
| **Alternative Tax Rates** | | | | | | | |
| (1) Historical | 0.3843 | 0.4615 | 0.5000 | 0.5144 | 0.4946 | 0.4815 | 0.4709 |
| (2) Capital maintenance | 0.4198 | 0.6016 | 0.5493 | 0.5642 | 0.5629 | 0.5304 | 0.5071 |
| (3) "SEC" | 0.3653 | 0.4234 | 0.6509 | 0.5287 | 0.5891 | 0.5448 | 0.4460 |
| (4) "FASB" | 0.3674 | 0.4189 | 0.6147 | 0.5233 | 0.5800 | 0.5371 | 0.4389 |
| (5) National Income Accounts | 0.3750 | 0.4386 | 0.5424 | 0.5282 | 0.5287 | 0.4875 | 0.4810 |
| (6) Real current cost | 0.3926 | 0.4329 | 0.5639 | 0.5476 | 0.5667 | 0.5942 | 0.3903 |
| (7) Nominal current cost | 0.4249 | 0.3930 | 0.4010 | 0.5008 | 0.5013 | 0.5177 | 0.3482 |
| (8) Nominal stockholder | 0.4079 | 0.3515 | 0.4360 | 0.5100 | 0.9436 | 0.1670 | 0.2491 |
| (9) Real stockholder | 0.3948 | 0.3648 | 0.5199 | 0.5355 | 1.0759 | 0.1707 | 0.2646 |
| **Alternative Rates of Return** | | | | | | | |
| (1) Historical | 0.1230 | 0.1498 | 0.1467 | 0.1055 | 0.1102 | 0.0917 | 0.1174 |
| (2) Capital maintenance | 0.0652 | 0.0540 | 0.0764 | 0.0552 | 0.0544 | 0.0504 | 0.0690 |
| (3) "SEC" | 0.0820 | 0.1110 | 0.0499 | 0.0637 | 0.0489 | 0.0476 | 0.0881 |
| (4) "FASB" | 0.0813 | 0.1131 | 0.0584 | 0.0651 | 0.0507 | 0.0491 | 0.0907 |
| (5) National Income Accounts | 0.1280 | 0.1644 | 0.1238 | 0.0998 | 0.0961 | 0.0895 | 0.1127 |
| (6) Real current cost | 0.0719 | 0.1061 | 0.0719 | 0.0582 | 0.0531 | 0.0384 | 0.1107 |
| (7) Nominal current cost | 0.0629 | 0.1251 | 0.1389 | 0.0702 | 0.0691 | 0.0524 | 0.1327 |
| (8) Nominal stockholder | 0.1609 | 0.3362 | 0.2341 | 0.1236 | 0.0073 | 0.5373 | 0.2819 |
| (9) Real stockholder | 0.1699 | 0.3172 | 0.1671 | 0.1116 | −0.0087 | 0.5233 | 0.2599 |
| **Alternative Measures of Tobin's $q$** | | | | | | | |
| (1) Traditional (net of fin. assets) | 0.4813 | 0.5572 | 0.5875 | 0.6052 | 0.5656 | 0.7802 | 0.8658 |
| (2) Net of inventories | 0.3300 | 0.4135 | 0.4454 | 0.4756 | 0.4264 | 0.7145 | 0.8253 |
| (3) Inventories at 90 cents | 0.3592 | 0.4460 | 0.4798 | 0.5084 | 0.4585 | 0.7444 | 0.8555 |
| (4) Inventories at 75 cents | 0.4029 | 0.4947 | 0.5315 | 0.5577 | 0.5065 | 0.7892 | 0.9007 |

b) 1956–63

| | 1956 | 1957 | 1958 | 1959 | 1960 | 1961 | 1962 | 1963 |
|---|---|---|---|---|---|---|---|---|
| **Alternative Tax Rates** | | | | | | | | |
| (1) Historical | 0.4577 | 0.4602 | 0.4574 | 0.4549 | 0.5053 | 0.4619 | 0.4213 | 0.4408 |
| (2) Capital maintenance | 0.5090 | 0.4983 | 0.5004 | 0.4791 | 0.5202 | 0.4750 | 0.4013 | 0.4177 |
| (3) "SEC" | 0.4221 | 0.5741 | 0.5399 | 0.5774 | 0:6919 | 0.5410 | 0.5253 | 0.5794 |
| (4) "FASB" | 0.4109 | 0.5473 | 0.5279 | 0.5601 | 0.6699 | 0.5329 | 0.5093 | 0.5630 |
| (5) National Income Accounts | 0.4785 | 0.4799 | 0.4792 | 0.4814 | 0.4873 | 0.4962 | 0.4725 | 0.4710 |
| (6) Real current cost | 0.3835 | 0.5492 | 0.5290 | 0.4845 | 0.7280 | 0.5479 | 0.5349 | 0.5597 |
| (7) Nominal current cost | 0.3230 | 0.4064 | 0.4475 | 0.4021 | 0.5850 | 0.4966 | 0.4437 | 0.4785 |
| (8) Nominal stockholder | 0.4184 | -0.9745 | 0.1299 | 0.4259 | 0.8688 | 0.1880 | -3.3225 | 0.2185 |
| (9) Real stockholder | 0.5069 | -0.6426 | 0.1339 | 0.5082 | 1.1765 | 0.1940 | -1.4368 | 0.2324 |
| **Alternative Rates of Return** | | | | | | | | |
| (1) Historical | 0.1137 | 0.0999 | 0.0800 | 0.0994 | 0.0708 | 0.0824 | 0.0985 | 0.0949 |
| (2) Capital maintenance | 0.0624 | 0.0567 | 0.0448 | 0.0608 | 0.0458 | 0.0547 | 0.0763 | 0.0758 |
| (3) "SEC" | 0.0886 | 0.0418 | 0.0383 | 0.0409 | 0.0221 | 0.0420 | 0.0462 | 0.0395 |
| (4) "FASB" | 0.0928 | 0.0466 | 0.0401 | 0.0439 | 0.0245 | 0.0434 | 0.0493 | 0.0422 |
| (5) National Income Accounts | 0.1046 | 0.0923 | 0.0733 | 0.0893 | 0.0760 | 0.0718 | 0.0800 | 0.0840 |
| (6) Real current cost | 0.1020 | 0.0449 | 0.0388 | 0.0578 | 0.0178 | 0.0394 | 0.0430 | 0.0415 |
| (7) Nominal current cost | 0.1330 | 0.0799 | 0.0538 | 0.0808 | 0.0338 | 0.0484 | 0.0620 | 0.0575 |
| (8) Nominal stockholder | 0.1033 | -0.1338 | 0.4445 | 0.0816 | 0.0080 | 0.2367 | -0.0626 | 0.2086 |
| (9) Real stockholder | 0.0723 | -0.1688 | 0.4295 | 0.0586 | -0.0080 | 0.2277 | -0.0816 | 0.1926 |
| **Alternative Measures of Tobin's q** | | | | | | | | |
| (1) Traditional (net of fin. assets) | 0.8422 | 0.6873 | 0.9066 | 0.9041 | 0.8833 | 1.0254 | 0.9153 | 1.0313 |
| (2) Net of inventories | 0.7952 | 0.5989 | 0.8819 | 0.8784 | 0.8520 | 1.0323 | 0.8924 | 1.0400 |
| (3) Inventories at 90 cents | 0.8250 | 0.6272 | 0.9084 | 0.9052 | 0.8788 | 1.0591 | 0.9195 | 1.0681 |
| (4) Inventories at 75 cents | 0.8697 | 0.6696 | 0.9481 | 0.9455 | 0.9190 | 1.0993 | 0.9600 | 1.1101 |

(Table continues on the following pages)

**Table 11.3** (continued)

c) 1964–71

| | 1964 | 1965 | 1966 | 1967 | 1968 | 1969 | 1970 | 1971 |
|---|---|---|---|---|---|---|---|---|
| **Alternative Tax Rates** | | | | | | | | |
| (1) Historical | 0.4186 | 0.4106 | 0.4135 | 0.4000 | 0.4467 | 0.4135 | 0.4548 | 0.4363 |
| (2) Capital maintenance | 0.3959 | 0.3887 | 0.3835 | 0.3699 | 0.4076 | 0.3814 | 0.4087 | 0.4025 |
| (3) "SEC" | 0.4798 | 0.4468 | 0.4809 | 0.4269 | 0.5855 | 0.4925 | 0.6666 | 0.7920 |
| (4) "FASB" | 0.4688 | 0.4324 | 0.4523 | 0.4037 | 0.5226 | 0.4359 | 0.5328 | 0.6226 |
| (5) National Income Accounts | 0.4377 | 0.4221 | 0.4242 | 0.4240 | 0.4672 | 0.4861 | 0.4936 | 0.4715 |
| (6) Real current cost | 0.4900 | 0.4211 | 0.3838 | 0.3705 | 0.5183 | 0.3363 | 0.8381 | 1.1847 |
| (7) Nominal current cost | 0.4316 | 0.3641 | 0.3154 | 0.3066 | 0.3667 | 0.2549 | 0.3917 | 0.4849 |
| (8) Nominal stockholder | 0.2612 | 0.3066 | −8.9087 | 0.1441 | 0.2400 | −0.8363 | 0.6210 | 0.1993 |
| (9) Real stockholder | 0.2823 | 0.3511 | −1.3288 | 0.1560 | 0.3056 | −0.4296 | 2.8589 | 0.2546 |
| **Alternative Rates of Return** | | | | | | | | |
| (1) Historical | 0.1044 | 0.1155 | 0.1163 | 0.1079 | 0.1016 | 0.1097 | 0.0710 | 0.0806 |
| (2) Capital maintenance | 0.0853 | 0.0954 | 0.0995 | 0.0924 | 0.0889 | 0.0926 | 0.0619 | 0.0652 |
| (3) "SEC" | 0.0606 | 0.0751 | 0.0668 | 0.0728 | 0.0433 | 0.0588 | 0.0214 | 0.0115 |
| (4) "FASB" | 0.0633 | 0.0796 | 0.0750 | 0.0801 | 0.0559 | 0.0739 | 0.0375 | 0.0266 |
| (5) National Income Accounts | 0.0966 | 0.1101 | 0.1112 | 0.0978 | 0.0935 | 0.0818 | 0.0608 | 0.0699 |
| (6) Real current cost | 0.0565 | 0.0814 | 0.0967 | 0.0877 | 0.0536 | 0.1060 | 0.0075 | −0.0064 |
| (7) Nominal current cost | 0.0715 | 0.1034 | 0.1307 | 0.1167 | 0.0996 | 0.1570 | 0.0605 | 0.0436 |
| (8) Nominal stockholder | 0.1482 | 0.1203 | −0.0591 | 0.3253 | 0.1628 | −0.0989 | 0.0257 | 0.1843 |
| (9) Real stockholder | 0.1332 | 0.0983 | −0.0931 | 0.2963 | 0.1168 | −0.1499 | −0.0273 | 0.1343 |
| **Alternative Measures of Tobin's q** | | | | | | | | |
| (1) Traditional (net of fin. assets) | 1.0985 | 1.1160 | 0.9505 | 1.1047 | 1.1628 | 0.9369 | 0.9121 | 1.0124 |
| (2) Net of inventories | 1.1267 | 1.1493 | 0.9357 | 1.1362 | 1.2112 | 0.9182 | 0.8870 | 1.0159 |
| (3) Inventories at 90 cents | 1.1552 | 1.1782 | 0.9656 | 1.1661 | 1.2410 | 0.9479 | 0.9156 | 1.0443 |
| (4) Inventories at 75 cents | 1.1980 | 1.2214 | 1.0104 | 1.2111 | 1.2856 | 0.9925 | 0.9586 | 1.0868 |

d) 1972–79

| | 1972 | 1973 | 1974 | 1975 | 1976 | 1977 | 1978 | 1979 |
|---|---|---|---|---|---|---|---|---|
| Alternative Tax Rates | | | | | | | | |
| (1) Historical | 0.4355 | 0.4016 | 0.2872 | 0.3544 | 0.3740 | 0.3788 | 0.3628 | 0.3499 |
| (2) Capital maintenance | 0.4060 | 0.4071 | 0.3210 | 0.3411 | 0.4104 | 0.3926 | 0.3755 | 0.3763 |
| (3) "SEC" | 0.4939 | 0.3506 | 0.2802 | 0.8558 | 0.4602 | 0.5098 | 0.4583 | 0.4375 |
| (4) "FASB" | 0.4332 | 0.3081 | 0.2368 | 0.5328 | 0.4033 | 0.4319 | 0.3801 | 0.3516 |
| (5) National Income Accounts | 0.4418 | 0.4283 | 0.4138 | 0.4002 | 0.4043 | 0.4145 | 0.4135 | 0.3937 |
| (6) Real current cost | 0.4559 | 0.2701 | 0.2007 | 0.8924 | 0.7140 | 0.3841 | 0.3215 | 0.3036 |
| (7) Nominal current cost | 0.3189 | 0.2043 | 0.1417 | 0.2521 | 0.3773 | 0.2551 | 0.2121 | 0.1904 |
| (8) Nominal stockholder | 0.2354 | −0.3230 | −0.3683 | 0.1628 | 0.2215 | 1.5153 | 0.4083 | 0.3147 |
| (9) Real stockholder | 0.3037 | −0.2294 | −0.2378 | 0.2025 | 0.2602 | −5.8144 | 0.6294 | 0.4563 |
| Alternative Rates of Return | | | | | | | | |
| (1) Historical | 0.0853 | 0.1087 | 0.1810 | 0.1101 | 0.1215 | 0.1238 | 0.1418 | 0.1492 |
| (2) Capital maintenance | 0.0678 | 0.0733 | 0.1000 | 0.0711 | 0.0618 | 0.0689 | 0.0785 | 0.0761 |
| (3) "SEC" | 0.0475 | 0.0932 | 0.1214 | 0.0062 | 0.0504 | 0.0428 | 0.0558 | 0.0590 |
| (4) "FASB" | 0.0606 | 0.1129 | 0.1524 | 0.0323 | 0.0636 | 0.0585 | 0.0770 | 0.0847 |
| (5) National Income Accounts | 0.0832 | 0.0974 | 0.1033 | 0.0906 | 0.1070 | 0.1066 | 0.1145 | 0.1237 |
| (6) Real current cost | 0.0532 | 0.1315 | 0.1788 | 0.0041 | 0.0163 | 0.0706 | 0.0974 | 0.1008 |
| (7) Nominal current cost | 0.0952 | 0.1895 | 0.2718 | 0.1011 | 0.0673 | 0.1286 | 0.1714 | 0.1868 |
| (8) Nominal stockholder | 0.1427 | −0.1880 | −0.2319 | 0.4135 | 0.2669 | −0.0237 | 0.1246 | 0.1899 |
| (9) Real stockholder | 0.1007 | −0.2460 | −0.3249 | 0.3165 | 0.2159 | −0.0817 | 0.0506 | 0.1039 |
| Alternative Measures of Tobin's q | | | | | | | | |
| (1) Traditional (net of fin. assets) | 1.0482 | 0.7718 | 0.5111 | 0.6075 | 0.6993 | 0.6201 | 0.5869 | 0.5733 |
| (2) Net of inventories | 1.0618 | 0.7050 | 0.3558 | 0.4945 | 0.6112 | 0.5069 | 0.4608 | 0.4358 |
| (3) Inventories at 90 cents | 1.0899 | 0.7342 | 0.3876 | 0.5233 | 0.6405 | 0.5367 | 0.4913 | 0.4680 |
| (4) Inventories at 75 cents | 1.1320 | 0.7781 | 0.4352 | 0.5665 | 0.6845 | 0.5814 | 0.5371 | 0.5164 |

are important, and not captured by any of our accounting measures. However, it should be pointed out that these adjustments are not due to price level changes but rather to specific price movements.

## 11.7    Conclusion

In this paper we have reviewed the basics of adjusting nonfinancial corporate profit figures for inflation, and have utilized a new data source to compute alternative measures of adjusted profits, corporate rates of return, and $q$ series. We have argued that partial procedures for adjusting income figures such as those required by the FASB and the SEC are misleading in terms of determining the difference between real and nominal profits. We propose using the balance sheet approach to systematically adjust income reporting.

We have found that real accrued corporate profits are far more volatile than those reported in the National Income Accounts. Further, and more interesting, perhaps, is the fact that real accrued profits have actually exceeded those presented by the NIA in the more recent inflationary years, reversing the relative relationship of the 1950s and 1960s. The most striking aspect of our new $q$ estimates, based on the new national balance sheet data, is that they are generally lower than those previously published.

# Notes

1. We would like to thank Larry Summers of MIT for making us aware of these data and Elizabeth Fogler of the Federal Reserve for helping us obtain the information.

2. Against the usefulness of inflation-adjusted corporate figures must be weighed the cost of obtaining them. There are no estimates of these figures to the best of our knowledge.

3. Bonds that never mature, termed "consols," need not return to par, however.

4. A similar argument can be made about depreciation deductions. When a firm purchases an asset, it also acquires a stream of depreciation deductions based on the historical cost of the asset and (perhaps) an investment tax credit. These depreciation deductions are thus nominal assets held by the firm. As with nominal debt obligations, the values of these deductions are affected by general inflation and by changes in nominal adjustments to a firm's balance sheet for depreciation. However, there are complications. First, it is difficult to separate the value of depreciation deductions from the rest of an asset's worth, based simply on currently available data. Second, if depreciation rules do not change from year to year, a decrease in the present value of depreciation deductions on new assets (in the presence of an increase in inflation and nominal interest rates) would make new investment less attractive, leading to a decrease in the amount of new investment and an increase in the present value of rents for assets already in place. Finally, the value of the depreciation asset depends on the present and future corporate tax rate.

5. The SEC rquires firms with inventories and gross property, plant, and equipment in excess of $100 million to submit the supplementary inflation accounting information. The

FASB regulations apply only to slightly larger firms—those having inventories, gross property, plant, and equipment of $125 million or more, measured at the beginning of the fiscal year. Further, even if these gross tangible assets do not meet this criterion, if total assets are over $1 billion, the reporting requirements must be met.

6. The recoverable amount is an estimate of the net realized value of an asset subject to near-term sale or the net present value of expected cash flows derived from an asset that is to be used in business operations.

7. Because of data limitations, we could not discriminate between current cost and replacement cost valuations.

# References

Beaver, W. 1979. Accounting for inflation in an efficient market. In *Impact of inflation on accounting: A global view*, pp. 21–42. Urbana: University of Illinois.

Bulow, J. I. 1979. Analysis of pension funding under ERISA. NBER Working Paper No. 402, November.

Deloitte, Haskins, and Sells. 1979. *Financial reporting and changing prices: Supplementary disclosure requirements of FASB Statement No. 33.* New York.

Federal Reserve System, Board of Governors, Flow of Funds Section, Division of Research and Statistics. 1980. Balance sheets for the U.S. economy. Unpublished data mimeo, June.

Financial Accounting Standards Board. 1979. Illustrations of financial reporting and changing prices: Statement of Financial Accounting Standards No. 33. Stamford, Conn., December.

Shoven, J., and Bulow, J. 1975. Inflation accounting and nonfinancial corporate profits: Physical assets. *Brookings Papers on Economic Activity* 3: 557–611.

———. 1976. Inflation accounting and nonfinancial profits: Financial assets and liabilities. *Brookings Papers on Economic Activity* 1: 15–66.

# 12 The Anatomy of Double-Digit Inflation in the 1970s

Alan S. Blinder

## 12.1 Introduction and Summary

The 1970s was the decade of inflation in the United States. While it may be surprising to some that the average inflation rate for the decade as a whole was only 6.8%, this rate is double the long-run historical average and nearly triple the rate of the previous two decades (see table 12.1). In addition to the high *average* inflation rate, we were plagued by extremely *variable* inflation rates during the 1970s. In both respects, the 1970s had much in common with the 1940s and were very different from the 1960s (see table 12.1 again).

This paper seeks to explain inflation in the 1970s, and especially the two episodes of "double-digit" inflation: 1974 and 1979–80. There are many parallels between the 1973–75 period and the 1978–80 period. The underlying nature of the two inflationary episodes was much the same; food and energy "shocks" precipitated both. In both periods, inflation was very uneven; some prices rose extremely rapidly while others rose moderately. Thus the inflation of the 1970s was accompanied by substantial changes in relative prices. The direction of causation here is not obvious; indeed, causation is unlikely to have been entirely unidirectional. While it is now part of the conventional wisdom that high rates of inflation cause changes in relative prices, I wish to propound the view here that the lines of causation during the 1970s ran mostly the other way: large unavoidable adjustments in relative prices bred inflation.

Alan S. Blinder is professor of economics at Princeton University and a research associate of the National Bureau of Economic Research.

The opinions expressed are those of the author and not the NBER or the National Science Foundation. Research assistance from Danny Quah and helpful comments from the members of the NBER Project on Inflation are gratefully acknowledged.

Table 12.1          Historical Inflation Data, 1930–80

| Period | Mean Inflation Rate | Standard Deviation |
|--------|---------------------|--------------------|
| 1930–40 | −1.10% | 5.73 |
| 1940–50 | 6.35% | 3.47 |
| 1950–60 | 2.38% | 1.52 |
| 1960–70 | 2.56% | 1.29 |
| 1970–80 | 6.85% | 2.20 |
| 1930–80 | 3.41% | 4.38 |

Source: Bureau of Economic Analysis.
Note: Based on implicit deflator for personal consumption expenditures, annual data.

The paper is organized as follows. After some general introductory remarks on analyzing inflation (section 12.2), section 12.3 offers a brief rundown of the major events that conspired to produce double-digit inflation in 1974. For the most part, this section is an overly terse summary of a recent book of mine on the Great Stagflation of the mid-1970s (Blinder 1979, especially chapters 5 and 6). Readers seeking further details are referred to the book. Section 12.4, by far the longest of the paper, chronicles in much more detail—because it has not been chronicled before—the burst of inflation in 1978–80, pointing out similarities to and contrasts with the earlier episode. Finally, section 12.5 deals with an objection that has often been raised to the type of inflation analysis presented here: if relative price shocks "caused" the inflation of the 1970s, why did they not also cause rapid inflation in the 1950s and 1960s? I will argue that, the theorist's desire for tidiness and uniformity notwithstanding, the 1970s really were different.

A list of some of the major conclusions may be useful at the outset.

1. The dramatic acceleration of inflation between 1972 and 1974 can be traced mainly to three "shocks": rising food prices, rising energy prices, and the end of the Nixon wage-price controls program. Each of these can be conceptualized as requiring rapid adjustments of some relative prices.

2. The equally dramatic deceleration of inflation between 1974 and 1976 can be traced to the simple fact that the three factors just named were not repeated. In other words, double-digit inflation went away "by itself."

3. The state of demand thus had precious little to do with either the acceleration or the deceleration of inflation between 1972 and 1976. This is not to say that aggregate demand management was irrelevant to inflation, but only that it effects were minor compared to the supply shocks.

4. While the rate of inflation as measured in the CPI rose about eight percentage points between 1977 and early 1980, the "baseline," or "underlying," rate may have risen by as little as three percentage points. The rest of the inflationary acceleration came from "special factors."

5. The initial impetus for accelerating inflation in 1978 came mainly from the food sector, with some help from mortgage interest rates. The further acceleration into the double-digit range in 1979 mainly reflected soaring energy prices and, once again, rising mortgage rates. Finally, mortgage interest carried the ball almost by itself in early 1980.

6. The 1970s really were different. Energy shocks are quite clearly a product of the brave, new post–OPEC world. Food shocks are not new. We experienced them in the 1940s, but somehow managed to get away without them in the 1950s and 1960s.

## 12.2   The Two Inflations

Before marshaling the evidence, it will be useful to outline a conceptual framework into which the facts can be fitted. I claim, and will try to document in what follows, that the data support a story about inflation in the contemporary United States that goes something like this.[1]

1. At any given moment, there is a normal, or "baseline," inflation rate toward which the actual inflation rate tends to gravitate. (This rate is also referred to as the "underlying," or "core," rate of inflation.) This baseline rate is determined by fundamental economic forces, basically as the difference between the growth rates of aggregate demand and aggregate supply.

2. On the demand side, the weight of the historical evidence is that the growth rate of money is the dominant factor in the long run. It is in this very limited sense that Milton Friedman's famous dictum "Inflation is always and everywhere a monetary phenomenon" has some validity. However, other factors like fiscal policy also influence the growth rate of aggregate demand. On the supply side, the fundamental long-run force is the trend rate of change of productivity, though occasional abrupt restrictions in aggregate supply (so-called supply shocks) can dominate the supply picture over short periods.

3. For empirical purposes, the baseline rate of inflation can be measured either by the rate of change of wages minus the trend rate of change of productivity[2] or by the rate of change of prices exclusive of food prices, energy prices, and mortgage interest rates. The latter measure of baseline inflation is relied upon here.

4. The observed rate of inflation can deviate markedly from the baseline rate over short periods. The major reasons for such deviations are obvious from the empirical definition of the baseline rate. Rapid in-

creases in food or energy prices, or run-ups in mortgage interest rates, can push inflation above the baseline rate for a while. Conversely, unusual moderation or declines in food or energy prices, or a serious recession, can pull inflation below the baseline rate. There are other special one-shot factors as well. For example, the Nixon price controls played a major role in the 1973–75 episode.

Despite the cacophony of complaints about "ruinous" budget deficits and "excessive" monetary growth, the headline-grabbing double-digit inflations of 1974 and 1979–80 were mainly of the special-factor variety. Only a minor fraction of each inflationary acceleration can be attributed to changes in the baseline rate; the rest came from supply shocks from the food and energy sectors, from mortgage interest rates, and from the end of price controls—a whole host of special one-shot factors. It is precisely this aspect of the recent inflation that this paper seeks to document.

Since the paper focuses on the special factors to the exclusion of the baseline rate, it is worth pointing out at the outset that the two inflations are not really independent. Inflation from special factors can "get into" the baseline rate if it causes an acceleration of wage growth. At this point policymakers face an agonizing choice—the so-called accommodation issue. To the extent that aggregate nominal demand is *not* expanded to accommodate the higher wages and prices, unemployment and slack capacity will result. There will be a recession. On the other hand, to the extent that aggregate demand *is* expanded (say, by raising the growth rate of money above previous targets), inflation from the special factor will get built into the baseline rate.

This analysis of the interaction between special factors and the baseline rate, I believe, helps us understand why baseline inflation, which was perhaps 1–2% in the early 1960s, rose to perhaps 4–5% by the early 1970s, and to perhaps 9–10% by 1980. But the evolution of the baseline rate is not the subject of this paper. My focus here is squarely on understanding the sudden accelerations of inflation into the double-digit range in 1974 and again in 1979, and the subsequent decelerations. For this purpose, I shall argue, it is almost unnecessary to worry about changes in the (slowly evolving) baseline rate.

## 12.3   The Inflationary Bulge of 1973–75

Though we have now become somewhat inured to such things, I think it fair to say that Americans were stunned by the first bout of double-digit inflation, the one that took place in 1974. The Consumer Price Index (CPI) is without a doubt the most closely watched barometer of prices, and the northwest quadrant of table 12.2 shows that inflation as measured by the CPI skyrocketed from only 3.4% in 1972 to 12.2% in 1974. Then it fell

Table 12.2    Inflation Rates in United States, 1972–80

|  | All Items | | Excluding Food and Energy | |
|---|---|---|---|---|
|  | CPI[a] | PCE[b] | CPI[a] | PCE[b] |
| 1972 | 3.4% | 3.7% | 3.0% | 3.3% |
| 1973 | 8.8% | 7.3% | 4.7% | 4.4% |
| 1974 | 12.2% | 11.0% | 11.3% | 9.6% |
| 1975 | 7.0% | 6.0% | 6.7% | 5.7% |
| 1976 | 4.8% | 5.0% | 6.1% | 6.0% |
| 1977 | 6.8% | 5.9% | 6.4% | 6.1% |
| 1978 | 9.0% | 7.8% | 8.5% | 6.8% |
| 1979 | 13.3% | 9.5% | 11.3% | 7.1% |
| 1980: |  |  |  |  |
| First half | 14.8% | 11.0% | 14.6% | 9.7% |
| Second half | 9.9% | 9.1% | 9.6% | 8.5% |

[a]Twelve months ending in December of given year.
[b]Four quarters ending in fourth quarter of given year.

almost as rapidly as it had risen, reaching 4.8% in 1976. The deflator for personal consumption expenditures (PCE) from the National Income Accounts exhibits similar behavior.

The reasons for this performance can be summarized in three words, none of which is "money": food, energy, and decontrol. The boom of 1972–73 and the bust of 1974–75 notwithstanding, these three shocks *alone* can account for almost all of the acceleration *and* deceleration of inflation in that period. While aggregate demand did play some role in the accelerating inflation of 1973–74 and the decelerating inflation of 1975–76, its role was minor compared with that of the three aforementioned factors.

## 12.3.1   The Food Shock

Bad weather conditions both in the United States and, more importantly, in much of the rest of the world sent retail food prices soaring in 1973. The CPI for food, which had risen less than 5% during 1972, increased 20% during 1973 and 12% during 1974. This constituted a major supply shock whose importance, I believe, has still not been adequately appreciated.

Compare, for example, the inflation rates in the northwest and northeast quadrants of table 12.2. Using the CPI, the inflation rate increased 5.4 percentage points from 1972 to 1973. But if food and energy prices are excluded, the remaining acceleration was only 1.7 percentage points. When we remember that energy prices became a factor only in the closing months of 1973, it becomes clear that food prices accounted for most of this large discrepancy. In fact, the impact of food price increases on overall inflation probably is even larger than table 12.2 suggests. Food price increases, we may assume, get reflected in higher wages, and the resulting wage-price spiral pushes prices still higher. In Blinder (1979), I made some rough estimates of the *total* effects of food prices on inflation, including both the *direct* effects that result from the fact that food is an important component of the CPI and the *indirect* effects operating through the wage-price spiral. These estimates suggest that food prices accounted for about 5 percentage points of the overall annual rate of inflation between mid-1973 and mid-1975. Some perspective on this is provided by recalling that a 5% *total* inflation rate was, until quite recently, considered extraordinarily high for the United States.

### 12.3.2   The Energy Shock

As is well known, the solidification of the Organization of Petroleum Exporting Countries (OPEC) following the Arab-Israeli conflict in October 1973 led to a quadrupling of the price of imported crude oil within a very few months. While this was an inflationary shock of the first rank, I think it important, especially in drawing comparisons with 1979, not to exaggerate the inflationary impact of the 1973–74 energy shock.

A direct comparison between the 1974 and 1979 OPEC shocks is postponed to section 12.4, but a hint that the direct inflationary consequences of the energy shock were not nearly as great as those of the food shock can be seen in table 12.2. Inflation rates with and without food and energy prices are much closer together in 1974 (when energy was the major factor) than in 1973 (when food was the major factor).

Having issued this disclaimer, I feel compelled to repeat the obvious: energy prices *were* a major engine of inflation in late 1973 and early 1974. Calculations I made in Blinder (1979) suggest that the *direct* effects of higher energy prices on the PCE deflator raised the latter about 2.4% between 1973:3 and 1974:3. Most of this effect came within two quarters. To this must be added an (admittedly crude) estimate of the energy costs "embodied" in other consumer goods. Perry (1975) estimated this to be another 1% or so, bringing the total energy shock to the overall price level up to about 3.5%. Indirect effects through the wage-price spiral appear to have been roughly canceled out by the downward pull of the recession on inflation, so that my final estimates of the effects of higher energy prices on the *level* of the PCE deflator were 3%, 3.5%, and 4.5% as of the third quarter of 1974, 1975, and 1976, respectively.[3] Other researchers have come up with similar estimates.

### 12.3.3   Wage-Price Controls

Despite their obvious importance, it is quite clear from table 12.2 that food and energy prices alone cannot explain the acceleration and deceleration of inflation in 1974–75; the ups and downs are just as pronounced when food and energy prices are excluded as when they are included. However, it is not hard to find the culprit behind the gyrating inflation rate for nonfood, nonenergy prices: the imposition and subsequent demise of wage-price controls.

The United States began its first, and up to now its only, experiment with mandatory controls over prices and wages in peacetime when President Nixon announced a three-month "freeze" on 15 August 1971. The controls subsequently evolved through several phases before lapsing at the end of April 1974.

William Newton and I (Blinder and Newton 1981) recently published a detailed econometric study of the effects of controls on nonfood, nonenergy prices. The results are easy to summarize. If we consider a four-year period beginning just before controls started and ending in mid-1975 (long enough after the end of controls to allow for a postcontrols "catch-up" period), it appears that controls had very little effect on the *average* rate of inflation. They did, however, alter the time pattern of inflation rates considerably—lowering inflation when it would otherwise have been low (especially in 1972) and raising inflation when it would otherwise have been high (especially in 1974). Specifically, we estimate that the rate of increase of nonfood, nonenergy prices was from 1.1 to 1.6 percentage points lower in 1972 and from 0.9 to 1.3 points lower in 1973 as a consequence of controls. Importantly, however, the end of controls then lifted inflation in 1974 some 1.7 to 3.1 percentage points *higher* than it would have been without controls, as artificially depressed prices snapped back. Since the extra catch-up inflation was concentrated in the period from February to October or November 1974, this phenomenon explains why the overall inflation rate remained in the double-digit range despite the rapid drop in the rate of increase of energy prices.[4]

The estimates cited above are based on a conventional econometric wage-price model, a tool whose validity has justifiably been questioned in recent years. In this case, however, the results of the econometric model can be buttressed by more impressionistic (but model-free) evidence.

If we study the detailed monthly time structure of the CPI purged of food and energy prices, it becomes quite apparent that double-digit inflation took place *only* during the nine-month period beginning in February 1974. During these nine months the annual rate of inflation was 13.4%. During the preceding nine months the annual rate of inflation was only 5.5%, and during the following nine months it was 6.4%. In a word, the rate of inflation of nonfood, nonenergy prices rose sharply and abruptly in February 1974, and fell almost as precipitously after November 1974. The symmetry of the rise and fall of the inflation rate is notable here, but is even more extreme if we look at quarterly data on the PCE deflator purged of food and energy. According to this index, the annual inflation rate during the period of peak inflation (1974:1 to 1974:4) was 10.4%, while the inflation rates of both the preceding and following three-quarter periods were 5.4%. If the end of controls was not the reason for this symmetry, we have quite a coincidence to explain.

More nails are added to the coffin by disaggregating the indexes to see which specific prices experienced the sharpest accelerations and decelerations during this period. This exercise singles out automobile prices (both new and used) and prices of certain "other nondurable goods," especially paper goods, as the main culprits.

Used car prices *fell* at an annual rate of 12% during the prepeak period, *rose* at an annual rate of 38% during the period of peak inflation, and then rose at only a 10% rate during the postpeak period. This remarkably volatile price performance, which was quite obviously a side effect of the oil crisis of 1974, accounts for a significant share of the total acceleration and deceleration of the nonfood, nonenergy CPI.

New car prices were virtually unchanged during the prepeak period, rose at a 14% annual rate during the peak period (February–November 1974), and then rose at only a 5% rate during the postpeak period. It is no coincidence, I suggest, that the auto industry was released from controls—subject to a pledge not to raise prices rapidly—in December 1973. The winter of 1973–74, when the oil crisis was at its height, was hardly a propitious time to raise car prices, so the automakers waited until spring and new car prices shot up between May and September 1974. Since sales were way down and inventories (relative to sales) were way up during this period, it seems most unlikely that this was a case of demand pulling up prices. Instead, it has all the earmarks of a postcontrols catch-up.

Various paper goods displayed even more dramatic price behavior. Noting that "the paper industry faced problems in early 1974 that went well beyond controls, " that "the most difficult problem was a severe world-wide shortage of raw materials, causing world prices to soar above controlled domestic prices," and that "new capacity was needed as well,"[5] the Cost of Living Council (COLC) lifted controls on the industry in March 1974. But COLC insisted on written commitments from the big producers that they would exercise restraint until summer. Then, between August and December 1974, retail prices of paper napkins rose at a 43% annual rate while prices for toilet tissue skyrocketed at a 77% pace.

I conclude from this that more than regression estimates implicate decontrol as the primary culprit responsible for the sharp acceleration and deceleration of nonfood, nonenergy prices in 1974.

12.3.4  Summary

The rate of inflation increased tremendously between 1972 and 1974. Three factors accounted for this stunning acceleration of inflation: food prices, energy prices, and the end of price controls. Then, from 1974 to

1976, the inflation rate tumbled almost as rapidly as it had climbed. The reasons for the deceleration were the mirror images of the reasons for the acceleration: food price increases slowed, the OPEC shock was not repeated, and the extra catch-up at the end of price controls was completed.

## 12.4   Accelerating Inflation, 1977–80

How does the recent experience compare with this history? Once again, inflation mounted rapidly from 1977 to early 1980.[6] Once again, three factors led the way, and none of them was money. Two of these were repeat offenders from 1972–74: food prices and energy prices. The third was a newcomer: mortgage interest rates. The "special factors" nature of the 1977–80 acceleration of inflation is every bit as clear as it was in 1972–74.

My examination of the recent inflation is organized as follows. First, I look briefly at each of the phenomena mentioned just above: food prices, energy prices, and mortgage interest rates, in each case stressing similarities and contrasts with the experience of the mid-1970s. Then I try to put the three culprits together in order to lay bare the anatomy of the recent recession.

### 12.4.1   The 1978–79 Food Shock

Table 12.3 presents data on the annual rate of increase of food prices, as measured in the National Income Accounts, for the period 1977–80. For comparison, corresponding data for the period 1972–75 are presented in the lower half of the table. This juxtaposition of the data illustrates two points:

**Table 12.3**      **Rates of Increase of Food Prices, 1977–80 and 1972–75**

|            | 1977 | 1978 | 1979 | 1980 |
|------------|------|------|------|------|
| 1st quarter | 6.1 | 10.9 | 15.2 | 3.6 |
| 2d quarter | 6.0 | 17.3 | 6.2 | 5.8 |
| 3d quarter | 4.5 | 9.6 | 4.9 | 16.7 |
| 4th quarter | 5.6 | 9.9 | 10.1 | 16.0 |
|            | 1972 | 1973 | 1974 | 1975 |
| 1st quarter | 6.7 | 14.0 | 16.8 | 5.0 |
| 2d quarter | 2.5 | 17.8 | 7.4 | 3.0 |
| 3d quarter | 5.4 | 18.3 | 5.9 | 12.2 |
| 4th quarter | 6.5 | 15.1 | 13.5 | 5.0 |

Source: Bureau of Economic Analysis.
Note: Quarter to quarter change, seasonally adjusted, expressed at annual rates.

1. The 1978–79 food shock, while it looked very similar at the outset, proved not to be nearly as severe as the 1973–74 shock. PCE food prices rose 22% between 1977:4 and 1979:4 versus 29% between 1972:4 and 1974:4.

2. While the 1978–79 food shock lasted about as long as its precursor (five quarters), the 1973–74 shock was followed by a period of blissful tranquillity in food prices. (Data for 1975 are in table 12.3. Food prices during 1976 were virtually constant.) By contrast the second half of 1980 was a bad one for food prices.

Another interesting aspect of the recent food price performance is concealed by the rather aggregated PCE data. It turns out that the problems emanating from the food sector were remarkably concentrated. The "food inflation" was in large part a "meat inflation." Meat prices as measured in the CPI rose at extraordinarily high and variable rates during 1978–79. During 1978 and the early part of 1979, the number of cattle on United States farms continued a decline that had started in early 1975. The size of the drop in the total cattle herd (over 16%) was the largest ever recorded. Expectations that falling beef production in 1978 would be offset by higher output of pork and poultry were dashed by severe weather in the winter of 1977–78, disease, rising feed costs, and uncertainty over government regulations on the use of nitrites. When ranchers finally started rebuilding their herds in 1979, their actions reduced current marketings even further and prices continued to soar.[7]

The result of all these goings on was that meat prices dominated the food price picture. During the eight quarters of 1978 and 1979, the mean annual inflation rate of food prices was 10.3% and the standard deviation was 4.9%. However, if we remove the extraordinary behavior of meat prices, the remaining index (for food exclusive of meat) displays a mean inflation rate of only 8.4%. More significantly, the standard deviation drops to only 1.6%.

One final point worth noting can be seen in table 12.3. While food prices played a substantial role in the acceleration of inflation in the first half of 1978, they played little role in the subsequent acceleration into the double-digit range in 1979.

## 12.4.2   The 1979 Energy Shock

The energy price run-up of 1979 had its origins in the political turmoil in Iran early in the year. The consequent disruption in supply, coupled with desperate efforts to build inventories, led to chaos in the world oil market and rapidly escalating spot-market prices in the second quarter. OPEC followed with a series of price increases in April, July, and December. Queues at gasoline stations were common in various locales in the spring and summer months.

Between December 1978 and March 1980, the average cost per barrel of imported crude oil to United States refiners rose from about $15 to over $33. On a dollars per barrel basis, this shock was far greater than the 1973–74 OPEC shock, though on a percentage basis the earlier shock was obviously much larger. The prices of retail petroleum prices responded with very little lag in both cases. The CPI energy component, for example, rose 26% (a 58% annual rate) between September 1973 and March 1974 and 56% (a 43% annual rate) between December 1978 and March 1980. Looking at the two shocks this way shows that while the earlier shock was more rapid and abrupt, the later shock was substantially more severe— driving retail energy prices up about twice as much.

This margin increases when we translate these hikes in energy prices into effects on the overall CPI. Because the relative importance of energy items in the CPI has increased greatly since 1973—averaging about 0.065 during the first OPEC shock and about 0.10 during the second—any given percentage increase in energy prices now has a far greater effect on the overall CPI.[8] In round numbers, the 26% increase in retail energy prices in 1973–74 pushed the all-items CPI up directly by about 1.5–2 points in six months while the 56% increase in energy prices in 1979–80 pushed the all-items CPI up by about 5–6 points in fifteen months.[9]

Another way to appraise the relative sizes of the two shocks is to ask how much the American consumer's oil bill would have increased in each case had consumption not declined. In 1973, United States petroleum consumption averaged 17.3 million barrels per day. Since refined petroleum products increased in price by about $5.50 per barrel between September 1973 and May 1974, the implied increase in the United States oil bill (the "oil tax") was roughly $35 billion. In 1978, United States petroleum usage averaged 18.8 million barrels per day, and the increase in product prices between December 1978 and March 1980 was roughly $21 per barrel. Thus the more recent oil tax was about $144 billion. Computed in this way, the first OPEC shock amounted to a levy of about 2½% of gross national product while the second shock amounted to about 6½%—quite a bit more.

### 12.4.3   Mortgage Interest Rates

It is hard to know what to say about mortgage interest rates, though it is impossible to discuss the 1978–80 inflation without them. Certainly the rise in home mortgage rates cannot be considered an exogenous inflationary shock, like food and energy. Mortgage rates, like all interest rates, are influenced in a fundamental way by inflation; so it is more than a little awkward to speak of rising mortgage rates as a "cause" of inflation. More likely, they are an effect.

Yet the way mortgage rates are treated in the CPI does make them an important component of inflation as measured by this index.[10] Since the CPI is an index of current transactions prices—not a "cost-of-living" index, as it is commonly treated—the mortgage rate included in it is a current market rate.[11] This rate, needless to say, is a price that precious few consumers pay. Yet it can have a dramatic effect on the CPI.

A simple back-of-the-envelope example will illustrate how this works. Suppose mortgage rates increase from 9% per annum to 10% per annum. Monthly payments on new mortgages will increase about 11%. If mortgage payments have a 9% relative importance in the overall CPI, this will increase the CPI by a full percentage point (0.09 times 11% = 0.99%). If this occurs within a few months, the effect on the *annual rate of increase* of the CPI can be astronomical.

Because of this, it is probably wise to pay more attention to the PCE deflator than to the CPI during periods in which mortgage interest rates are rising (or falling) rapidly. Yet it is far from clear that the PCE deflator is the "right" index to look at. Certainly mortgage interest rates should get *some* weight in any proper index of the prices actually paid by consumers, even though these rates do not count in the GNP.[12]

Mortgage interest rates were quite stable throughout 1977, holding at about 9% per annum.[13] Consequently, the CPI excluding mortgage interest rates rose at almost the same rate as the all-items CPI (see table 12.4). Things changed dramatically in 1978. Mortgage rates rose throughout the year, reaching roughly 10% by December, and the overall CPI rose noticeably faster than the CPI excluding mortgage interest (table 12.4). Then mortgage rates rose even more rapidly in 1979 and early 1980, and this surge had correspondingly dramatic effects on the CPI. As table 12.4 shows, by the first half of 1980 the gap between the inflation rates of the CPI and the CPI excluding mortgage interest rates reached 3.7 percentage points. But rates peaked in May 1980 and fell rapidly through August. As a result, the whipsaw effect of mortgage rates on the CPI became extreme in mid-year: the seasonally adjusted CPI actually recorded a *zero* rate of inflation between June and July! For the second half of 1980 as a whole, the CPI including mortgage interest rates rose slightly slower than the CPI excluding them.

**Table 12.4     Alternative Annual Inflation Rates, 1977–80**

| Period | All-Items CPI | CPI Excluding Mortgage Interest |
|---|---|---|
| Dec. 1976–Dec. 1977 | 6.8 | 6.6 |
| Dec. 1977–Dec. 1978 | 9.0 | 8.2 |
| Dec. 1978–Dec. 1979 | 13.3 | 11.6 |
| Dec. 1979–Jun. 1980 | 14.8 | 11.1 |
| Jun. 1980–Dec. 1980 | 9.9 | 10.9 |

## 12.4.4   The Anatomy of Inflation in 1978–80

We are now in a position to put the pieces together and analyze the 1978–80 acceleration of inflation. But first a word on methodology.

By some simple arithmetic it is possible to decompose the overall inflation rate into the parts contributed by food, energy, and all other factors.[14] In making this split, 1977 provides a useful reference point because in that year "special factors" inflation was unimportant, so the actual and baseline rates of inflation coincided (see table 12.1). By comparing the years 1978–80 with 1977, we can get an impression of how much of the recent acceleration of inflation was due to special factors and how much represented an increase in the baseline rate. I should stress that the analysis that follows is not "causal"; there is no model behind it. However, as we shall see, the data seem to be consistent with a model in which inflation from special factors passes directly into the overall inflation rate on a one-for-one basis in the short run.[15]

Consider first the composition of inflation according to the CPI, the index most in the public eye. As row 1 of table 12.5 shows, inflation mounted steadily from 6.8% during 1977 to 14.8% during the first half of 1980 (over 18% during the first quarter). The food and energy shocks we have discussed can be seen quite clearly in rows 2 and 3. The contribution of food price increases to overall inflation rose by 0.7 points from 1977 to 1978, and then stayed almost level between 1978 and 1980 (though the two halves of 1980 were quite different in this respect). As suggested earlier, and in marked contrast to 1973–74, the food shock was transitory and rather minor.

The same cannot be said of energy. Energy inflation made only "normal" contributions to overall inflation in 1977 and 1978, but then really took off. Fully 2.5 points of the total 4.3 point acceleration of inflation from 1978 to 1979 can be traced directly to energy prices, as can a fraction

**Table 12.5**     **Composition of CPI Inflation, 1977–80**

|  | 1977 | 1978 | 1979 | 1980 (first half) | 1980 (second half) |
|---|---|---|---|---|---|
| 1. Rate of inflation of CPI | 6.8% | 9.0% | 13.3% | 14.8% | 9.9% |
| Contributions of |  |  |  |  |  |
| 2.   Food | 1.4 | 2.1 | 1.9 | 0.8 | 2.8 |
| 3.   Energy | 0.6 | 0.7 | 3.2 | 3.9 | 0.1 |
| 4.   Mortgage interest cost | 0.7 | 1.4 | 2.5 | 4.6 | 0.5 |
| 5.   Everything else | 4.1 | 4.8 | 5.8 | 5.5 | 6.4 |
| 6. Rate of inflation of "everything else" | 6.0% | 7.2% | 8.7% | 8.7% | 10.1% |

of the further acceleration in early 1980. Stable energy prices then played a major role in the deceleration of inflation in the second half of 1980. Further disaggregation (not shown in the table) reveals that gasoline prices accounted for the lion's share of the total contribution of energy.

Row 4 shows what many observers believe to be a serious measurement problem in the CPI—its extreme sensitivity to changes in mortgage interest rates. Mortgage rates, we see, accounted for about one-third of the total acceleration from 1977 to 1978 (0.7 points out of 2.2), about one-quarter of the acceleration from 1978 to 1979 (1.1 points out of 4.3), and more than 100% of the acceleration from 1979 to early 1980 (2.1 points out of a total of 1.5). The situation was just as extreme on the downside. The contribution of mortgage interest rates to inflation declined by 4.1 percentage points from the first to the second half of 1980, whereas the overall inflation rate declined by 4.9 percentage points.

Looking at the acceleration period as a whole, we see that while the overall inflation rate increased by 8 percentage points (from 6.8% to 14.8%) between 1977 and the first half of 1980, fully 7.2 of these points can be traced directly to energy prices and mortgage interest costs. Fewer than 1½ points can be attributed to the catchall "everything else" category that constitutes about two-thirds of the index. On the downside, the deceleration of mortgage costs and energy prices was so extreme that they alone were sufficient to bring the inflation rate down about 8 percentage points from the first half of 1980 to the second half. The actual deceleration was limited to 5 percentage points by the misbehavior of food prices and by an ominous rise in the inflation rate of "everything else." This latter rate, which I take to approximate the baseline rate, rose gradually from 6% in 1977 to 8.7% in 1979, remained at that level during the first half of 1980, and then accelerated to a 10.1% annual rate during the second half of 1980.

Table 12.6 shows a similar decomposition for the PCE deflator, and its conclusions are similar in most respects (except, of course, for the absence of mortgage interest). The predominant role of food in the 1977–78 acceleration (1.2 points out of 1.8)[16] and the even more predominant role of energy in the 1978–79 acceleration (2.3 points out of 2.5) come shining through in these data. However, differences emerge in the first half of 1980, when the PCE deflator registers substantial acceleration in the prices on "everything else" while the CPI does not (compare the bottom rows of tables 12.5 and 12.6). According to the PCE numbers in table 12.6, the baseline rate of inflation, which had risen only 1.7 percentage points from 1977 to 1979, jumped 2 points from 1979 to the first half of 1980 and then receded slightly in the second half to 9%. Though the quarterly patterns are quite different, both indexes yield an estimate of the baseline rate of inflation for 1980 of about 9.4%.

**Table 12.6    Composition of PCE Inflation, 1977–80**

|  | 1977 | 1978 | 1979 | 1980 (first half) | 1980 (second half) |
|---|---|---|---|---|---|
| 1. Rate of inflation of |  |  |  |  |  |
|    *a*) PCE deflator | 5.9% | 7.8% | 9.5% | 11.0% | 9.1% |
|    *b*) PCE chain index | 6.0% | 7.8% | 10.3% | 10.8% | 10.0% |
|    Contributions of |  |  |  |  |  |
| 2.  Food | 1.2 | 2.4 | 1.8 | 1.0 | 3.3 |
| 3.  Energy | 0.6 | 0.6 | 2.9 | 3.0 | 0.4 |
| 4.  Everything else | 4.3 | 4.8 | 5.5 | 6.8 | 6.3 |
| 5. Rate of inflation of |  |  |  |  |  |
|    "everything else" | 6.0% | 6.7% | 7.7% | 9.7% | 9.0% |

Note: Except for rounding error, rows 2, 3, and 4 add up to row 1*b*.

The lesson to be learned from this exercise is pretty apparent. To the extent that inflation was propelled upward by special factors, we would expect the inflation rate to fall of its own accord. This appears to be just what happened from the first half of 1980 to the second half: the "special factors" contributed $-6$ points to the *change* in the inflation rate ($-8$ points from energy and mortgage rates, $+2$ points from food). A diminution of inflation of this type should be expected even in the absence of a recession. We should strive to avoid in 1980–81 the *post hoc, ergo propter hoc* fallacy into which so many observers fell in 1975. In 1974–75 a steep recession followed a sharp acceleration of inflation, and a stunning drop in the inflation rate quickly followed the recession. Many people continue to this day to give credit to the recession for breaking the back of the double-digit inflation whereas, in fact, it was the waning of special factors that did the trick. A similar scenario seems to have unfolded in 1980. For reasons just outlined, the inflation rate fell from the dizzying 18% rates of early 1980 back to the 8–10% baseline range. Simultaneously, we experienced a recession. We ought to avoid the temptation to credit the recession with knocking 8–10 points off the inflation rate—something no recession can do so quickly. Furthermore, to the extent that a recession works on inflation, its effects ought to show up in the baseline rate. This is something that at this writing (March 1981), it is still too early to see.

## 12.5  Were the 1970s Really Different?

A common criticism of the analysis of inflation presented here, in my book (Blinder 1979), and elsewhere,[17] runs as follows. There are "special factors" every year. In every year, some components of any price index are rising faster than the average. Thus, would it not be possible to use this methodology to brand all inflation as "special factor" inflation?

I have two answers to this criticism, one brief and one protracted. First, my concern here and in my 1979 book is with the *acceleration* of inflation well above the economy's "baseline" rate. No attempt is made to explain why the baseline rate itself increased. Such an explanation would focus on excessive aggregate demand (from money creation and other sources), lagging productivity growth, and so on, and there is little doubt that the rate of growth of money would play a prominent role. But there is equally little doubt that the behavior of the money supply tells us almost nothing about the bursts of double-digit inflation in 1974 nd 1979–80.

Now for the longer rebuttal. The explanation of inflation in the 1970s that I and others have propounded fundamentally revolves around food shocks (in 1973–74 and 1978) and energy shocks (in 1973–74 and 1979).[18] But have there not been food shocks and energy shocks before? It there were, why was there not double-digit inflation then?

In the case of energy shocks, the answer is straightforward: we simply did not have them until 1973. It is well known that the postwar period through 1972 was characterized by cheap energy growing cheaper. From January 1957 (when it starts) until January 1973, the CPI energy index rose at an annual rate of 1.7% while the all-items CPI rose at an annual rate of 2.7%. The greatest year-to-year change in the energy index was 4.5% in 1970. By contrast, the annual rate of increase of CPI energy prices from December 1972 to December 1979 was 15.2% (versus 8.8% for the all-items CPI). Energy prices rose 21.6% during 1974 and 37.4% during 1979. The 1970s really *were* different, and I fail to see why a theory of inflation is more "scientific" if it ignores this fact.

Things are far less clear with respect to food shocks, however. We have no OPEC to latch on to as a watershed, and it is difficult to understand what made weather conditions so much more adverse in the 1970s than in the 1960s and 1950s. Using CPI data since 1940, it is in fact possible to identify several earlier "food shocks" (see table 12.7).

In 1941 and 1942, for example, the rates of increase of food prices were respectively 16.4% and 17.5%. (It is probably no mystery why this occurred!) As a consequence, the rate of increase of the all-items CPI exceeded that of the CPI stripped of food items by 3.2 and 5.4 percentage points respectively. The *acceleration* of inflation between 1940 and 1942 was 8.3 percentage points in the overall CPI, but only 3.3 points if food items are excluded. Similarly, the *deceleration* between 1942 and 1943 was 6.1 percentage points including food but merely 0.5 percentage points excluding food.

Another severe food shock apparently occurred in late 1946 and early 1947 as the wartime controls over food prices were dismantled.[19] In 1946, the rate of inflation including food exceeded the rate of inflation excluding food by 9.1 percentage points. From 1945 to 1946, the CPI inflation rate accelerated by an astounding 15.9 percentage points. But without

**Table 12.7**        **Rates of Change of the CPI**
                      **and Selected Components, 1940–51**

| Year | Food Prices | All-Items CPI | CPI less Food |
|------|-------------|---------------|---------------|
| 1940 | 2.6   | 1.0   | 0.6   |
| 1941 | 16.4  | 9.7   | 6.5   |
| 1942 | 17.5  | 9.3   | 3.9   |
| 1943 | 3.1   | 3.2   | 3.4   |
| 1944 | 0.2   | 2.1   | 3.5   |
| 1945 | 3.0   | 2.3   | 1.8   |
| 1946 | 31.5  | 18.2  | 9.1   |
| 1947 | 11.2  | 9.0   | 7.5   |
| 1948 | −0.8  | 2.7   | 5.5   |
| 1949 | −3.7  | −1.8  | −0.8  |
| 1950 | 9.6   | 5.8   | 4.1   |
| 1951 | 7.4   | 5.9   | 5.0   |

Note: From December of previous year to December of stated year.

**Table 12.8**        **Rates of Change of the CPI**
                      **and Selected Components, 1952–72**

| Year | Food Prices | All-Items CPI | CPI less Food |
|------|-------------|---------------|---------------|
| 1952 | −1.1  | 0.9   | 1.7   |
| 1953 | −1.3  | 0.6   | 1.7   |
| 1954 | −1.6  | −0.5  | 0     |
| 1955 | −0.9  | 0.4   | 0.9   |
| 1956 | 3.1   | 2.9   | 2.6   |
| 1957 | 2.8   | 3.0   | 3.2   |
| 1958 | 2.2   | 1.8   | 1.6   |
| 1959 | −0.8  | 1.5   | 2.3   |
| 1960 | 3.1   | 1.5   | 1.0   |
| 1961 | −0.9  | 0.7   | 1.1   |
| 1962 | 1.5   | 1.2   | 1.2   |
| 1963 | 1.9   | 1.6   | 1.6   |
| 1964 | 1.4   | 1.2   | 1.0   |
| 1965 | 3.4   | 1.9   | 1.6   |
| 1966 | 3.9   | 3.4   | 3.3   |
| 1967 | 1.2   | 3.0   | 3.5   |
| 1968 | 4.3   | 4.7   | 4.9   |
| 1969 | 7.2   | 6.1   | 5.7   |
| 1970 | 2.2   | 5.5   | 6.5   |
| 1971 | 4.3   | 3.4   | 3.1   |
| 1972 | 4.7   | 3.4   | 3.0   |

Note: From December of previous year to December of stated year.

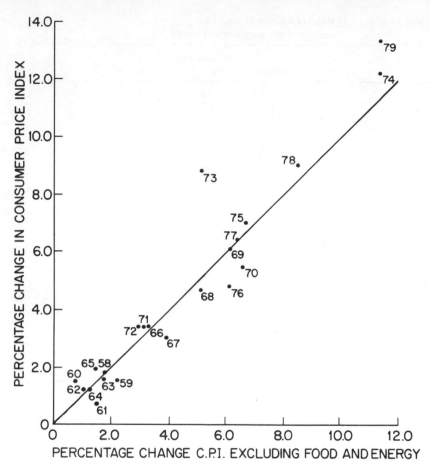

**Fig. 12.1a**      Percent change in CPI (excluding food and energy) versus percent change in CPI.

food prices this acceleration was only 7.3 points. Similarly, the deceleration from 1946 to 1948 was 15.5 points when food is included versus 3.6 points when it is not.

A similar shock in 1950–51 can be dimly perceived in table 12.7. During the winter of 1950–51, food prices rose at a 32% annual rate for a single quarter. In a word, shocks emanating from the volatile food sector have indeed been with us in the past.

What is striking in the data is the total absence of such shocks between 1952 and 1972 (see table 12.8). During these twenty-one years, the rate of increase of food prices exceeded 5% only once. The maximum amount by which inflation in the all-items CPI ever exceeded inflation in the CPI excluding food was 0.5 percentage points in 1960. I do not claim to know

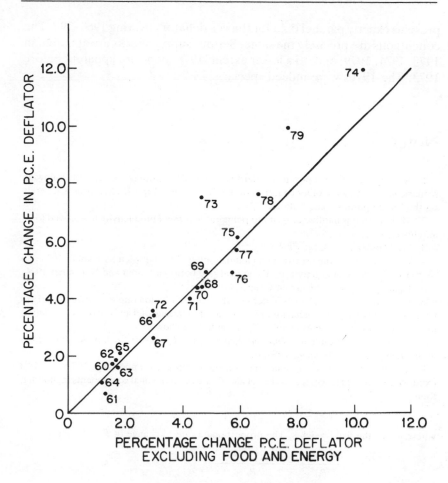

**Fig. 12.1b**    Percent change in PCE (excluding food and energy) deflator versus percent change in PCE deflator.

which state of affairs is the norm and which is an aberration—the volatile decades of the 1940s and 1970s, or the calm decades of the 1950s and 1960s. What is clear, however, is that food-price behavior was very different during the 1970s than during the 1950s or 1960s. It is not obvious that we get a better understanding of inflation by ignoring this fact.

More evidence that the 1970s differed dramatically from the 1960s in this regard is presented in figure 12.1. In panel *a*, which pertains to CPI data from 1958 through 1979, I have plotted percentage changes in the all-items CPI on the vertical axis and percentage changes in the CPI excluding food and energy on the horizontal axis.[20] Food and energy "shocks" thus stand out as vertical displacements from the 45 degree line in the diagram, and it is clear that these are a phenomenon of the 1970s. Panel *b* presents exactly parallel data for the PCE deflator covering 1960–79.[21] The conclusions are precisely the same. Serious supply shocks are apparent in 1973, 1974, 1979, and, to a lesser extent, 1978; none are apparent before 1973. The 1970s were indeed special.

# Notes

1. Although there are important similarities, it would be a mistake to apply the following scenario mechanically to other countries or to other historical epochs. My focus is squarely on the contemporary United States.

2. These days it is hardly necessary to point out that *trend* productivity has proved to be an elusive concept.

3. See Blinder (1979), pp. 78–88.

4. Energy prices in the CPI rose at an annual rate of 58% between September 1973 and March 1974, and then at only a 10.3% annual rate between March and November 1974.

5. United States Cost of Living Council (1974), p. 54.

6. I start in 1977 rather than 1976 because the overall inflation rate was distorted in 1976 by the unusually moderate behavior of food prices. Excluding food and energy, the inflation rate was essentially constant in 1975–77, as table 12.2 shows.

7. United States President, *Economic Report of the President, 1979*, p. 40; ibid., *Economic Report of the President, 1980*, p. 33.

8. This is a good place to define the concept of "relative importance." The CPI is a fixed-weight index. Hence, if $P_t$ is the CPI and $P_{it}$ are the individual components in month $t$, then

$$P_t = \sum_i w_i P_{it},$$

where $w_i$ are the fixed weights. The proportionate rate of change of $P$ is therefore

$$\frac{P_t - P_{t-1}}{P_{t-1}} = \frac{\sum_i w_i (P_{it} - P_{i,t-1})}{P_{t-1}}$$

$$= \sum_i \left( w_i \frac{P_{i,t-1}}{P_{t-1}} \right) \left( \frac{P_{it} - P_{i,t-1}}{P_{i,t-1}} \right).$$

The *relative importance* of item $i$ at time $t$ is defined as

$$r_{it} = w_i \frac{P_{i,t-1}}{P_{t-1}},$$

and hence it can be seen that the rate of change of the CPI is a weighted average (with weights $r_{it}$) of the rates of change of its individual components. The useful point to note is that an item's relative importance in the CPI automatically increases (decreases) as its price rises (falls) relative to the CPI as a whole.

9. These calculations measure only the direct contribution of energy prices to the CPI. They do not include either the indirect effects of increased energy costs on nonenergy products (e.g. higher gasoline prices make the cost of transporting food higher) or the eventual reverberations through the wage-price spiral.

10. For a fuller treatment of the issue, see Blinder (1980).

11. Because of certain economic and accounting lags, the rate actually used is a weighted average of market rates quoted in recent past months.

12. This is not quite true. Imputed rents on owner-occupied housing are included in the GNP, and hence the "price" of this service is tacitly part of the PCE deflator. Imputed rents depend on observed rents, which in turn depend on mortgage rates (and many other factors). So the mortgage rate creeps in through the back door, though very slowly. The issue is really one of timing.

13. The mortgage rate cited in this paragraph is the Federal Home Loan Bank Board's series on yields on new conventional mortgages. Monthly data can be found in United States President, *Economic Report of the President, 1980*, table B-64, p. 279.

14. When using the CPI, a fourth component is distinguished: mortgage interest costs.

15. This is quite different from the implications of a classical quantity theory model in which the overall inflation rate is controlled by the growth rate of money and special factors cause changes only in *relative* prices.

16. Reference is to the PCE chain index.

17. See, for example, Gordon (1975, 1977) or Eckstein (1980).

18. The Nixon price controls of 1971–74 also played a role, but primarily one of distorting the time pattern of inflation in 1971–75. See above, section 12.3.3.

19. I am grateful to Walter Salant for useful information on the decontrol process.

20. Inflation rates recorded are from December of the previous year to December of the stated year.

21. Inflation rates here are for the four quarters ending in the fourth quarter of the stated year.

# References

Blinder, A. S. 1979. *Economic policy and the Great Stagflation.* New York: Academic Press.

Blinder, A. S. 1980. The Consumer Price Index and the measurement of recent inflation. *Brookings Papers on Economic Activity* 2: 539–65.

Blinder, A. S., and Newton, W. J. 1981. The 1971–1974 controls program and the price level: An econometric post-mortem. *Journal of Monetary Economics* 7 (July): 1–23.

Eckstein, O. 1980. *Tax policy and core inflation.* Study prepared for the Joint Economic Committee, United States Congress, 96th Congress, 2d session, April.

Gordon, R. J. 1975. The impact of aggregate demand on prices. *Brookings Papers on Economic Activity* 3: 613–62.

―――. 1977. Can the inflation of the 1970s be explained? *Brookings Papers on Economic Activity* 1: 253–77.

Perry, G. L. 1975. The United States. In E. R. Fried and C. L. Schultze, eds., *Higher oil prices and the world economy*, pp. 71–104. Washington: Brookings Institution.

United States Bureau of Economic Analysis. 1976. *The National Income and Product Accounts of the United States, 1929–1974.* Washington: Government Printing Office.

————. *Survey of current business.* Various issues.
United States Cost of Living Council. *Economic Stabilization Program Quarterly Report.* Various issues.
United States President. *Economic Report of the President together with the Annual Report of the Council of Economic Advisors*, various issues.

# Contributors

Robert J. Barro
Department of Economics
University of Chicago
Chicago, Illinois 60637

Alan S. Blinder
Department of Economics
Princeton University
Princeton, New Jersey 08544

Jeremy I. Bulow
Graduate School of Business
Stanford University
Stanford, California 94305

Dennis W. Carlton
Department of Economics
University of Chicago
Chicago, Illinois 60637

Martin Feldstein
National Bureau of Economic
  Research
1050 Massachusetts Avenue
Cambridge, Massachusetts 02138

Stanley Fischer
Department of Economics
Massachusetts Institute of Technology
Room E52-280
Cambridge, Massachusetts 02139

Jacob A. Frenkel
Department of Economics
University of Chicago
Chicago, Illinois 60637

Robert J. Gordon
Department of Economics
Northwestern University
2003 Sheridan Road, Room G-180
Evanston, Illinois 60201

Robert E. Hall
Herbert Hoover Memorial Building
Stanford University
Stanford, California 94305

Douglas A. Hibbs, Jr.
Department of Government
Harvard University
Littauer M 35
Cambridge, Massachusetts 02138

Thomas J. Sargent
Department of Economics
University of Minnesota
Minneapolis, Minnesota 55455

John B. Shoven
Department of Economics
Fourth Floor, Encina Hall
Stanford University
Stanford, California 94305

# Author Index

# Subject Index